DAREDEVILS OF THE ATLANTIC OCEAN

DAREDEVILS OF THE ATLANTIC OCEAN

Unusual Crossings in Unlikely Vessels

Peter Firstbrook

SEAWORTHY PUBLICATIONS, INC. • MELBOURNE, FLORIDA

Daredevils of the Atlantic Ocean
Unusual Crossings in Unlikely Vessels
Copyright ©2023 by Peter Firstbrook

Published in the USA by:
Seaworthy Publications, Inc.
6300 N Wickham Rd.
#130-416
Melbourne, FL 32940
Phone 321-610-3634
e-mail orders@seaworthy.com
www.seaworthy.com - Your Bahamas and Caribbean Cruising Advisory

All rights reserved. No part of this book may be reproduced, stored in a retrieval system, or transmitted in any form, or by any means, electronic, mechanical, photocopying, recording, or by any storage and retrieval system, without permission in writing from the publisher.

Maps and illustrations are by the author

Library of Congress Cataloging-in-Publication Data

Names: Firstbrook, P. L., author.
Title: Daredevils of the Atlantic Ocean : unusual crossings in unlikely
  vessels / Peter Firstbrook.
Description: Melbourne, Florida : Seaworthy Publications, Inc., [2022] |
  Includes bibliographical references and index. | Summary: "Daredevils of
  the Atlantic" chronicles the exploits of a relatively new breed of
  adventurers and fortune-seekers who sometimes succeed and sometimes fail
  at crossing the Atlantic Ocean in all sorts of unlikely vessels and
  contraptions, including a few who even tried to swim across. Some were
  powered by motors, some by sails, currents, or just raw human power and
  athletic stamina. Many were outlandish attempts that only a madman could
  have conceived. These are their stories. The ocean separates two great
  continents, and men (and it has usually been the male species) have
  always sought new ways to cross 'the pond'-and not all of them in boats.
  This book is about these people: some wise and thoughtful, others
  reckless and frankly crazy; some well-prepared, others impetuous and
  disorganized; some skilled and proficient who understood the risks,
  while others were hot-headed, inexperienced and impulsive; some voyages
  were carefully planned, while others seemed to be cooked up on little
  more than a whim. In the world of trans-Atlantic sailing, as in life, it
  takes all sorts... What all these adventurers have in common, however,
  is that they launched themselves on a voyage of personal challenge and
  discovery, during which they put their lives on the line. For that
  reason alone, we should take our (sailing) hats off to them"-- Provided
  by publisher.
Identifiers: LCCN 2020002887 (print) | LCCN 2020002888 (ebook) | ISBN
  9781948494342 (paperback) | ISBN 9781948494359 (ebook)
Subjects: LCSH: Adventure travel--Atlantic Ocean. | Aquatic
  sports--Atlantic Ocean. | Ships--Atlantic Ocean. | Extreme
  sports--Atlantic Ocean.
Classification: LCC G516 .F57 2022 (print) | LCC G516 (ebook) | DDC
  910.9163--dc23
LC record available at https://lccn.loc.gov/2020002887
LC ebook record available at https://lccn.loc.gov/2020002888

Dedication

In memory of
Captain Simon Culshaw, 1939 – 2020
Master Mariner, BSc, MPhil, FRICS, FIMarEST, FRIN
Mentor and good friend

Introduction

Every year more than 200 sailing boats and over 1,200 crew members descend on Las Palmas in the Canary Islands to join the Atlantic Rally for Cruisers (ARC). This annual transatlantic sailing event for cruising yachts has been held every year since 1986. The "race" starts in early November, which gives even the slowest boat ample time to reach the finish in St. Lucia for Christmas parties. The direct sailing distance is a little over 2,500 nautical miles (4,630 km) and the voyage usually takes between 10 and 24 days, depending on the weather and the speed of the very different boats.

Modern yacht design and sophisticated navigational aids now make crossing the Atlantic from east to west a relatively easy and safe passage—it is often referred to as the "milk run." Even so, winds can be unpredictable, and although storms are rare if you cross towards the end of the year, you are still likely to encounter sudden squalls, strong winds, and torrential rain. The wise sailor never takes crossing the North Atlantic lightly—an ocean that covers an area greater than North America and Europe combined.

Over the years there have been many crossings that do not fit into the category of a "milk run." The ocean separates two great continents, and men (and it has usually been the male species) have always sought new ways to cross "the pond"—and not all of them in boats. This book is about these people: some wise and thoughtful, others reckless and frankly crazy; some well-prepared, others impetuous and disorganized; some skilled and proficient who understood the risks, whilst others were hotheaded, inexperienced and impulsive; some voyages were carefully planned, whilst others seemed to be cooked up on little more than a whim. In the world of transatlantic sailing, as in life, it takes all sorts...

What all of these people have in common, however, is that they launched themselves on a voyage of personal challenge and discovery, during which they put their lives on the line. For that reason alone, we should all take our (sailing) hats off to them.

Table of Contents

Dedication v

Introduction vi

Notes on Measurements viii

Big Ocean, Little Boats 1

The Great Space Race 33

Steam Across the Atlantic 61

The First Atlantic Yacht Race 88

The Arms Race 113

The History Men 143

The Atlantic Auto Route 174

The Heretics 198

Stranger Things Have Happened at Sea 222

Glossary 232

Bibliography 237

About the Author 247

Notes on Measurements

This book has always been intended for a lay reader, and I have made every attempt to simplify and explain maritime terminology; a glossary is also included at the end. One problem remains, however, over the use of nautical measurements—further complicated by the use of different measurements on opposite sides of the Atlantic.

Traditionally, horizontal distance at sea has always been measured in nautical miles, and speed knots; I have retained this convention in this book. For those unfamiliar with these measurements, a nautical mile is based on the circumference of the earth and is equal to one minute of latitude; it is 1-1/7th or 1.15 of a statute (land) mile, or 1.85 km; a knot is one nautical mile an hour (never expressed as knots per hour). The other long-established maritime distance measurement (that I have generally tried to avoid), is the fathom—traditionally a measurement of depth; one fathom is 6 ft or 1.83 m.

The origin of the term "knots" goes back to the early days of sail when a wooden log and line was used to measure the speed of a ship. The line was marked at regular intervals by knots; each interval or knot was 47 ft (14.3 m) long. The floating log was tossed overboard and acted as a drogue, remaining more or less stationary in the water, dragging the line out as the vessel sailed on. After 28 seconds had elapsed (measured using a sand timer), the number of knots that passed overboard was counted, giving the speed in knots, or nautical miles per hour.

For other measurements (such as the length of boats), I have used Imperial measurements followed by its metric equivalent in parentheses. For weights, one Imperial ton is 2,240 lbs and is virtually equivalent to a metric tonne. (I have avoided using the U.S. "short ton," which is 2,000 lbs or about 12 percent smaller than an Imperial ton). For volumes, I have used U.S. pints, quarts, and gallons, equivalent to 0.83 Imperial pints, quarts, and gallons.

Big Ocean, Little Boats

In 1787, just three and a half years after the end of the American War of Independence, a young sea captain and veteran of the Revolutionary War sailed for France in a trading ship. When he returned to South America—this time alone—he became the first person to cross the Atlantic Ocean single-handed, yet had no idea that he had actually sailed himself into the history books.

Josiah Shackford proved to be a better sailor than he was a husband. Born in Portsmouth, New Hampshire, around 1747, he went to sea as a young man and returned home to find his widowed father had remarried. Shackford took an immediate fancy to his new stepsister, Deborah Marshall (daughter of his father's new wife Eleanor and her first husband Samuel Marshall). Deborah was already betrothed to another, but Shackford persevered and the couple was married in February 1771. The newlywed husband soon went back to sea, leaving his wife back in Portsmouth.

According to British shipping records, Shackford became master of several vessels trading mainly in the West Indies, and he is known to have taken his ship, the *Squirrel*, as far north as Nova Scotia in 1775. That was the year the American War of Independence began, and Shackford was offered a commission in the fledgling American Navy as a Second Lieutenant. He served on the *USS Raleigh* and sailed for Europe and Africa, capturing a British ship off the coast of Senegal. The next year the *Raleigh* was seized by the British Navy off the coast of Maine, but young Lieutenant Shackford and most of the crew escaped capture.

Then in 1780, Shackford became master of a New Hampshire Privateer, the 10-gun *USS Diana*, and he distinguished himself by capturing the British gunship *HMS Adventure*. (Privateers were little more than semi-legitimate pirate ships, authorized by their government to attack and loot any vessel that was not on their side during a war.)

After the war, Shackford found his marriage was "on the rocks," to use a nautical term. According to one newspaper account, Shackford: "... wanted his wife to move to New York, but she refused to leave Portsmouth, and then she did not hear from him for several years before he returned suddenly to Portsmouth. He put up at the hotel, took tea with his wife, and left town the next morning, never to return."

The ESSEX JOURNAL AND NEW HAMPSHIRE PACKET reported that "A Mr. Shackford ... having the misfortune of discontent with his wife, left that place for Surinam [sic]."

Josiah Shackford – Commissioned Lieutenant of the frigate Raleigh July 1776; oil on canvas by John Singleton Copley (1735-1815).

Shackford left his wife without any financial support, so she petitioned the courts to be allowed to collect her husband's rents from his land because he had been "absent in a disordered, deranged state of mind and that the resources left by him for her subsistence are exhausted and have failed."

Clearly, all was not well in the Shackford household.

By 1786, Shackford was in Suriname, then a mosquito-infested Dutch colony that survived by selling slaves, coffee, and sugar cane. He was given command of a French trading ship and sailed for Bordeaux in France; on his arrival, the vessel's owner was so pleased with the safe return of his vessel that he gave the American a small sloop of 15 tons—a sailing boat around 36-39 ft (11-12 m) long. Shackford decided to return to Suriname with his new acquisition, and he engaged a crewman to sail with him across the Atlantic.

This fishing boat is typical of its day and similar to Shackford's vessel. The boat has a four-sided gaff mainsail, a jib set at the end of the bowsprit, and a foresail set at the front of the boat (the bow).

Things did not quite go as planned. On leaving the harbor, Shackford's companion deciding that an Atlantic crossing was not for him, so he jumped ship—literally straight into the pilot boat. Shackford was left with a seaworthy vessel and his dog, but no paid hand. They say he was "a man of too stern materials to turn about," so rather than take the sensible course and return to find a replacement crewman, he decided that his dog was enough. Shackford laid a course west to Cape Ortegal in Portugal, then down the Portuguese coast until he picked up the Trade Winds off the Canary Islands to take him across the Atlantic.

Sailing solo (even with a dog for company) makes great demands on a sailor, apart from just loneliness. You cannot anchor in the open ocean as the water is too deep, so you have three options of what to do at night. Shackford could probably balance the sails on his boat to keep it sailing in a straight line, for as long as the wind or sea conditions did not change; this lets you catnap while your ship continues on course, but you risk running into other vessels.

Alternatively, you can lower the sails and lay out a sea anchor—a funnel-shaped canvas drogue attached to a long rope that stops you from drifting too far off course. However, a sea anchor is hard work to haul in the next day, especially if you are alone.

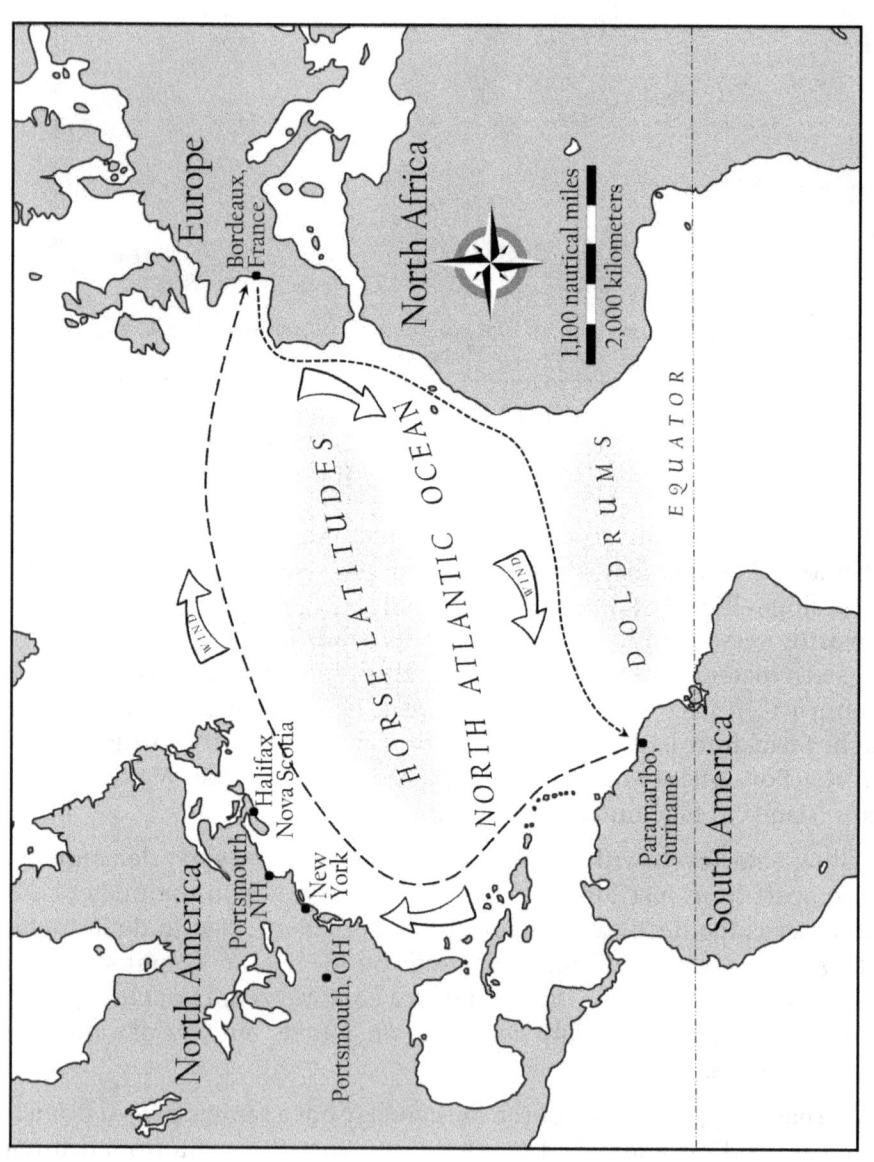

Shackford's routes to and from Bordeaux in 1786/87. Sailing ships need to avoid the Horse Latitudes and Doldrums if possible.

The third option is to drop all the sails and allow your boat to drift, although the incessant rolling does not allow for much sleep. Whether lying to a sea anchor or not, there still remains the danger of being run down by another vessel.

Shackford's two passages across the Atlantic in 1786/87 followed a time-tested route used by sailors since Columbus sailed from Spain to the West Indies and back. The winds and currents in the ocean form a huge gyre, rotating clockwise. Ships in Shackford's day could not sail at a close angle to the wind and were best suited with the wind at right angles or behind them. Shackford chose a long route to France, north up the east coast of America, before turning east across the North Atlantic. This was much faster than trying to sail directly to Europe against the winds; this route also avoided an area of light winds in the center of the ocean called the Horse Latitudes.

The prevailing wind directions in the Atlantic and their related ocean currents are always important considerations in any crossing in a sailing vessel.

On his solo return passage, Shackford again made use of favorable winds and currents by sailing south down the coast of Portugal until he picked up the Trade Winds that carried him west from the Canaries. He would also have avoided the Doldrums, another area of calm winds that lie north of the equator. His return voyage was about 4,320 NM (8,000 km) and took him 35 days. This was impressively fast, averaging 123 NM a day, or about 5 knots. As he was alone, he must have sailed at night to maintain this average.

His achievement has gone largely unacknowledged, yet this is the earliest account of a single-handed passage across the Atlantic in a sailing vessel. On his arrival, the authorities were suspicious and doubted his ability to cross the Atlantic without a crew. The American ESSEX JOURNAL AND NEW HAMPSHIRE PACKET of May 2, 1787, reported:

> "When he arrived, the novelty of the expedition excited unusual surprise, so far as to induce the government to take notice of the fact. Suspicions prevailed of his having dealt unfairly by the people who were supposed to have come out with him. But he produced his papers and journal, and proved his integrity so far to the satisfaction of his examiners, that they permitted him to take another man aboard and proceed to St. Bartholomews, where he arrived in safety, and now follows the coasting business from that island."

After a lifetime at sea, Shackford retired and purchased a large tract of land in Ohio (then practically a wilderness). Here, 500 miles (804 km) from the ocean, he built mills, stores, and several houses. He lived alone except for a serving boy, and reportedly never allowed a woman ever to enter his house.

His wife attempted a reconciliation after her mother died, and she wrote several letters to her estranged husband but never received a reply. When Shackford died at the age of 93, he left his substantial estate to strangers. His obituary claimed he was:

> *"A studious man, intelligent, but of an eccentricity which to some minds bore marks of insanity—but those who recollect him in Ohio will not allow that he was any other than a sane man."*

≈≈≈≈≈≈≈

They say that size is not everything, but in a sailing boat it certainly has its advantages. Bigger boats have more room for provisions, water, and creature comforts; generally they are also faster and more comfortable at sea. There is an old sailor's maxim that says never go to sea in a boat smaller than the seas you are likely to encounter, and remember that waves over 20 ft (6.1 m) high are common in the deep ocean. Riding out a storm in a small boat is like being inside a washing machine on a cold wash—and it can last for days at a time.

Despite their obvious advantages, big boats do not appeal to everyone. Shackford would have had plenty of room on his 15-ton sloop, especially as he only had to share it with a dog. However, from the second half of the nineteenth century, sailors began competing with each other to sail the Atlantic in the smallest of boats—and by "small," I mean any boat 20 ft (6.1 m) or less.

Nikola Primorac was the first. He was born in Dubrovnik in 1840; as he approached his thirtieth birthday, he came to England searching for a better life. What he stumbled upon were some of the most notorious drinking haunts in the port of Liverpool, where he drunkenly accepted a bet to sail across the Atlantic. Perhaps surprisingly after sobering up, he honored his £100 wager and set about converting a ship's lifeboat for the voyage.

On the surface, a lifeboat might seem a sensible option, as they are designed to keep you safe in the event of a shipwreck. These early lifeboats, however, were rudimentary open craft that were only really designed to keep you afloat for a short time until you were rescued. At best they could be rowed, but they were not really designed to sail efficiently, nor did they have much of a keel, that would have prevented them from being blown sideways

The Citta di Ragusa with a traditional gaff rig. A jib is set on the bowsprit, with a foresail at the bow. The boat also carries a mizzen sail on a small mast, aft. This keeps any single sail relatively small.

when trying to sail close to the wind. Primorac's lifeboat was also small; 20 ft (6.1 m) long (without bowsprit), with a beam of 6 ft (1.8 m) and a freeboard (height of the deck above the waterline) of just 2 ft 10 in (0.86 m). The boat came from a whaling ship that had foundered the previous year, so the omens for an easy crossing of the Atlantic were not auspicious.

Primorac built a cabin on the boat, rigged it as a gaff cutter in the common style of the period, and named her *Citta di Ragusa*—Ragusa was the Italian name for Dubrovnik. He wanted to sail under the flag of St. Blasius, the patron saint of the Dubrovnik Republic, but the Austro-Hungarian authorities (who controlled the region at the time) thought better of the idea and declined his request. He chose instead to sail under the British Merchant Navy flag. Inevitably, the English newspapers got hold of the story and THE TIMES of London claimed that it was "…an incredible brave and crazy adventure ever made that could turn into tragedy or triumph."

Like Josiah Shackford nearly 100 years before, all that Nikola Primorac needed now was a crew member to share the doubtful pleasures of the crossing. I suppose trawling the waterside pubs of Liverpool docks might have seemed a sensible idea at the time, but the consequences were all too predictable.

The next morning, June 2, 1870, Nikola Primorac sailed from Liverpool with an American by the name of J. C. Buckley. The *Citta di Ragusa* was cheered on by hundreds of excited spectators watching from the riverbanks. By all accounts, Buckley was still blind drunk and the word in Liverpool that day was that the only member aboard who was not still completely inebriated from the debauched night of drinking was their dog, Bosun.

When Buckley finally sobered up and realized what he had let himself into, he begged Primorac to let him leave the ship, promising to find a replacement. The *Citta di Ragusa* made it as far as Queenstown on the south coast of Ireland, a distance of just 300 NM miles (555 km) before Buckley was able to disembark. True to his word, he persuaded a Dutch sailor, E. R. W. Hayter, to take his place.

Not surprisingly, the crossing to North America was not without its memorable moments. The two intrepid sailors started with a couple of days of calm and pleasant weather, before strong winds and high seas forced them to take in all sail and run before the storm. This was a perfectly seamanlike response to the severe conditions, and they set out their sea anchor, trailed on a long length of rope to keep the boat facing into the wind; this allowed all but the worst of the waves to pass harmlessly on either side and prevented the boat from being rolled over in the big seas. Primorac and Hayter wisely stayed below, but their dog Bosun apparently went on deck during the night in search of a "lamp post," and was lost overboard.

Primorac and Hayter now faced a real challenge. By sailing east to west across the North Atlantic, they were sailing against the prevailing winds. Even in summer, low pressure systems bring strong headwinds that create huge waves. Their converted lifeboat only had a shallow keel and a low freeboard, and the vessel was not built to cope with these testing conditions.

Their voyage became notorious, and the maritime authorities in both Britain and the United States advised all ships sailing the Atlantic route to render assistance to the *Citta di Ragusa* if needed. The *Emma L. Rich*, an American fishing schooner, encountered the sailors off Newfoundland when they were already three-quarters of the way across. The skipper generously offered them help, which Primorac politely refused—and the two men sailed on. On July 27th, Nikola Primorac celebrated his 30th birthday at sea.

Word of the imminent arrival of the *Citta di Ragusa* was reported back to the mainland; by the time they arrived in Boston on September 8, 1870, journalists were waiting to report the sensational news. The crossing against the prevailing winds and currents had taken the two men 92 days. Once you include diversions and zig-zagging because of contrary winds, they probably sailed 3,000 NM (5,556 km) from Liverpool, averaging 33 NM

E. R. W. Hayter and Nikola Primorac (right) with their dog Bosun in Southern Ireland, before leaving for their Atlantic crossing.

(60 km) a day. An average speed of 1.5 knots was very slow progress, even for a relatively small sailing boat.

The crew of the *Citta di Ragusa* continued on to New York, where they received another triumphal reception. Primorac and Hayter basked in their glory for just 20 days before deciding to sail back to Europe. This time the return voyage to Liverpool with the wind and waves behind them took just 38 days. Soon after their arrival, Queen Victoria congratulated the two sailors on their achievement, and the *Citta di Ragusa* was exhibited in the Liverpool Museum until close to the end of World War II when the boat was destroyed during a bombing raid.

Primorac and Hayter's achievement is considered to be the first genuinely small boat crossing of the Atlantic; they are also recognized as being the first to sail the ocean in both directions in such a small boat.

≈≈≈≈≈≈≈

It is unlikely that Nikola Primorac ever realized what he had started, but his voyage set a trend for small boat crossings of the Atlantic. The early challenges to Primorac's record came from the hardened fishermen of New England, who understood the harsh reality and risks of sailing the Atlantic Ocean. For example, between 1866 and 1890 in the fishing harbor of Gloucester, Massachusetts, more than 380 schooners and 2,450 men were lost over the Atlantic fishing grounds. On August 24, 1873, nine vessels and 128 sailors were lost in a single storm, and Gloucester's dependence on the North Atlantic meant their seasoned fishermen developed a close relationship with tragedy and death.

Despite the risks, it was less than six years before a new challenger stepped into Primorac's seaboots. Alfred Johnson was a Grand Banks fisherman from Gloucester; although Danish by birth, he had run away as a teenager and worked his passage on sailing ships before finding his way to New England. Although only 29 years old when he made the crossing he was already an experienced sailor, well used to spending many days fishing for cod over the foggy Grand Banks. In 1876, he took on the Atlantic in his 20 ft (6.1 m) gaff-rigged dory, sailing single-handed from his home port to commemorate the first centennial of the United States; in honor of the anniversary, he named his boat *Centennial*.

Johnson's dory was not built especially for the crossing, but he made it as seaworthy as possible. He added a centerboard to improve sailing—this is a drop-down wooden keel that helps a boat to sail closer to the wind; Johnson also fitted watertight compartments to keep *Centennial* afloat in the event of a capsize. Despite these sensible improvements, the boat had

*Alfred Johnson at sea with Centennial, 1876.
The boat carried a gaff cutter rig.*

Centennial is on display in the Cape Ann Museum in Gloucester, Massachusetts.

no cabin and very little storage space and was wholly unsuited for an open ocean crossing.

Grand Banks dories are double-ended boats, which means they are more-or-less pointed at both ends. This is a very seaworthy shape, but it significantly cuts down on carrying capacity. Like all dories, *Centennial* also had a narrow hull with a flat bottom that slams in waves, and no guardrails to give protection at sea. The boat also had only a tiny cockpit and a completely flat deck, leaving only the smallest crawl-space below to get away from bad weather.

Despite these limitations, Alfred Johnson sailed on June 15, 1876, stopping briefly in Nova Scotia to make adjustments to the boat's ballast. On June 25th, he headed east alone. He was sighted several times by passing ships, most of which tried to rescue him. One vessel passed him two bottles of rum, which at least helped to while away his long evenings at sea. Johnson made good progress and averaged around 60 NM (111 km) a day. *Centennial* capsized once during a gale, but his buoyancy compartments kept the boat afloat. Even so, anybody in this situation knows the monumental effort needed to right a boat in rolling seas, unaided.

Johnson made landfall in the small harbor at Abercastle in Wales, on Saturday, August 12th. He rested for a couple of days, then continued to Liverpool, where he arrived on August 21st to a rapturous reception. When asked later in life why he made the crossing, he simply said: "I made that trip because I was a damned fool, just as they said I was."

Despite the boat's limitations, Johnson became the first person to cross the Atlantic, single-handed, from west to east. His boat was brought back to North America intact and is now on display at the Cape Ann Historical Society Museum in Gloucester, Massachusetts.

≈≈≈≈≈≈≈

There is no doubt that the American East Coast fishermen were a hardy lot. Johnson had thrown the gauntlet into the ring, and Thomas Crapo of New Bedford, Massachusetts, picked it up and tried it for size. Crapo was another experienced seaman, but also an opportunist. He had long dreamed of crossing the Atlantic in a small boat, and now he reasoned that: "If I could manage to eclipse all others [then] I could make considerable money by doing so."

Crapo knew exactly what he needed—a boat built along the lines of the local seaworthy whaleboats. He took his ideas to Samuel Mitchell, a local builder, who constructed *New Bedford* according to Crapo's detailed instructions. The sailor tried to keep his plans secret, but once his boat was finished it was difficult to hide his intentions. Once he handed in his notice at work, word spread around New Bedford: "It was the topic of the day, and many shook their heads as much as to say, he must be crazy…"

The *New Bedford* was 19 ft 7 in long (6 m), carefully built to be just a little smaller than Johnson's *Centennial*. The boat was rigged as a two-masted ketch, with leg-of-mutton sails that were easy to handle; it was a well-considered design. Had Crapo succeeded with his plan, he would have set a new record for a solo Atlantic crossing in the smallest boat; with a bit of luck, his dream of making "considerable money" might have been realized.

Thomas Crapo had, however, not considered the formidable Mrs. Crapo. You might have expected her to throw up her hands in horror and do everything she possibly could to stop her husband from embarking on such a hair-brained scheme. But no, Joanna Crapo insisted on coming along. Having a crew member was never part of Crapo's original plan; all along, he had intended to break the Atlantic record for a single-handed crossing. Besides, he had always been worried about the lack of space for one person on the boat—now he had two. But Joanna Crapo was not to be dissuaded; if her husband was going, then she was going too.

Crapo loaded his provisions: 90 lbs of ship's biscuits, 75 lbs of canned meats, 100 gallons of fresh water, plus tea, coffee, and sugar. On May 29, 1877, the husband and wife team set sail from New Bedford. Initially, they made a good start, but stopped briefly in Chatham, Cape Cod, to make minor

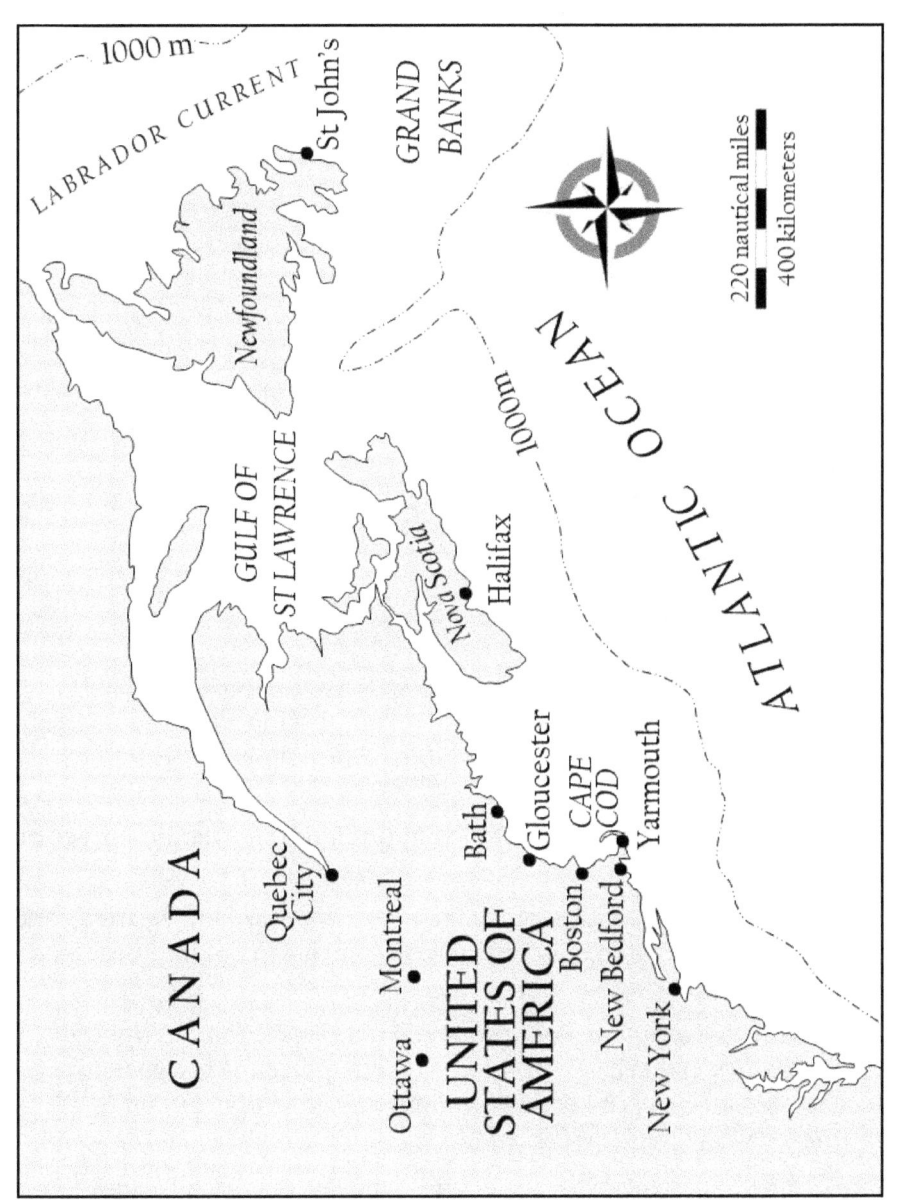

New England and Eastern Canada, showing ports of arrival and departure.

The strongly curved, sheer, shallow draft, and flush deck of the New Bedford are typical of New England whaleboats. The boat had two small cockpits, but no guardrails.

repairs and adjustments. They finally committed to the Atlantic proper on June 2nd.

Ocean sailing in a small open boat is not for the faint-hearted, and Crapo wrote how even the simplest of tasks, such as cooking, becomes a test of nerve and skill:

"As the motion of the boat rendered it unsafe to leave a lighted lamp stove anywhere unattended, my wife placed it between my feet, so the motion of the boat would not have any effect upon it, as no one knows when it will explode."

The Crapos experienced the usual unnerving events that all transatlantic sailors face, regardless of the size of their vessel. They had dense fog over the Grand Banks in the first two weeks, with the haunting sound of horns from ships passing close. They were later visited by a large pod of sperm

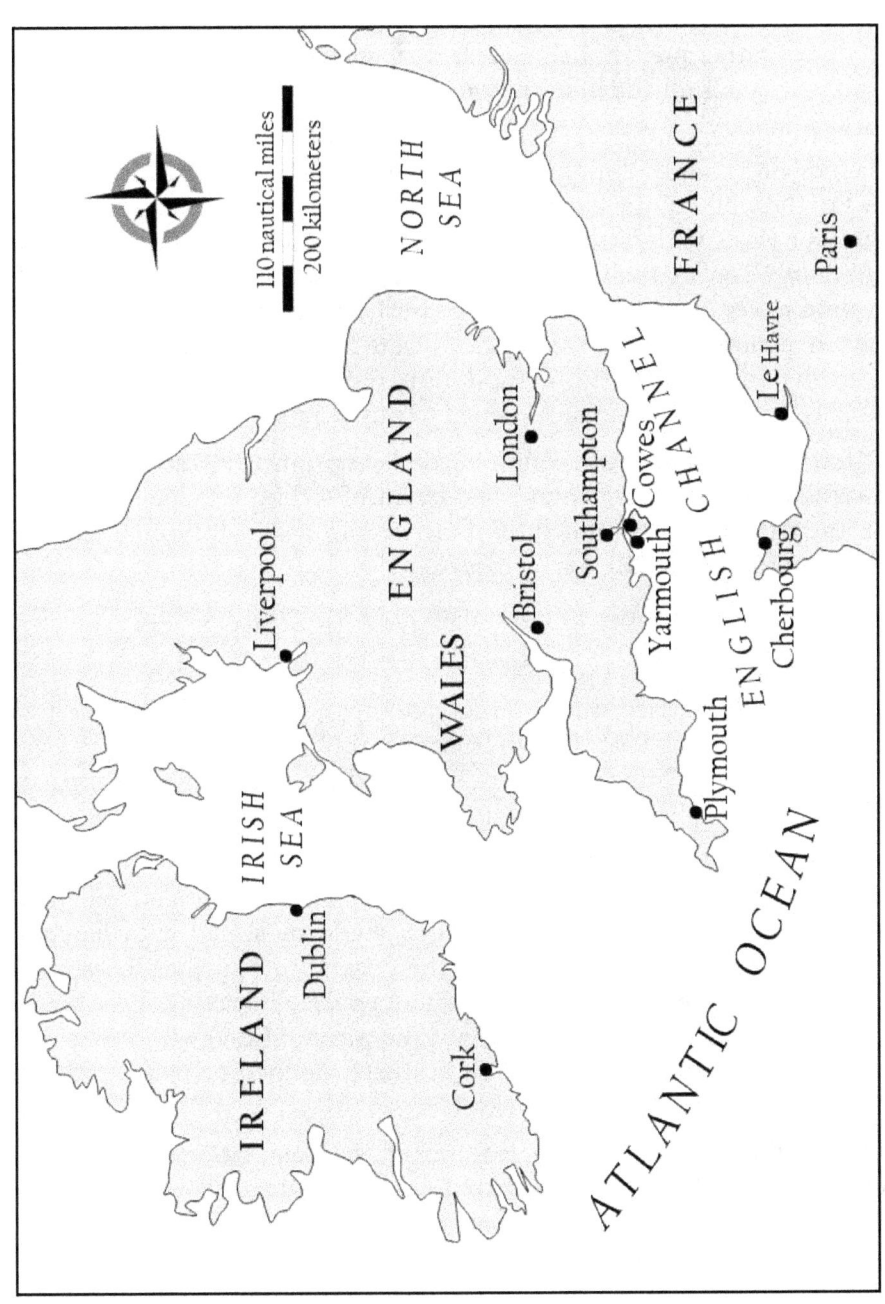

North-western Europe showing ports of arrival and departure in Ireland, England and northern France.

whales; adult males can grow up to 67 ft long (20.5 m) and weigh more than 57 tonnes, and the Crapos understandably became worried: "My wife was very much frightened, and she was not to blame for being so, as our position was rather precarious." Gale force winds, thunderstorms, sunburn, and saltwater boils all added to their discomfort.

It is worth remembering that these open sailboats were intended for day-fishing or a couple of nights at sea at most. With no cabin, the crew was subject to the worst of the weather, 24 hours a day. Their clothing was made of cotton or wool, with oilskin jackets and trousers to keep off at least some of the water. Even so, their clothing underneath became saturated with salt and would never dry properly without a freshwater rinse. Sunburn too was a problem; commercial sunscreen lotions were only developed in the 1930s. Prior to that, sailors relied on zinc lotion and a hat and grew a beard if possible (protection presumably denied to Mrs. Crapo).

After 49 days at sea, the couple made landfall in Penzance, Cornwall. Thomas Crapo never did achieve his dream of sailing the smallest vessel across the Atlantic alone, but his wife went into the history books as the first woman to sail a small boat across.

Clearly Mrs. Crapo was not a woman to be underestimated.

≈≈≈≈≈≈≈

Another year passed and another attempt began, this time by two brothers, William and Asa Andrews from Beverly, Massachusetts. They were determined to beat Crapo's two-handed record by sailing an even smaller boat and commissioned Higgins and Gifford of Gloucester to build a vessel that was shorter by just 7 in (18 cm).

The *Nautilus* too was built specifically for the crossing and was fully decked except for two small cockpits that could be sealed with hatches. This allowed both the helmsman and the crew sitting further forward to stay on deck in bad weather in relative safety, while still leaving space below for provisions and sleeping. Surprisingly, she was not fitted with watertight buoyancy compartments; instead, the brothers pumped or bailed out any water that found its way below decks.

One of the most innovative features of the boat was the sailing rig, which comprised a lateen sail similar to an Arab Dhow. The lateen made sense in a small boat built for the open ocean, for the sail could be reefed or taken in completely from the relative safety of the cockpit, without the need for the crew to go on deck. Nor did the boat fly a foresail from a bowsprit, making the rig much simpler to handle than a gaff rig. However, the very shallow rudder must have made the boat difficult to control in heavy seas.

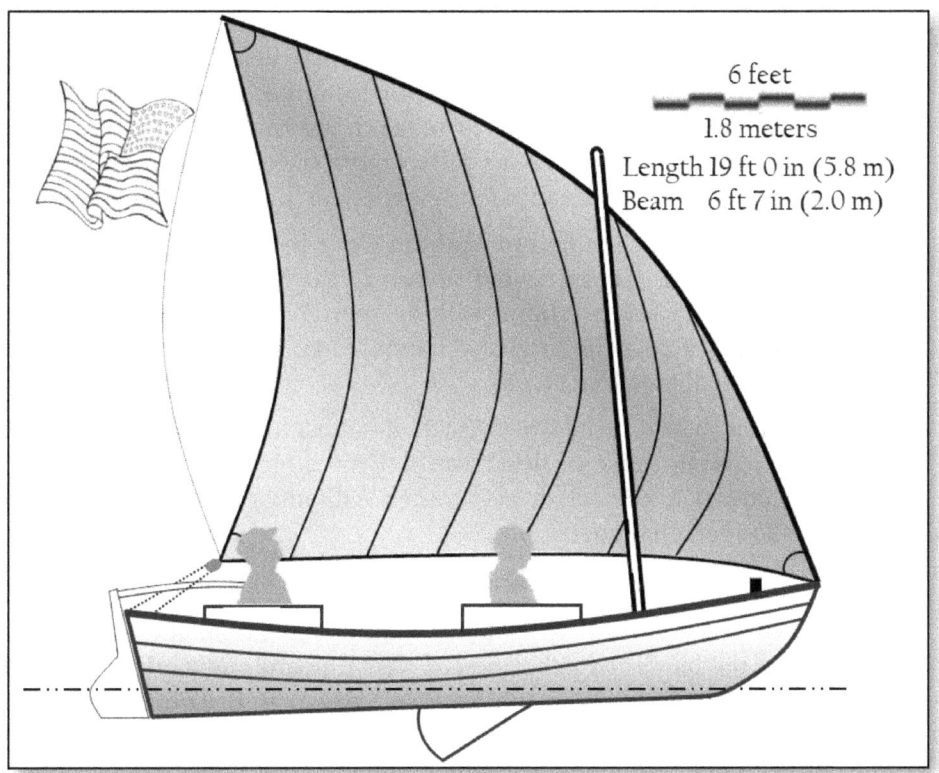

The novel single-mast lateen rig of Nautilus, with twin cockpits. The drop-down centerboard prevented the boat from being blown sideways when sailing.

The brothers left Boston, Massachusetts, on June 7, 1878. This is an ideal time to cross the North Atlantic, for gales are less frequent and the days are at their longest. Despite their perfect start with a light offshore breeze, they experienced a gale on their first night and put into Beverley for repairs. They finally left for the open ocean on June 12th.

William and Asa Andrews experienced the usual challenges in the first few weeks, including gales and whales. William was struck on the head by the heavy wooden boom and claimed he was fortunate not to be killed.

The sailors carried a sextant and were able to take sun sights to determine their position. However, it is not easy taking an accurate positional "fix" when rolling in a small boat at sea, and especially when you are close to sea level. When the opportunity arose, they hailed passing ships to get a precise position.

The brothers reached the halfway stage on July 8th, and a few days later Asa began to cough up blood. A passing ship offered them a bottle of "Friar's

Balsam," which seemed to do the trick and brought immediate relief to his symptoms. Friar's Balsam can still be bought today as an inhalant to help relieve nasal congestion, and as an antiseptic for minor cuts, abrasions, and chapped skin, but it is not intended to be taken internally. It's not clear how the tincture could have helped Asa's rather more serious symptoms but the brothers continued, with Asa apparently experiencing no ill-effects.

The *Nautilus* made landfall in Mullion Cove in Cornwall on July 21st, after 44 days at sea, having sailed about 2,700 NM (5,000 km) at an average speed of 2.5 knots (about walking speed). The brothers sailed on to Falmouth, then across the English Channel to Le Havre in France, where they were reportedly well-received.

Shortly after their return home, Asa died—most likely from tuberculosis that was the leading cause of death in the United States at the end of the nineteenth century. Undeterred, his brother William began to prepare for a new, single-handed challenge.

≈≈≈≈≈≈≈

Until 1880, the contest to sail the Atlantic in the smallest boat was dominated by the hardened fishermen of New England; now others entered the contest. Frederick Norman was born in Norway to British parents, and was a professional seaman who teamed up with his friend, George P. Thomas from Halifax, Nova Scotia; together they bought *Little Western*.

The boat had been built by Higgins & Gifford (the same builder chosen by Thomas Crapo). *Little Western* cost £100 and was 16 ft 7 in (5 m) long, with a relatively wide beam of 6 ft 8 in (2.0 m) and a draft of 2 ft 5 in (0.76 m). The boat was cutter-rigged (with two foresails before the mast) and carried 460 sq ft (43 sq m) of sail—something that would be considered today to be grossly over-canvased, and contemporary drawings show her carrying too much sail for such a small boat.

Like many previous contestants, *Little Western* was another traditional New England lapstrake double-ender with 500 lbs (227 kg) of ballast; lapstrake is a method of building strong but light boats with wide overlapping hull planks. It made sense to use a local design because the New England builders knew how to build these boats well, but these East Coast fishing boats were never designed to make extended voyages at sea.

The crew was experienced and well-prepared. Frederick Norman had served aboard the American warship *USS Trenton*, and George Thomas was also an experienced sailor. They shared the cost of buying and equipping their little cutter; the provisioning included 50 gallons of water, 100 lbs of bread, 50 lbs of canned beef and tongue, 48 cans of canned fruit, 12 of

The lapstrake hull of the Little Western is made from wide overlapping planks, and the cutter rig had twin foresails.

condensed coffee, plus chocolate, milk, corn, oatmeal, dried fruit, and port wine. They cooked with kerosene as well as alcohol and brewed hot coffee twice a day. Quite where they stowed all this food in a boat under 17 ft (5.2 m) is something of a mystery.

The two friends left Gloucester on June 12, 1880. Word soon got around and they were reportedly cheered on by a crowd of around 36,000 people. This is about the capacity of the Fenway Park baseball stadium in Boston and more than the entire population of Gloucester today; this gives you some idea of just how popular these transatlantic voyages had become with the general public.

In the late nineteenth century, many more ships were crossing the Atlantic than today, and it was common for small boat sailors to encounter fishing boats and steamships en route. The unwritten rule of the transatlantic challenge was that you could not leave your boat, but you could pick up supplies and freshwater, get an accurate positional "fix" or simply report that all was well. This was the case with *Little Western* when a week into the voyage, the Cunard steamer *Gallia* came alongside and spoke to the crew. They reported all was well and were making good progress.

Unfortunately, they had spoken too soon. The next day, they encountered headwinds and lost 54 NM (100 km), or about a day's sailing. On June 30th, 17 days into the crossing, they spoke to the steamship *SS Bulgaria*; the captain offered to take them aboard, but they politely declined. Nearly a month later on July 26th, they sighted land—Land's End in Cornwall. They had covered 2,500 NM (4,630 km) in 46 days, an average speed of 2.3 knots. The two friends continued up the English Channel as far as the Isle of Wight, where they disembarked in Cowes on July 28th.

Little Western was taken to London, where she was exhibited at the London Aquarium. Frederick Norman and George Thomas stayed in England for nearly a year, displaying *Little Western* and basking in their glory. These Victorian touring exhibitions certainly pulled in the crowds, and hopefully a little income as well.

On June 15, 1881, the men set sail from London to return to Gloucester. It was reported that: "The Thames embankment was crowded with interested spectators." After a slow passage down the English Channel, they began to realize that sailing east to west against the prevailing winds was a very different proposition, and the limitations of the small, flat-bottomed dory soon became apparent. On July 12th, after weathering a storm for two days, they caught a huge breaking wave broadside, that tossed their little boat on to her side and both men into the water. After this brutal treatment, the boat leaked badly, and they spent hours every day pumping her out. They finally made landfall in Halifax, Nova Scotia, after a tough passage taking 62 days, sailing an average speed of just 1.6 knots (about half walking speed).

The two men succeeded in breaking several records: they beat the Andrews brothers' time for sailing the smallest boat across the Atlantic from west to east, knocking three days off their crossing; when they eventually made it home on September 16, 1881, they became the first to sail both ways across the Atlantic in a boat under 20 ft (6.1 m), beating the size record set by Nikola Primorac in *Citta di Ragusa* by 4 ft (1.2 m).

≈≈≈≈≈≈≈

Public interest in eccentric transatlantic exploits showed little sign of abating and more attempts soon followed. By now, we are getting into boats that were less than 15 ft (4.6 m) long, or what we might call micro-cruisers.

It is worth considering for a moment exactly what this involves:

Boats this small have to be specially designed and built to survive the rigors of an Atlantic crossing, but this was still the late nineteenth century and boatbuilding materials and techniques had changed little for hundreds of years. These micro-cruisers were still built from solid timber (making them heavy for their size), the mast and boom were still cut from solid pine (making them top-heavy), and the sails were hemp or canvas—stiff to handle when dry and a struggle when wet.

There is also the matter of space; small boats are ... well ... small. A 15 ft (4.6 m) long boat will typically have a beam less than 5 ft 6 in (1.7 m), and such low freeboard that you cannot even sit upright below deck. Imagine the physical discomfort of living for weeks on end in a boat smaller than a family station wagon—but without the headroom. A space where you are constantly damp and the incessant motion is unpredictable and jerky.

You can never carry enough water to have the luxury of washing in fresh water, let alone being able to rinse your salt-ridden clothing in anything but seawater. If you are lucky, you can shower and rinse your clothes in the rain, but in the North Atlantic it is going to be a cold shower, and wet clothes take days to dry. Everything you wear and touch becomes salty, damp, and moldy, including your clothing and bedding. The consequences are acute discomfort, leading to painful saltwater boils and a variety of skin complaints. These are the realities of trying to sail the Atlantic in ever smaller boats.

In 1877, Thomas Crapo took 100 gallons of fresh water, 90 lbs of ship's biscuits, and 75 lbs of canned meats. This would have taken up all his space below decks and would also have made his boat heavy; water is by far the heaviest—100 U.S. gallons weighs 836 lbs (380 kg) or more than a third of a tonne (even without the weight of the wooden casks, which each weigh around 100 lbs (45 kg). Crapo must have carried well over half a tonne of provisions, but his boat was 19 ft 7 in (6 m) long. Now try squeezing that into a smaller, lighter boat...

In July 1881, John Traynor and Ivar Olsen managed to do exactly that, together with their kitten. Traynor (a Maine seaman) convinced Olsen (a Scandinavian) that they "could make millions" by sailing the Atlantic in the smallest boat. Together they planned the *City of Bath*, with high hopes.

The boat was another East Coast dory, this time 14 ft (4.27 m) long, 5 ft (1.52 m) wide, and 1 ft 9 in (0.53 m) deep. The boat was built in Georgetown, Maine, and was fully decked over and rigged with a single mast. Traynor and Olsen sailed from Bath, Maine, on July 5, 1881, stopping briefly in Trepassey, Newfoundland; they made landfall in Falmouth, Cornwall, on August 24th with a crossing that took 50 days. From there,

Transatlantic dory City of Bath, Havre, France, 1881, a watercolor by Eugene Grandin (1833-1919), now at the Maine Maritime Museum, Bath.

the two friends sailed to Le Havre in Northern France, where they were met with great excitement before exhibiting the *City of Bath* in Paris, Barcelona, and other European cities.

History does not record what happened to their kitten.

≈≈≈≈≈≈≈

William Andrews was determined not to lose the limelight. He had previously crossed the Atlantic with his brother Asa in *Nautilus*, their 19 ft (5.8 m) dory. Asa died shortly after their return from Europe, but William was determined to continue the small boat challenge alone. He did so in *Dark Secret*, and he found a novel way to finance his voyage by naming his vessel after the theatrical production of his main sponsor.

Andrews was a showman and an astute businessman. He was paid $500 for naming *Dark Secret,* and he signed a contract with his sponsor to tour the United States for 47 weeks at $100 a week plus expenses once he returned from the voyage—that is about $2,500 a week in today's money, so it was a lucrative deal.

Capt. Andrews in the "Dark Secret," at Point of Pines.

He left Point of Pines in Boston on June 17, 1888, and managed to strike a deal with the owners of the pier there to share the revenue from the admission receipts, where he netted himself another $1,400, or around $35,000 at today's inflated prices.

Dark Secret was exceptional, even by the crazy standards of microcruisers of the time. She was just 12 ft 9 in (3.9 m) long and leaked. Not surprisingly, Andrews' 1888 attempt ended prematurely after 61 days at sea when he ran out of water and was taken aboard a passing ship. On September 11, 1888, the BOSTON DAILY GLOBE ran a front-page article that summed up his epic ordeal. What is most telling about the headline is that trouble from barnacles merited a mention on the same line as sharks and whales. In fact, barnacles and growths of other animals and weeds on the bottom of boats are a sailor's nightmare.

Today, sailors paint the bottom of their boats with a copper-rich anti-fouling paint that inhibits unwanted growth. In the nineteenth century, wooden ships were covered with thin copper sheets below the waterline, but this was rarely used on small boats. William Andrews may have used a mixture of pitch, tar, and brimstone, or even various compounds of copper, arsenic, or mercury on the bottom of *Dark Secret*. Whatever he might have used to prevent fouling (if anything at all), it obviously did not work and a colony of marine crustaceans growing on the bottom of his boat would have significantly slowed him down.

Undeterred, Andrews built a new dory, this time a little longer at 15 ft (4.57 m) and named it the *Mermaid*. He intended to have a like-for-like race with Josiah Lawlor, sailing the *Sea*

> **ABANDONED.**
>
> ------
>
> **Captain Andrews and the Dark Secret**
>
> ------
>
> **Return to New York on a Norwegian Bark**
>
> ------
>
> **The Mariner's Story of His Unsuccessful Trip.**
>
> ------
>
> **Two Months and One Day on the Ocean.**
>
> ------
>
> **Sharks, Whales and Barnacles Cause Lots of Trouble.**

The Boston Globe, September 11, 1888.

Sea Serpent (above) and Mermaid (below) were both 15 ft (4.57 m) long. Like many small boats of the period, they both look grossly over-canvassed for such small craft.

Serpent of the same length; this was, of course, all good for publicity and for making money. The boats left the Ocean Pier in Boston on June 17, 1891, and more than 28,000 people came out to watch. As darkness fell, the two men lost sight of each other.

The lookout on the steamship *SS Sobraon* spotted a small boat, 37 days into their voyage. Thinking it held survivors from a shipwreck, the captain closed on the boat, and to his astonishment, he found the *Mermaid* under full sail; William Andrews explained that he was racing from Boston to Land's End in, England. He declined any assistance but asked the captain to forward his logbook to the BOSTON HERALD. (Good for publicity, in the circumstances). Andrews was reported to be in good health and spirits. He did, however, mention that a shark had followed the *Mermaid* for several days.

Meanwhile, Josiah Lawlor was also having close encounters with a marine visitor. That same night, he was woken by a grinding noise coming from outside the hull. Looking over the side, he saw a large fish rubbing itself against the boat. He had encountered sharks before and its presence did not bother him at first, but then it began to gnaw at the back of his boat. Lawlor had a harpoon, but he was afraid he would lose it if he succeeded in stabbing the shark; instead, he lashed a knife to the harpoon thinking that the knife was at least dispensable. By now, the fish was doing serious damage to the *Sea Serpent*, so as a last resort, he wrapped a patent yacht signal (a pyrotechnic rather like a Roman candle) in newspaper, lit it, and threw it at the shark. As soon as the parcel hit the water, the shark let go of the boat and swam towards the pyrotechnic. As the shark seized the package, it ignited; the shark did not bother Lawlor or his boat again.

Sea Serpent made landfall at Coverack, near the Lizard Point in Cornwall, on August 5, 1891. William Andrews was not so fortunate. After the *Mermaid* capsized several times in the mid-Atlantic he decided not to continue, and asked the steamship *SS Elbruz* out of Antwerp in Belgium to take him and his boat aboard. He arrived safely in Europe, where he sold the *Mermaid* for a tidy profit.

A rare early photograph: William Andrews and Sapolin in 1898 after his successful transatlantic crossing to Portugal.

The two adversaries met up in England and planned another race for the next year in even smaller boats, each 14 ft 6 in (4.42 m) long. They left in 1898 with their new boats; Andrews was sailing *Sapolin* and Lawlor was aboard *Christopher Columbus*. However, time was running out for both adventurers; Lawlor was lost at sea, and nothing was ever found of either him or his boat.

Andrews completed the race in *Sapolin*, sailing from New Jersey to Portugal and setting a new west to east record that lasted for a remarkable 73 years. He tried again in the even smaller 14 ft (4.27 m) *Phantom Ship*, but he failed after 27 days; it is difficult to believe, but he shortened the boat to 12 ft (3.66 m) and renamed her the *Doree*; in 1899 he aborted his voyage after just three weeks.

William Andrews was not a man to give up lightly. He married in 1901 and started another transatlantic passage—this time with his bride. His new boat, the *Flying Dutchman*, was another dory 16 ft 5 in (5 m) long, but it proved to be his last voyage. 85 NM (158 km) out from Boston, the couple encountered the *SS Durano* and they reported that all was well; that was the last sighting of William Andrews, his bride, or the *Flying Dutchman*.

≈≈≈≈≈≈≈

A remarkable single-handed Atlantic crossing was made in 1899 by another Gloucester fisherman, Howard Blackburn. He sailed from west to east in his 30 ft (9.14 m) sloop, *Great Western*, and reached Gloucester in England after 62 days.

Howard Blackburn (1859–1932)
An indefatigable veteran of Cape Horn and two Atlantic crossings, Blackburn's 30 ft sloop Great Western that he sailed alone to Gloucester, England.

What makes Blackburn's achievement especially noteworthy is that 16 years previously, he lost all his fingers, several toes, and both thumbs to the first joint from frostbite after losing contact with his mother ship while fishing in winter over the Grand Banks. Blackburn also took a vessel around Cape Horn to the Klondike gold fields, and later successfully sailed the

Atlantic again. His sloop *Great Republic* and dory *America* are now on display at the Cape Ann Museum, in Gloucester.

The most famous of the early sailors was undoubtedly Joshua Slocum. While his boat is really too big to be considered making a "small boat" crossing of the Atlantic, it is difficult not to acknowledge his remarkable achievements in long-distance solo sailing. He was born in Nova Scotia, Canada in 1844, but later became a naturalized U.S. citizen. As a young boy, he ran away from home at age 14 and signed on a fishing schooner as a cabin boy, then worked as an ordinary seaman on merchant ships. By the age of 25, he was a ship's captain sailing the Pacific out of San Francisco. He married and had seven children.

After many adventures and narrow escapes at sea, he was given a derelict 36 ft 9 in (11.2 m) gaff-rigged oyster boat by a friend in Fairhaven, Massachusetts; the boat was called the *Spray*. Slocum was out of work at the time and broke, so he rebuilt the boat over a 13-month period for just $553.62. After he sailed the *Spray*, he found that one of her remarkable features was the boat's ability to sail a straight course unattended.

Slocum found that he could balance the boat on most points of sailing by adjusting or reefing the sails, then lashing the helm fast. A boat that kept

Joshua Slocum's Spray sailed a straight course for long periods.

a straight course was a huge advantage for a solo sailor who was about to embark on a long and ambitious voyage.

Slocum left Boston on April 24, 1895 and visited his boyhood haunts in Canada over the early summer. He finally left Sambro Island near Halifax, on July 3rd, and headed for Gibraltar, which he reached on August 4th. He intended to sail alone around the world in an easterly direction and he left Gibraltar in late summer for the Mediterranean. He soon found that pirates made that route too dangerous, so he backtracked to Gibraltar, then sailed across the Atlantic again to South America. He arrived in Rio de Janeiro on November 5, 1895, and deservedly takes the record for a solo double-crossing of the Atlantic within a little over 6 months.

Slocum went on to become the first person to sail alone around the world, a voyage that took him more than three years. He sailed over 40,000 NM (74,080 km) but his return to Newport, Rhode Island went almost unnoticed. He published his book, *Sailing Alone Around the World* in 1899 to enthusiastic reviews. Arthur Ransome (the English author of *Swallows and Amazons* among others) declared that: "Boys who do not like this book ought to be drowned at once."

Slocum embarked on successful and lucrative speaking tours, but after a few years, he found he was unable to settle ashore and he sailed the *Spray* to the Caribbean every winter. His mental health began to deteriorate in old age and on November 14, 1909, he sailed again for his winter sojourn; he was never heard of again and was declared legally dead in 1924.

≈≈≈≈≈≈≈

As the world moved into the twentieth century, attempts to sail the Atlantic in ever-smaller boats seemed to dwindle to a halt. People were certainly making the crossing in bigger boats, but the appetite to sail across in the smallest of boats seems to have been satiated—at least for a few decades.

There are probably several reasons why this should be the case. The loss of Josiah Lawlor in 1898, of William Andrews and his wife in 1901, and Joshua Slocum in 1909, brought home to the tightly-knit coastal community of New England that sailing the Atlantic, especially in small boats, is a perilous pursuit. Sponsors too became wary of becoming associated with the demise of some of their protégés, and they would certainly have mourned the loss of their investment.

By the early twentieth century, sailors were also up against the limits of the materials and technologies of the day. Smaller boats could certainly be built, but they became proportionally heavier as they became smaller, therefore you inevitably reach a point where the boat is simply too heavy to be seaworthy, and too small to carry adequate provisions. Freshwater, for example, still had to be carried in traditional wooden or metal casks, rather than in today's plastic tanks and bottles. It is difficult to see how all this could fit into a boat that was no more than 13 ft (3.9 m) long.

Nobody sailed in the sub-5-meter category in the early years of the twentieth century, but in 1904, the Norwegian Ole (Abe) Brude took his home-built boat from Norway to Gloucester, Massachusetts. The *Vraad* was made from ⅛ in (3 mm) boilerplate, 18 ft (5.5 m) long and 8 ft (2.4 m) wide, and was completely decked over and looked more like a submarine than a sailing boat. The helmsman steered from inside the hull and the crew rarely came out on deck for fear of slipping into the water. Brude managed to squeeze a crew of three into the boat and they carried enough provisions for six months, including 450 gallons (1,703 liters) of water, which alone weighed more than 2 tonnes.

The Vraad under full sail crossing the Atlantic (left), and (right) looking a little worse for wear, having been washed up on a beach in Gloucester in January 1905.

The *Vraad* left Norway on June 27, 1904 (a good month for sailing) and arrived in America in January 1905 (a terrible month for sailing). A few days before they arrived, their rudder fell off during a storm and they sat out the brutal conditions, rolling and pitching in their floating tube until the *Vraad* was washed up on the beach. They waited for the tide to go out, then the crew crawled out of the hull onto dry land. They sailed more than 3,240 NM (6,000 km), at an average speed of less than 1 knot—at that speed, they certainly qualify for some sort of slow-boat small-boat cruising award.

≈≈≈≈≈≈≈

The second decade of the twentieth century also brought the reality of a global war, and a dark cloud loomed over Europe for years, casting its long shadow across the Atlantic to the United States. In time, World War I became a distant memory, and other European sailors were tempted to make the crossing.

One remarkable voyage was made by Teresia Fava, an Italian. He sailed from Naples to Newfoundland in 1926 in his home-built 20 ft (6.1 m) cutter; the boat was completely decked over except for a small center cockpit. What is remarkable about this crossing was not the boat, but the sailor; Fava had lost both legs during World War I.

Another European was the German, Franz Romer. On the last day of March 1928, he cast off from the Canary Islands for a 58-day voyage to St Thomas in the Virgin Islands. His choice was not a sailing boat, but a sailing kayak. The 29-year-old adventurer had wanted to be the first to fly solo across the Atlantic, but Charles Lindbergh beat him to that record the previous year. Instead, Romer decided to become the first person to cross the Atlantic in a kayak.

His Klepper kayak was 21 ft 6 in (6.6 m) long, 3 ft 3 in (1 m) wide, and just 1 ft 6 in (0.46 m) deep. It was made from a rubber sheet stretched over a wooden frame and sported a small mast, 8 ft (2.4 m) high with a simple square sail. With only 6 in (15 cm) of freeboard, he knew it would be a wet trip. Romer packed practically all the space below deck with provisions,

Franz Romer at sea in his Klepper sailing kayak.

including 75 gallons (284 liters) of water, 600 cans of food, and a sack of lemons. He only had room to sit, and when he needed to stretch his legs, he had to stand up in this very unstable craft.

The voyage started in Lisbon, Portugal; by the time Romer arrived in the Canary Islands, the muscles in his legs had atrophied and he had painful boils on his lower limbs and backside. This was only a foretaste of much worse to come. The kayak offered no protection from the elements, and he was soaked for practically the whole crossing. On arrival in the West indies, his legs were so stiff that he could barely move them. He had no shade sitting in the canoe, and by the time he made landfall in St Thomas, every exposed piece of skin was blistered.

Romer landed in the Virgin Islands, then sailed on to Puerto Rico. In September 1928, he was caught at sea in a category 5 hurricane, with sustained winds of 140 knots (260 km/h). Hurricane San Felipe Segundo was one of the most destructive in North American history and over 2,500 people lost their lives. Franz Romer had no chance offshore in these conditions in a lightweight kayak, and neither he nor his craft was ever found.

≈≈≈≈≈≈≈

In the late spring of 1939, a 38-year-old Briton called Harry Young set out from New York in his home-built boat, just 13 ft 9 in (4.2 m) long. It is not clear exactly why he made the passage, but there were rumors that Young had got into trouble in New York and needed to leave town quietly. It does not seem a very convincing justification for his voyage because there are many other ways of leaving town quietly that would have been quicker, easier, and safer than building a boat and setting off across the Atlantic. But what we do know is that he did not even bother to give his boat a name, neither was it registered nor insured. Maybe he just did not like paperwork.

On leaving New York City, Young sailed into easterly winds—they were "on the nose" in sailor-speak. This is always the most challenging angle, and sailing "close to the wind" always highlights a boat's weaknesses. His homemade hull was so skewed when it was built that he found it almost impossible to turn into the wind to tack. Even though the boat had an iron keel, it weighed only 200 lbs (90.7 kg), or about 10 percent of the weight of the boat. The inadequate ballast caused the boat to be "tender"; in other words, it heeled excessively in anything more than a light breeze—not an encouraging feature for a sailing boat facing the Atlantic. Even so, Young stuck it out for 21 days before turning back.

There was clearly something wrong with the design and construction of his boat. He could have altered the sail plan or increased the weight of the keel, or perhaps even added a short bowsprit; any of these changes would have improved the sailing qualities of his boat. Instead, he relied on liquid ballast. Harry Young's innovative solution was to store large quantities of red wine and cans of beer under the cabin sole, which was then firmly screwed in place in case of a capsize.

Young set out again from New York City in the summer of 1940; this was at the height of the German blockade of the United Kingdom, with U-boats keeping a close eye on anything that floated in the North Atlantic. His boat still did not sail or steer well, so when the wind picked up, he simply lowered the sails, deployed his sea anchor to limit drifting, and retired below to check his wine and beer cellar until the wind abated. This of course used up his ballast, so the more he drank, the less seaworthy his boat became.

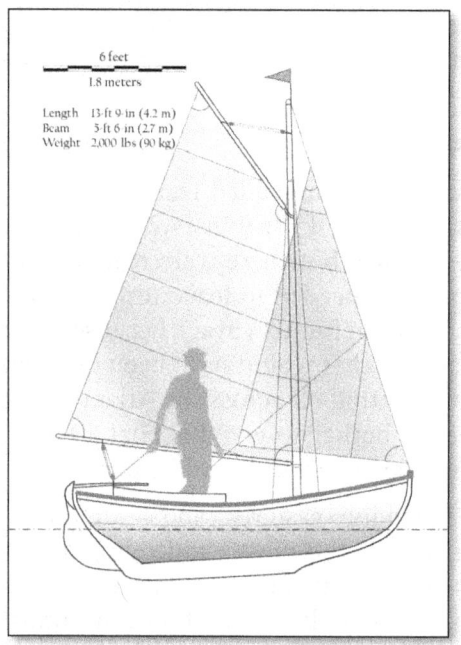

Unlike other boats that have attempted the Atlantic, Harry Young's boat seems under-canvased.

On July 13th, he sighted the island of Flores in the Azores. Young had sailed over 2,300 NM (4,260 km) in 39 days, an average speed of under 2.5 knots. He decided (perhaps wisely) not to sail across the Bay of Biscay, so he loaded his boat onto a Portuguese freighter and continued to war-torn England in a bigger and much safer vessel; sadly, there is no record of what happened to him next.

It was a bold (if rather foolhardy) venture; Harry Young did not complete a full transatlantic crossing, so he does not strictly qualify for the record books. Nevertheless, he matched the determination and resolve of the earlier pioneers, and his pocket-sized sloop opened the doors after World War II for many more attempts across the Atlantic in ever-smaller boats.

The Great Space Race

The post-war years saw a boom in private boat ownership in Europe and North America. Most people were happy to potter around on the weekends with maybe a two-week cruise in summer. But this was not for everyone, and the late 1940s and early 1950s saw more attempts to sail the Atlantic in ever-smaller boats.

The first was in 1949 in *Nova Espero*, "New Hope" in Esperanto (and Spanish for that matter). The brothers Stanley and Colin Smith were British Royal Air Force pilots during World War II and based in Canada for their flight training. After hostilities were over, they decided to return with ambitious ideas. They sailed from England on the *SS Aquitania* in March 1949 and spent most of the crossing in their tiny cabin designing a boat to make their planned return voyage across the Atlantic. Their father was a boatbuilder in Yarmouth on the Isle of Wight in southern England, so they had grown up with small boats and had a good idea of what was involved.

The brothers arrived in Halifax, Nova Scotia, with £500 (worth US $665 in 1949) and immediately started to build their boat in the basement of a local chapel—it took them just three months. The boat was 20 ft (6.1 m) long, with a beam of 6 ft 3 in (1.9 m), and a shallow draft of 2 ft 10 in (0.86 m). *Nova Espero* was strongly built with a clinker (lapstrake) hull and carried a 110 lb (50 kg) cast iron keel. They ran out of money before they finished, so they left the boat open and lashed an upturned dinghy on deck to act as a make-shift cabin; this gave them 3 ft 6 in (1.1 m) of headroom in the "cabin."

Nova Espero was really more of a day sailer, best suited to cruising protected waters such as the Western Solent where they grew up—she was certainly not a boat that most sailors would choose to cross an ocean. But the brothers were young, keen, and experienced—and besides, they had no money left to pay for a passage home.

Stanley and Colin Smith left Halifax in July 1949 with 28 U.S. gallons (106 liters) of water, powdered milk, dried biscuits, potatoes, and lots of sugar. They slept on the floor of the cabin in sleeping bags that were wet most of the time. As Thomas Crapo had done previously, they cooked with a simple Primus stove wedged between their knees. They had a sextant for navigation and an old aircraft compass; they also took a portable radio for time checks—but it never worked, so they tossed it over the side. Because they were short of funds, they could not afford a sea anchor, a chronometer (an accurate ship's clock used for navigation), or even oilskins, making themselves woefully under-equipped for an Atlantic crossing.

The summer of 1949 in England is known for its record-breaking temperatures, marred only by thunderstorms in mid-July. Unfortunately, the same balmy conditions did not extend to the mid-Atlantic, and the two brothers experienced bad weather for much of their crossing, including a full-blown violent storm.

Traditionally, conditions at sea are graded on the Beaufort Scale based on wind speed, which also defines the likely sea state according to the speed of the wind. This is particularly useful because it is the sea conditions and not the actual wind speed that poses the greatest risk to vessels at sea. A full gale is classified as a force 8, with wind speeds between 34 and 40 knots (62-74 km/h). A force 11 is classified as a violent storm, just one scale below hurricane-strength winds, with wind speeds of 56-63 knots (103-117 km/h), accompanied by waves 37-52 ft (11.5-16 m) high. These were the conditions experienced by Stanley and Colin Smith in the mid-Atlantic, with waves building to the height of a four-story apartment block.

The winds moderated as they approached the Irish coast; Colin was knocked overboard during a squall, but Stanley skillfully turned the boat around and picked him up. They were then becalmed for five days off southern Ireland and were down to their last 2.6 U.S. gallons (10 liters) of water. They were sighted by a French trawler, that generously topped up their tanks and gave them fresh fish and bread.

Unbelievably, the two sailors had not told anyone of their intentions, not even their family: "We didn't want anyone to know we were sailing across the Atlantic because we didn't want to worry our parents." Colin later admitted. "It never occurred to us that anyone would be interested in our journey."

By the time they got to England, it turned out that a lot of people became extremely interested. As they sailed up the English Channel, they were met by a Royal Navy destroyer flying a huge banner saying "Welcome Home." They arrived in Dartmouth, Devon, on August 18th, after 43 days; they had sailed 2,390 NM (4,426 km) at an average speed of 2.3 knots. Thousands of people lined the harbor wall to greet them. They later sailed up the English Channel to their home port of Yarmouth—the two local boys had finally returned.

Stanley later admitted that they were "never more frightened in our lives" than when they saw the huge number of people who greeted them wherever they stopped. The tabloid newspaper, the DAILY EXPRESS, made them their "News Story of the Year," and the paper took *Nova Espero* up to Fleet Street to show to the public.

The Nova Espero arrives off Yarmouth, Isle of Wight.
The dinghy used as a cabin can be seen lashed on deck.
Photo © Colin Smith

After the voyage, Colin settled down on the Isle of Wight where his father and grandfather had been boatbuilders. He lectured in yacht design and built the popular 15 ft (4.6 m) pug-nosed pocket sailing cruiser called the West Wight Potter. He died in February 2018. In 1951, Stanley sailed back to Canada in *Nova Espero* with a friend, Charles Violet. They re-rigged the boat with two masts and built a proper cabin—a wise decision; the return trip took them nearly 18 weeks. Stanley eventually settled in Denmark, where he died in 1979.

≈≈≈≈≈≈≈

The year the Smith brothers returned to England, the German research chemist Paul Müller was living in East Berlin, then under Russian occupation. He complained there was "no work, no money, and little food" so he decided he would start a new life in Argentina with his 18-year-old daughter Aga (Agatha). He planned to get there by sailing.

Müller had "form" in transatlantic adventures. In 1928, he sailed his 18 ft (5.5 m) boat, *Aga*, from Hamburg to Cuba, and then on to Florida. It was an inauspicious arrival, and he was blown ashore at New Smyrna.

He repaired *Aga* and continued, but was caught in a storm off the coast of Charleston, South Carolina, where he was blown ashore again. This time the damage was profoundly serious, and he decided that his boat was irreparably damaged. Fearing he might not be rescued, Müller burned the wreck to attract attention, and he was picked up by a Government liquor patrol vessel—this was at the height of alcohol prohibition in the United States. The generous people of Charleston took pity on Müller and raised enough money to allow him to build a replica. He headed for New York in *Aga II,* but the boat lost its mast off Cape Hatteras, and he was towed ashore.

When Müller left on his second Atlantic crossing in 1949, he was 63 years old and in poor health. Together with his daughter, he sailed his 16 ft (4.88 m) boat, *Berlin,* out of the Baltic, into the North Sea, and south into the English Channel. It was a voyage fraught with risk as the region had not been fully cleared of mines from World War II. In fact, the authorities believe there are roughly 80,000 unexploded mines still in just the Baltic Sea today. However, the real danger came not from the unexploded military ordinance, but from himself; Müller was rescued nine times in the 260 NM (481 km) section between Weymouth in southern England and Waterford in southern Ireland. Here they were towed into the harbor by the local lifeboat on January 8, 1950. It was certainly an achievement to have survived the 130-mile (241 km) open stretch of water between England and Ireland in mid-winter in such a small boat. But overall the voyage had been a disaster—with Müller falling overboard twice.

Undeterred, father and daughter sailed south to Portugal and on to West Africa. Just 13 days out of Freetown in Sierra Leone, Müller became seriously ill; as he lay in his bunk unable to move, local villagers came aboard and stole everything they could carry. To escape, the indefatigable Aga cut the anchor rope and headed back out to sea. That night, July 3rd, Müller died aboard; with no anchor, Aga was forced to run the boat up on a beach on the Liberian coast and seek help.

Afterward, she returned to Ireland and was reunited with her mother, and she later became a journalist with the IRISH PRESS in Dublin.

≈≈≈≈≈≈≈

The end of World War II brought a range of new materials and technologies into popular use, and boat building was revolutionized. Plywood and glass reinforced polyester (GRP) was used for hulls, extruded aluminum for masts and booms, stainless steel produced rust-free fittings, Terylene and Dacron were great improvements over canvas for sails, nylon and polypropylene replaced cotton and hemp ropes that tended to stretch and rot. Freeze-dried food took up less space, and even water could be carried in lightweight stainless steel or plastic tanks. Intrepid adventurers were able to use these new materials to build ever-smaller and ever-lighter boats to tackle the North Atlantic.

In 1952, Patrick Ellam and Colin Mudie set off east to west in the *Sopranino*, 19 ft 1 in (5.8 m) overall with a beam of 5 ft 9 in (1.75 m), and weighing just 0.7 tonne. The perceived wisdom of the day was that boats should be strongly built to withstand the enormous forces of the sea. Ellam theorized that if you built a boat light enough, then it would rise over the waves and yield to heavy seas, and would therefore not have to be so heavily constructed; *Sopranino* was his experiment.

The boat was designed by the well-established yacht designer, Laurent Giles, and it became famous as the first example of an offshore micro-cruiser/racer. The boat was light enough to be towed behind a family car and many of its revolutionary design features have since found their way into mainstream yacht construction. For example, instead of a weighted swinging or lifting keel (to give the boat stability), the "fin and bulb keel" was made removable; the cockpit was self-draining and could empty quickly if any water found its way aboard; the boat was also rigged as a Bermudian cutter, which was a modern style rig using a triangular-shaped mainsail.

On the morning of September 6, 1951, Ellam and Mudie slipped quietly out of Falmouth Harbor on the west coast of England and laid a course south for the Canaries, then picked up the Trade Winds to the West Indies. They intended to sail to New York, with frequent stops along the way. Their successful voyage took over a year and they sailed approximately 8,600 NM (15,927 km); they inevitably encountered gales, calms, and even waterspouts. Ellam proved his theory that has helped revolutionize the construction of small boats that can safely cross oceans in the hands of a competent crew.

Ellam went on to become a leading figure in offshore racing, and Mudie made a successful career as a boat designer. Some years ago, *Sopranino* was discovered decaying in a boatyard in Newport, Rhode Island; she was bought for $1 and shipped back to the UK. The boat has since been restored and when not sailing in the Solent, she can be seen in the Classic Boat Museum in Cowes on the Isle of Wight.

Another micro-cruising pioneer was Jean Lacombe, a Parisian leather worker with no sailing experience. In 1955, he made a solo crossing from Toulon, France in his 18 ft (5.5 m) *Hippocampe* ("Seahorse"). He first sailed

Golif used the relatively new glass reinforced polyester (GRP).

to Gibraltar, then to the Canaries, and finally Puerto Rico. The crossing took him 68 days before sailing on to New York.

Lacombe entered the first Observer Single-handed Transatlantic Race (OSTAR) in the 21 ft (6.4 m) *Cap Horn* in 1960—he was the smallest of five entries and came last after a 74-day crossing. He sailed four years later in the second OSTAR in a boat of the same length, *Golif*, which was the first production small cruiser to be made from GRP. Again, Lacombe was the smallest entrant, but this time he placed 7th out of 14 boats on corrected time. Thousands of *Golif* cruising sailboats were built during the 1960s and Lacombe did a lot to popularize sailing in France.

≈≈≈≈≈≈≈

The exploits of Patrick Ellam, Colin Mudie, and Jean Lacombe did much to introduce modern materials and new design ideas into sailboat construction during the '50s and '60s, but the Atlantic space race took on a whole new perspective with Robert Manry, a copy editor on a newspaper in Cleveland, Ohio.

By all appearances Manry was a regular kind of all-American guy; he was happily married to Victoria, they had a daughter, a son, a dog, a cat, and a car. He also had a boat, which he saw advertised in 1958 in his local paper: "SAILBOAT, 13½ ft. *Old Town*, needs some repair, cheap." Those critical words, "needs some repair," can mean very different things with boats. In Manry's case, they really meant "needs a considerable amount of rebuilding." The hull had two long splits above the waterline, two dozen broken hull ribs, dry rot in the hull and the centerboard case, the deck was worn, and the sails too threadbare to be usable. Surprisingly, Bob Manry decided this really was the boat for him and he haggled the price down to $160; the boat was nearly 30 years at the time and even in 1958 dollars, this seems quite a lot of money for a small, derelict sailboat.

The *Whitecap* sailboat is 13 ft 6 in (4.1 m) long with a beam of 5 ft 6 in (1.7 m) and weighs just 500 lbs (226 kg); they named her *Tinkerbelle*. The construction was overlapping plywood panels (lapstrake) with a hinged wooden centerboard that could be lowered to improve sailing abilities; this took her shallow draft of 9 in (0.23 m) to 2 ft 6 in (0.76 m). The boat had no weighted keel to help keep her upright, but this was unnecessary as this was a small dinghy only ever intended to be used for a gentle afternoon's sail in protected waters, preferably on a lake or (very) sheltered coastal waters.

Courtesy: Cleveland Memory Project

The original Whitecap dinghy used in Bob Manry's "cruiser" conversion.

Manry worked for nine months over the winter of 1958/59 before *Tinkerbelle* was ready for day-sailing on their local lake. It gave the family huge enjoyment for three seasons, then he decided to make the boat more suitable for camping trips. He converted *Tinkerbelle* logically, with thoughtfulness and care. He built a small cabin, but this added weight and windage to what was designed to be a very light boat. It was not the prettiest of conversions, but it allowed his family to sit inside the cabin. He also rebuilt the boat's cockpit to make it self-draining in the event of a capsize. In fact, he took great care to make sure the boat would remain watertight even if it rolled completely over; in his words, he wanted the boat "to have the storm-weathering properties of a corked bottle."

He next replaced the wooden centerboard with a steel plate weighing 100 lbs (45 kg) to give *Tinkerbelle* more stability, but this also added weight and stress to the lightweight hull. He fitted a new mast, sails, rigging, navigation lights, compass, and countless other pieces of gear that turned his day sailer into … well … a day sailer with a cabin and lots of new equipment. With a freshly-painted white hull, red deck, and varnished cabin, Manry was proud of his transformation; he was undoubtedly right when he declared: "no other boat like her existed anywhere in the world."

He only sailed the transformed *Tinkerbelle* for one summer before a friend suggested to Manry that they should sail his 25 ft (7.6 m) sloop across the Atlantic together. This had always been one of Manry's lifelong dreams and he jumped at the chance. He wrote to his executive editor requesting a leave of absence, which was granted. Unfortunately, his friend was only half-serious, and Manry was totally disheartened when the plan fell through. But this started him thinking and he looked at *Tinkerbelle* with new eyes. As he once said: "There is no dream so large that it cannot fit into a tiny boat…"

Well, Bob Manry had a big dream and a very small boat.

Manry was familiar with the voyages of the *Little Western* and *Sea Serpent* two generations before (see chapter *Big Oceans, Little Boats*), with Atlantic crossings in rowing boats, an inflatable dinghy, and even an amphibious jeep (see chapter *Atlantic Auto Race*). He reasoned that if an aquatic auto could traverse the broad ocean, *Tinkerbelle* could do it too. His lightweight dinghy was totally unsuitable for what he proposed, and it was a hare-brained idea. But he only had to remind himself of what others had achieved to reassure himself that it was possible to make a safe crossing in a totally unsuitable vessel.

Manry left Falmouth, Massachusetts, on June 1, 1965. It was a good time to leave but he suspected there would be trouble over the horizon—in his naiveté, he just did not realize exactly how much trouble. He was awakened one morning by the *USS Tench*—the submarine had surfaced dangerously close to his boat; he was badly stung by a Portuguese-man-of-war and swept overboard on more than one occasion. He also suffered the usual list of gear failures and had to repair a broken rudder in mid-ocean—something which is notoriously difficult to do, especially when alone. (It took him two days whilst drifting to his sea anchor).

The mind can play powerful tricks and single-handed sailors have long experienced fantasies. During long voyages, sleep deprivation, loneliness, fear, and exhaustion can wreak havoc on a lone sailor, and Manry had his share of visions and hallucinations. He wrote about seeing an imaginary island in mid-ocean that was so real that he tried to steer around it. One evening he was convinced that two convicted murderers were in his cabin, waiting to shoot him. He became distraught when he thought he heard the voice of his young son below. Convinced that he had to save his son, he threw open the cabin hatch armed only with a spotlight, hoping to blind his attackers and wrestle their gun away before they could kill him.

Robert Manry sailing Tinkerbelle

Other solo sailors recall having imaginary shipmates shaking them awake at night, only to find they are minutes away from running aground or on a collision course with a freighter. Gerry Spiess sailed the Atlantic solo in 1978 (see page 49) and went on to make a five-month single-handed crossing of the Pacific in 1981. To help him overcome the crippling loneliness of his long voyage, he created an imaginary shipmate to sail with him. Spiess recalls that his companion disappeared the moment he docked in Sydney, and years later he still became emotional when recalling the experience.

Back in the real world, Manry was astonished to be tracked down in mid-ocean by an enterprising journalist who cleverly "scooped" his story, to the chagrin of his colleagues on his local Ohio newspaper, the PLAIN DEALER. On his arrival in Falmouth, England after 78 days, *Tinkerbelle* became the smallest boat to cross the Atlantic. His story became a media frenzy. He was accompanied by an armada of small boats and reportedly 50,000 cheering spectators. Manry had embarked on his voyage with only his family knowing his full intentions and he had not expected his adventure to change his whole life.

After a brief stay in England with his family, they returned home aboard the *RMS Queen Mary*. Manry made several appearances on TV shows, but never went back to his job as a newspaper copy editor. Instead, he concentrated on writing his book and giving speaking tours. In this respect, his life of traveling and lecturing differed little from what his New England countrymen had experienced nearly a century previously. Tragically four years after his voyage, his wife Virginia was killed in an automobile accident and Manry lost all interest in writing a second book.

Manry re-married, but died of a heart attack on February 21, 1971, just four months after his wedding; he was 52 years old. A small park in Willowick, Ohio, where he lived is named after him. *Tinkerbelle* is now on display at the Crawford Auto Aviation Museum of the Western Reserve Historical Society, in Cleveland, Ohio.

≈≈≈≈≈≈≈

John Riding was an experienced sailor from Southport in Merseyside, England with grand plans to beat Manry's record. He applied to enter the 1963 Transatlantic Yacht Race from Newport, Rhode Island to the Nab Tower off the Isle of Wight, but the organizers refused his entry on the grounds that his boat was too small.

Riding had built his 12 ft (3.66 m)-sloop himself and her name described her shape perfectly. The *Sea Egg* could not have been more different from Bob Manry's *Tinkerbelle*. Riding's boat was beamy, pug-nosed, and with a pronounced "tumblehome" (where the maximum beam of the hull curves inwards at deck level). Even the cabin was rounded, making the boat look for all the world like a giant egg, capable of shrugging off the worst of seas. Small windows, plenty of grab rails, and a well-designed self-steering system added up to a carefully designed micro-cruiser, ready to take on the Atlantic.

Riding left Plymouth in Cornwall on September 1, 1964 and laid a course south and then west for Bermuda. His diet comprised a limited menu of canned meat, canned porridge, and occasional sausages. His long voyage across the Atlantic was broken with a stopover in the Azores and it passed without much incident until three days before the end when his boat was surrounded by three inquisitive whales. "They looked to me as if they meant business." he wrote. "I took out a World War I .32 revolver and fired shots in front of them. Then I took out a 6-foot harpoon I picked up in the Azores and prodded them until they went away." Fortunately, the cetaceans did not take offense and left him alone.

He was spotted by a U.S. Navy research ship off the coast of Bermuda; the crew radioed ashore for assistance, and his engineless *Sea Egg* was taken in tow by a local boatman. Riding had broken the world record for the smallest boat crossing of the Atlantic. Unfortunately, it was not the only thing he broke—after surviving the voyage unscathed, he slipped in a shower while ashore and fractured his leg.

Riding continued into the Pacific, and by 1973, he had sailed as far as Kawau Island on the north-east coast of New Zealand. He expected to cross the Tasman Sea in about 66 days. However, he never arrived in Sydney, Australia. Riding and his little sloop had disappeared without a trace. The seaworthiness of the *Sea Egg* was not in doubt and Riding was an experienced sailor. So, what could have happened? Possibilities include being run down by a ship or attacked by a predator, or becoming disabled through losing the mast, a keel, or the rudder and drifting helplessly until food and water ran out; mental instability, hallucinations, or suicide are possible but considered unlikely given Riding's proficiency and past achievements.

≈≈≈≈≈≈≈

Two years after Riding set his new Atlantic record, an Irish-American named Bill Verity took on the challenge, sailing west to east. Verity was inspired by the fabled story of St. Brendan and his fellow monks, who some historians believe might have sailed to North America in the eighth century (see chapter *The History Men*). Verity knew that academics had no proof that the saintly sailor had made the crossing, but he wanted to show it was at least possible. This seems a flimsy justification for his voyage because there had been plenty of crossings in small vessels to show that a transatlantic crossing was perfectly possible. But being of Irish descent, he felt a close affinity with the mariner-monk, a fellow Kerryman.

Verity drew up a list of priorities for his boat: it should be small, seaworthy, and comfortable. You can usually get any two of these in a sailing boat, but all three are difficult, especially as he settled on an overall length of 12 ft (3.66 m) and a beam of 5 ft (1.5 m). He built the hull himself using grooved mahogany strip planks that slotted into each other, then glued and nailed; he reinforced the outside of the hull with ⅛ in (3 mm) glass cloth, saturated with epoxy resin; it was a massively strong hull.

Like most Atlantic sailors before him, Verity did not have an engine because of space and weight. A substantial 650 lbs (295 kg) lead keel brought the displacement to 1,750 lbs (794 kg)—a lot for a 12 ft boat, but she was a proper little yacht and certainly strongly built and very seaworthy. The boat had a modern sloop rig with a modest 19 ft (5.8 m) aluminum mast, and he also chose strength over sea views and fitted very small, circular windows.

Verity was aware of the dangers of fatigue for solo sailors and he fitted an innovative "Hasler" wind vane self-steering system. "Blondie" Hasler was one of the entrants in the single-handed 1960 OSTAR (in which Jean Lacombe sailed *Cap Horn*) and he had designed a self-steering system to keep his own boat on course using wind and water power. In keeping with his design philosophy to make the boat as comfortable as possible, Verity also cleverly modified an aluminum lawn chair to act as a steering seat and bunk.

Verity called his boat *Nonoalca*, which translates to "those who do not speak our language." After a shake-down cruise to Mexico, he pronounced himself ready. He left Florida on May 8, 1966, but three days out he was caught off the notorious Cape Hatteras by a sudden squall that slammed his boat down horizontally three times before he was even able to lower the sails. This was followed by a near collision with a tanker. In fact, he had several near collisions, despite carrying a large radar reflector on top of the mast. Solo sailors cannot keep watch at all times, and the possibility of being run down at sea is a constant worry for anyone sailing alone or short-handed.

After several days of good sailing, Verity faced the worst 24 hours of his voyage with strong winds and mountainous seas from the fringe of Hurricane Alma, a rare June hurricane and the earliest for 15 years. He wrote that he "could only hang on and listen to the roaring seas crash against the hull." It was too rough to eat, sleep, or even rest as *Nonoalca* was tossed around like a bath toy. In these conditions, all you can do is ride out the conditions and hope the hull will survive the pounding.

More gales, a visit by sperm whales, and gear failures stopped the voyage from becoming boring. After 65 days, Verity picked up the loom from the lighthouse on Brendan's Head in County Kerry, Ireland. He had sailed 4,550 NM (8,427 km) and survived a hurricane, seven gales, and had crossed the Atlantic at an average speed of 2.9 knots.

Verity proved that a boat smaller than St. Brendan's could sail the Atlantic, although *Nonoalca* was nothing like the monk's medieval boat, reputedly made from hides stretched over a wooden frame. Nevertheless, Verity put himself firmly into the record books by crossing the Atlantic in the smallest boat—but in less than two years, that record would be spectacularly shattered.

≈≈≈≈≈≈≈

Hugo Vihlen was from Homestead, Florida, a former Korean War fighter pilot who later became a Delta Airlines captain. In 1968, he swapped his aircraft cockpit for something much smaller when he decided to break the "smallest sailboat" record for crossing the Atlantic. His boat, named *April Fool*, was a quantum change from anything that had sailed before.

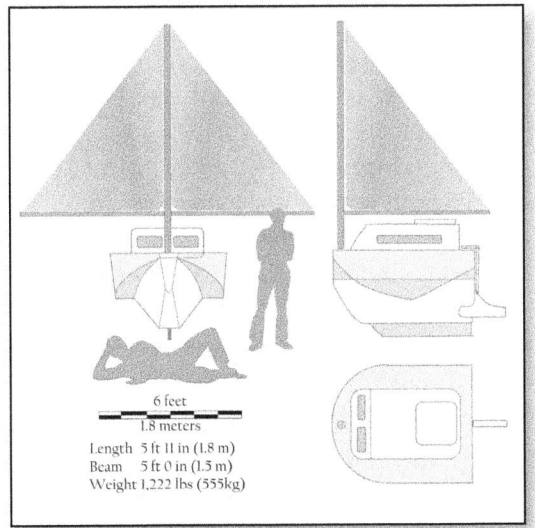

April Fool: the twin booms helped the boat sail the Trade Wind route.

Vihlen (his Swedish name is pronounced Va-lyn) made careful preparations. He had a yacht designer draw up plans, and his boat was professionally built in Coconut Grove, Florida. *April Fool* was radical because she was almost inconceivably small, just 5 ft 11 ⅞ in (1.8 m) long, 5 ft (1.5 m) wide, with a draft of 1 ft 7 in (.48 m); the boat weighed 1,222 lbs (554 kg).

Sailing boats typically have a length to beam ratio of about 3 to 1, so a boat 18 ft (5.5 m) long would have a beam of about 6 ft (1.8 m). By contrast, *April Fool* had a ratio of 6 to 5—it looked more like a hot tub with a cabin than a sailboat. However, there was no other way the designer could get enough capacity in such a small hull.

April Fool was made from plywood and fiberglass, with an aluminum mast and twin mainsails. Vihlen chose this unusual configuration for the Trade Winds route to make the most of "downwind" sailing, with the wind behind him. He also carried a small outboard, but he only had room for limited fuel. He only intended to use the engine to get out of the harbor, or possibly to move away from the path of a ship. This was one of his main concerns, for *April Fool* was so small that she was difficult to see from the bridge of a large ship.

On March 29, 1968, Vihlen left Casablanca in Morocco, intending to sail west and pick up the Trade Winds. His first problem—as with others in small boats leaving from North Africa—was breaking away from the coast. Small boats sail slowly and if the winds are not ideal, the strong Canary Current can sometimes sweep a small craft south towards the Cape Verde Islands faster than it can sail.

Vihlen persevered and eventually clawed his way out of the grip of the southerly current and sailed west, beyond the Canary Islands in search of the trade winds. By leaving in spring, he hoped to be in the West Indies before the arrival of the Atlantic hurricane season that starts in June. He was blessed with (mostly) fine weather and easterly winds from behind. This was just as well because *April Fool* could not sail close to the wind. Even so, the ocean swells along the Trade Winds can exceed 20 ft (6.1 m) high, nearly twice the height of *April Fool's* mast, and it was a daunting experience to be alone in the open ocean in such a tiny craft.

Vihlen endured rolling seas for 85 days, sleeping on his back with his knees bent and his feet wedged firmly in the bow. The boat was so small that he was unable to stretch out unless he stood up or took a swim. Three months is a long time at sea, and Vihlen listened on his shortwave radio to the world changing around him. The late 1960s was a time of great social turmoil: the Vietnam war polarized America (and much of the rest of the world); Martin Luther King Jr was assassinated on April 4, 1968, when Vihlen was somewhere west of the Canary Islands; news of Robert Kennedy's assassination came to him on June 5th, somewhere off Puerto Rico. Alone at sea, Vihlen sunk into despair, wondering what kind of country he would find when he got home.

The inability to keep a constant watch is a worry for any solo sailor. Fortunately, ocean-going ships follow tight shipping lanes; as long as you know where you are, then you can predict when you are likely to cross these shipping routes. Even so, Vihlen wisely set his alarm to go off every hour so he could check his heading, weather, and the sailing conditions. Inevitably, this routine brings chronic exhaustion.

Long-distance small boat sailors also have to cope with a variety of privations. There is no spare fresh water to wash, and anyone who has used seawater knows how unsatisfactory it can be—you never really feel fresh and clean. Food is in short supply, cooking is difficult, and eating becomes boring; Vihlen coped with all this, and more. On June 9th, after 71 days at sea, he wrote in his logbook with wry humor: "Catastrophe. I ran out of toilet paper today. Thank God for Reader's Digest."

There is never enough space to carry everything you need for a long voyage in a boat like *April Fool,* and there are only so many fish you can catch or rainwater to collect. Towards the end of the voyage, Vihlen was running short of more than just toilet paper. North of Cuba, a U.S. submarine surfaced close-by, and he sailed alongside to ask for supplies. However, small yachts and big ships do not mix well at sea, and the swell hurled the tiny *April Fool* against the hull of the submarine. As *April Fool* made impact, the radio antenna snapped; he remained out of contact for the rest of the voyage.

Vihlen planned to make landfall in Miami, but the Gulf Stream carried him north. By June 21st he was within six miles of the shore—close enough to see the hotels of Fort Lauderdale, but currents pushed him back out to sea. He tried sailing close to the wind to claw back the miles, but *April Fool* was not designed for this. He had long given up hope that his little outboard would ever burst into life again, and besides, he was long out of fuel. He was now at the mercy of an offshore wind and a current pushing him north, and nobody knew his whereabouts.

The next morning land was nowhere to be seen. Shortly after midday, a 60 ft (18 m) motor cruiser hove into view. It was the motor yacht *First Edition* belonging to the Gore family, owners of the FORT LAUDERDALE NEWS. Vihlen asked if they would report his position to the Coast Guard who had, apparently, been searching for him. Now everybody would know he had arrived; he also gratefully accepted supplies from the crew. Then the radio on the motor yacht came alive—the Coast Guard wanted to know if he wanted to be towed to shore? Vihlen firmly declined—he had been at sea for a long time, and he was going to make it ashore alone. The Coast Guard, however, had other plans.

Unknown to Hugo Vihlen, a tropical depression was forming south of Key West and squalls continued to push *April Fool* north. Unperturbed, he was happy to make landfall somewhere in North Carolina. His worried family, however, had asked the U.S. Coast Guard to find him. Soon, the USCG Cutter *Cape Shoalwater* arrived to give him safe passage back to Florida. Vihlen declined the offer, but the captain of the Coast Guard cutter had clear orders—he was to bring Vihlen and his boat home.

On arrival in Florida, he was treated like an amiable but certifiable hero and honored with a gun salute, a public parade, and lucrative endorsements. President Lyndon Johnson sent him a signed photo and the Governor of

Florida made him a "commodore." The Miami Seaquarium even named their killer whale "Hugo" after him—that at least was a "first" for a transatlantic sailor.

Vihlen's maximum daily run was 73 NM (135 km) and he never drifted more than 8.6 NM (16 km) off course. It had been a bumpy three months and a boat this small becomes almost unbearably uncomfortable in big seas. It was a remarkable achievement and Vihlen set a new record for the smallest boat to cross the Atlantic that would hold for a generation.

April Fool is now on public display at the International Small Craft Center in Newport News, Virginia.

≈≈≈≈≈≈≈

Before Vihlen had even landed in Florida, William Wallis attempted to sail west to east in his appropriately named 11 ft (3.35 m) *Little One*. Wallis was a life-long adventurer; at the age of 15, he left home in Hamburg to sail around Cape Horn. During his first solo voyage, he sailed 5,800 NM (10,741 km) from South America to American Samoa. On his second voyage 10 years later (on a raft), he sailed 9,560 NM (17,705 km) across the Pacific.

This was now Wallis's third great adventure; he was 77 years old when he left Montauk Point on Long Island, New York, on May 2, 1968. *Little One* was later found abandoned 345 NM (639 km) off the Irish coast; the cause of his death is not known. His log showed a final entry dated July 21st, so Wallis had certainly survived for 11 weeks, suggesting he was on the final leg of his voyage.

Another attempt was made seven years later by the Dutch conceptual artist, Bas Jan Ader, sailing a production fiberglass Guppy 13, *Ocean Wave*. Ader left Falmouth in England in June 1975, to sail the Atlantic as part of his artistic work "In Search of the Miraculous." His 13 ft (3.96 m) sailboat was found by a Spanish fishing boat 10 months later, still floating but with its bow submerged, 130 NM (240 km) off the Irish coast. The crew hoisted the *Ocean Wave* on deck and searched its cabin. Among spoiled food cans and navigational gear, they found his passport, driver's license, health insurance card, and a University of California, Irvine ID card.

Based on the size of the barnacles attached to the side of the hull, the trawler's captain concluded the *Ocean Wave* had drifted for around six months, which suggests that Ader might have sailed for four months and could easily have covered a distance of over 860 NM (1,5902 km). The *Ocean Wave* was taken to La Coruña in Spain for an investigation; a few weeks later the boat was stolen and has never been recovered.

Bas Jan Ader's body was never found, and the rumor mill cranked into life with people wanting to know what happened to him. The concepts of risk, failure, and disappearance were all regular features of his artistic work. Was he really dead? Or had he staged his own disappearance? Did he commit suicide? If so, had he planned this from the beginning? These questions became more relevant than ever due to the artistic nature of Ader's voyage. He was the artist who died for his art.

The next attempt in 1979 was sailing from west to east by a schoolteacher and experienced sailor, Gerry Spiess. He built his 10 ft (3 m) plywood and fiberglass boat in his garage at home in White Bear Lake, Minnesota. *Yankee Girl* weighed 750 lbs (340 kg) and carried a mainsail set on a 14 ft (4.27 m) mast, two jibs, and a spinnaker. He also had a self-steering mechanism, a VHF radio, navigational equipment, a small Evinrude outboard motor, and took 60 U.S. gallons (227 liters) of fuel; his big regret was that he did not take a good pillow.

Spiess slipped quietly away from Virginia Beach, Virginia—nobody was there even to see him off. During his 54 days at sea, he encountered sharks and whales, survived close shaves with passing ships, and his little sloop was hammered by 20 ft (6.1 m) waves and 40-knot winds (gale force 8). When he arrived in Falmouth, England on July 24th, he had successfully shaved 2 ft (0.61 m) off the west to east record for the smallest boat. He had a tough crossing and declared: "I wouldn't do it again or advise anybody to do it. The first two weeks were sheer hell." But some people never seem to learn. Indeed, he did not sail the Atlantic again, but two years later he took *Yankee Girl* on a 153-day voyage across the Pacific from Long Beach, California to Sydney, Australia. His little boat was later donated to the Minnesota Historical Society.

Irishman Tom McClean served with the British Army in the Parachute Regiment and in the Special Air Service (the SAS are an elite special operations force similar to the U.S. Delta Force). McClean later became a professional adventurer and survival expert. In 1969, he became the first person to row solo across the North Atlantic from west to east (see chapter *The Arms Race*). He also spent 39 days in 1985 living on Rockall, an uninhabited islet 160 NM (296 km) off the west coast of Scotland. He claimed he did it to reaffirm the United Kingdom's territorial claim to the island.

In 1982, McClean entered the transatlantic sailing history books; on June 9th, he left St John's, Newfoundland, in his 9 ft 9 in (2.97 m) *Giltspur*. He found the experience was grueling, sailing in very demanding conditions. He landed in Oporto, Portugal, 62 days later on August 10.

His record, however, was short-lived. Bill Dunlop had previously sailed the Atlantic in 1980 in his 34 ft (10.4 m) sailboat, *Enchantress*. Now he followed the same route in a boat a fraction of that size—the 9 ft 1 in (2.77 m) *Wind's Will* (the name was taken from a poem by Longfellow). 40-year-old Dunlop used a $16 plastic sextant and received time signals by radio, but he had no engine. He left Portland Harbor marina in Maine on June 13, 1982, but experienced problems with his rudder, and hand-steered for 16-17 hours a day. He also suffered badly from seawater sores, his boat was capsized 15 times, and he encountered fog so dense that he could not see beyond the front of his boat. Dunlop arrived in Falmouth, Cornwall after 78 days at sea, just three weeks after McClean had set his new record in *Giltspur*. Now Dunlop claimed the honors with a boat that was 8 in (20 cm) shorter.

Dunlop took *Wind's Will* back home to Mechanic Falls in Maine where he rebuilt the self-steering system. In 1984, he set off on his most ambitious challenge yet—a solo circumnavigation. He was seen leaving Aitutaki atoll in the Cook Islands on June 23rd and was never seen again. The official report concluded Dunlop and his boat had perished in near hurricane-force winds. Some sailing friends believe that a large outboard motor given to Dunlop in Tahiti might have upset the balance of his small boat. The only clue to what might have happened to him was found late in October 1984—a handwritten note inside a bottle washed up on a beach in Queensland. A new search was organized of the Great Barrier Reef area, but no further clues were found.

Meanwhile, Tom McClean was not going to allow Dunlop's Atlantic record to go unchallenged. He took a chainsaw to *Giltspur* and cut 2 ft (0.61 m) off his boat, shipped it back to Newfoundland, and repeated the voyage. Both his mast and steering broke during a storm, but McClean showed survival ingenuity: "I overlapped the mast and tied it together, shortened the sails, cut them up, [and] floated in the last 400 miles." People pleaded with him by radio to give up, but he kept going. By the time he landed, he had lost 40 lbs (18 kg) and was running low on supplies.

The next attempt came from Wayne Dickinson, a computer technician from Satellite Beach, Florida, who planned a new record attempt. His 8 ft 10 in (2.69 m) *God's Tear* looked more like a sailing submersible than a sailboat, enhanced by bright orange paintwork. Surprisingly for an electronics engineer, he had no onboard radio. Dickinson left Hull, Massachusetts for Falmouth in Cornwall, but returned for repairs; he finally left on October 30, 1982. A winter crossing of the North Atlantic in such a tiny boat was tempting fate, and the consequences were all too predictable.

After a punishing crossing that took 142 days sailing 17.6 NM (32.6 km) a day (an average speed of just 0.7 knots), *God's Tear* was driven onto rocks on Ireland's unforgiving west coast on March 25, 1983, during a gale. The lighthouse keeper was on a routine check of Arranmore Island when he found Dickinson crawling up the cliffs, unable to walk, dazed, and in shock; it took two hours to restore normal circulation to his arms and legs. Dickinson told his rescuer that he thought he had landed on the Outer Hebrides off Scotland—320 NM (592 km) north of his position. His $150,000 boat was wrecked beyond repair.

That same year, 1983, the British sailor Eric Peter (43) claims to have crossed the Atlantic in his tiny 5 ft 8 in (1.73 m) *Tonikay Nou*, 4 in (10 cm) shorter than Hugo Vihlen's *April Fool*. What made Peter's crossing unusual was that it was achieved in a barrel on which he fitted a rudder, keel, and sail. Peter said he survived on a diet of almonds, Spanish olive oil, bran, and a pint of water a day, although he collected more water during a 5-day squall.

Peter claims not to have had even a compass and crossed from the Canary Islands to Guadeloupe—a distance of a little over 2,600 NM (4,815 km)—in just 46 days. Before leaving, he declared "It's never been done before in a barrel, what a terrific publicity stunt!" Yet he never wrote a book, nor did he draw much attention to what would—if true—have been a remarkable crossing and a new record.

It is difficult to get independent verification of Eric Peter's voyage and his passage time of more than 56 NM (104 km) a day was nearly twice Vihlen's speed over the same route. The maximum displacement speed of any boat is limited by its waterline length, and Eric Peter's barrel could physically not sail faster than 3 knots, even in perfect conditions. However, conditions are often not ideal on the Trade Wind route and sailors experience many days of calms or contrary winds. So, an average speed of 2.3 knots for the whole voyage is remarkably fast for such a small boat, but theoretically not impossible. Without independent confirmation, it remains conjecture whether the voyage ever took place quite as Eric Peter claims.

≈≈≈≈≈≈≈

1983 was a bumper year for attempts to sail the smallest boat across the Atlantic, and none was more eccentric than the efforts by Tom McNally, a fine arts lecturer from Kirby, near Liverpool in England. McNally brought a touch of the absurd to the battle royale in the "space race" to cross the Atlantic in the smallest boat.

McNally's life on the ocean wave had more than the usual ups and downs. As a young man, he scraped together enough cash to buy a 17 ft 6 in (5.3 m) twin keel day boat, that he named *Anisor* (pronounced an-eye-sore). It was totally unsuitable for a transatlantic crossing—so, for that matter, was McNally, who had no sailing experience at all. Unfazed, he set course for the West Indies ... and ended up in Recife, Brazil, much wiser for the ordeal. But he had caught the sailing bug, and he later made four successful Atlantic crossings with friends.

His next solo attempt was in the micro-cruiser *Vera Hugh*, 12 ft 6 in (3.8 m) on deck, that he sailed from Liverpool to the Canary Islands and then towards Anguilla in the Caribbean. He lost his mast on the way and that led him to develop an innovative "A" frame design for his later boats.

This brought him to 1983, sitting in the harbor in St John's, Newfoundland, aboard his 6 ft 9 in (2.06 m) *Big C*, named after his long-running commitment to raise money for cancer research. He almost had not made it that far, as the shipping company had "temporarily misplaced" his boat on its delivery from England. It eventually arrived and he was keen to leave. As always, McNally was totally broke, but a friendly grocer back home had stocked his boat for the voyage—with food cans with missing labels.

Two months into the voyage, fierce gale-force winds blew out his sails and he was left drifting for two weeks. A Russian trawler, the *Yuri Kostikov*, came to his rescue. The radio operator had picked up a message, "Look out for a man in a 6-foot boat." but assumed it meant "Look out for six men in a boat." When the trawler found McNally, the wind was gusting over 35 knots (gale force 8) and the seas were running high. It is never easy for a large ship to rendezvous with a small boat at sea, and McNally found himself bouncing down the rusty sides of the trawler towards the churning blades of the propellers. He crouched on the tiny, pitching deck, desperately trying to push his boat away from the trawler.

At the last minute, the captain shut down the roaring engines and the propellers stopped turning, but the *Big C* continued to scrape down the trawler's side and under its towering stern—it then crashed into a stationary propeller blade, gashing the side of the tiny sailboat. The *Big C* began to sink, and the Russian crew shouted for him to jump free. McNally would have none of it, and he clambered around the pitching deck, desperately tying ropes to the boat as best he could. Any language communication was non-existent, so using hand signals, he got the Russians to lower him more ropes that he passed under the hull to keep his boat afloat. A boom with heavy lifting tackle was swung over the side, McNally maneuvered the *Big C* underneath, and as a wave lifted the boat up, he quickly looped the rope strops over the huge steel hook.

The *Big C* was snatched from the surface, McNally lost his balance and toppled over the side—fortunately still attached to his lifeline. As he floundered in the icy waters, his pants (now with the pockets full of water) were dragged from his waist. His dignity was taking as much of a knocking as the *Big C;* the trawler hoisted the hull up with McNally dangling from the boat, swinging in circles from his lifeline, and naked from the waist down. Bruised and bloodied, he was unceremoniously dumped onto the trawler's deck, shaken, frozen, but grateful still to be alive.

After a warm bath and fresh clothes McNally went to thank the captain and asked to be allowed to repair the *Big C* so he could be dropped back at the same coordinates to continue his voyage. The captain was horrified and rolled his eyes: "Now I know why they call the English crazy!" The skipper eventually relented, and McNally spent the next few weeks recovering from his ordeal and repairing the *Big C*. When the boat was eventually re-launched, she continued to leak; he reluctantly agreed to be dropped off in Plymouth, Cornwall.

McNally was determined to have another crack at the transatlantic space record, and he built an even smaller boat on the upper floor of a local shop. Once complete, he had only to lift the hull out through a window, lower it to the ground, and bolt on the keel. That night the building caught fire and the interior collapsed—along with his boat.

Undismayed, he started work on *Vera Hugh-Pride of Merseyside* (a name that was almost as long as the boat). As ever, he was short of funds, so he used a discarded wardrobe as the central support for his new craft. He molded foam around it in the shape of the boat, then covered the hull with fiberglass cloth. Once hardened, he dug out the foam and built the inside. Innovative as ever, he used a Perspex door from a washing machine as a deck hatch. Little wonder he became known as "the crazy sailor." By the spring, McNally was ready to have another crack at the record in the 5 ft 4 in (1.63 m) *Vera Hugh*.

McNally was not aware that another micro-cruiser enthusiast was planning his own attempt on the Atlantic—it was none other than Hugo Vihlen. It was 24 years since Vihlen took *April Fool* across from Morocco to Florida, and he was now 61 years old and had retired as a commercial pilot. With time to spare, Vihlen set about building a new micro-cruiser called *Father's Day*, 5 ft 6 in (1.68 m) long and nearly 6 in (15.24 cm) shorter than his previous boat. To make things a little more challenging, he decided to tackle the stormy northern route across the Atlantic, west to east.

Vihlen knew what he was up against and had spent two years meticulously planning the voyage. Technology had moved on and his new boat was a significant improvement over *April Fool*. The hull was more rounded and built strongly from fiberglass and Airex (a lightweight foam). He also had a Global Positioning System (GPS) that allowed him to know his exact position, a water-maker, short-range VHF radio, and a long-range SSB/Ham radio.

Vihlen had prepared well and took his boat to Cape Cod in Massachusetts as his chosen point of departure. He had not, however, taken account of the U.S. Coast Guard (who had, of course, plucked him out of the water against his will in Florida at the end of his last voyage). With four days to go before his departure, Rear Admiral W. Ted Leland of the U.S. Coast Guard declared that *Father's Day* was too small for the crossing and would ultimately need rescuing. He was refused permission to sail.

The authorities had not inspected the boat and Vihlen vehemently argued that size had nothing to do with seaworthiness. Leland would not budge, and Vihlen's only option was a legal challenge. He was furious: "They haven't even seen it, but just because of its size, the boat is [considered] unseaworthy," he fumed. "There's nothing I can do but pursue this through the courts, dealing with the two people I hate most—the Coast Guard and lawyers!"

Vihlen decided on a simpler and cheaper solution—he put *Father's Day* back on her trailer and drove to St John's in Newfoundland. Here the sailing distance was shorter, the favorable currents closer inshore, and the U.S. Coast Guard had no jurisdiction; Vihlen was now a much happier man. When he arrived at his waterside motel, the clerk took one look at *Father's Day* and declared: "Why it's just a teacup, it is," shaking her head in amazement, "I can't imagine anyone crossing an ocean in this." Her sentiments seemed in tune with those of Rear Admiral W. Ted Leland of the U.S. Coast Guard.

While preparing for his departure, a stranger came up to Vihlen on the quayside at St John's and introduced himself: "I'm Tom McNally, your competition." Vihlen knew about the English sailor, but they had never met. McNally took Vihlen down to the harbor and pointed out his own miniature boat on its mooring. McNally had just shipped *Vera Hugh* from Liverpool and was preparing his early summer departure. After waiting 24 years, there were now two boats bobbing less than a hundred feet apart, each capable of taking the record. Vihlen was stunned, to say the least, but there was more in store—McNally's *Vera Hugh* was 1.5 inches (3.8 cm) shorter than *Father's Day*.

The two men standing on the quay in St John's could not have been more different. Vihlen, the fighter pilot turned commercial pilot was cautious, meticulous, and methodical, used to checking every small detail before committing himself to either air or sea. McNally was a free-spirited, likable mischief-maker who seemed to bounce from one life-crisis to the next, always living by the seat of his pants.

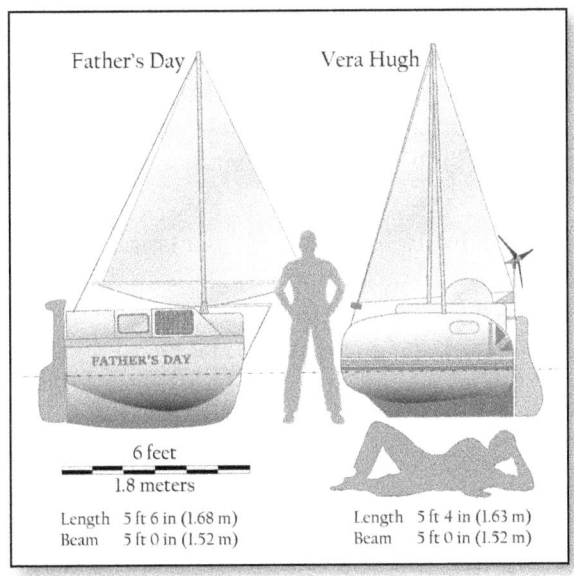

Micro-cruisers need to be short, beamy, and rounded. Both boats carried twin sails, Vera Hugh had twin masts. To generate electricity, Vihlen used solar panels and McNally a wind generator.

Their boats reflected their owners; *Father's Day* was carefully designed and professionally built using modern materials and fitted with the latest equipment. *Vera Hugh* looked as if it had been knocked together in McNally's back garden, using rocks for ballast, and with an ancient water-maker that lacked spares.

The two men became good friends but remained resolute rivals.

The summer sailing season had already begun and Vihlen had little choice but to carry on with his longer boat. On the evening of June 29th, Vihlen and McNally dined together as they had done most evenings since meeting a few days previously. Vihlen kept a poker face all night, not wanting to let McNally into his plans.

The next morning, Vihlen pushed *Father's Day* off from the quayside, accepted a tow to get safely out of the harbor, and then set full sail heading east. Frustratingly, the wind dropped and the next day it swung around to the east, pushing him back towards the rocky Newfoundland coastline. These ultra-small sailboats cannot sail well to windward, so Vihlen had no choice but to call for a boat to pull him clear of the shoreline. The wind continued to blow from the east and Vihlen reluctantly decided to put *Father's Day* back on her trailer and head home to Florida, disappointed but unbowed.

Tom McNally stayed in St. John's, waiting for his chance. The same adverse winds plagued his departure, and he too gave up and shipped *Vera Hugh* home. They were both lucky for that August, Hurricane Andrew (the most destructive hurricane for decades) hammered the eastern seaboard of the United States. The North Atlantic was no place to be that summer in a small boat.

≈≈≈≈≈≈≈

Despite their obvious differences, Vihlen and McNally had much in common. They were both resolute, tenacious, and very determined men. Once Hugo Vihlen had recovered from the damage wreaked back home in Florida by Hurricane Andrew, he set about preparing *Father's Day* for a new attempt. His first job was to cut 2 in (5 cm) off the boat, making it a fraction smaller than *Vera Hugh*.

Meanwhile in England, Tom McNally had his own plans; he was not prepared to wait a whole year for another attempt, so he shipped *Vera Hugh* to Lisbon to sail the Trade Wind route. But things never seemed to go smoothly for McNally. Unused to the Portuguese traffic, he stepped out to cross a road, looked the wrong way, and was hit by a van. The driver stopped, checked he was still alive, and quickly drove off. Inevitably, McNally soon became a local celebrity.

Late one afternoon, two hefty, inebriated locals decided to inspect his boat. Before McNally realized what was happening, they jumped aboard and broke into a drunken song at the top of their voices. The inevitable happened—with the extra weight on deck, the boat tipped over and sunk to the bottom of the harbor. All of his electrical equipment and supplies were ruined by salt water.

Undaunted, McNally raised his micro-cruiser and trucked her west to Sagres on the south-western tip of Portugal, which was an easier departure point for an Atlantic crossing. Unfortunately, the Portuguese Guardia Fiscal would not permit him to leave in what they considered to be an unsuitable craft. McNally was determined to sail before the end of 1992 to commemorate the 500th anniversary of Columbus' voyage. It was a stalemate, with the Guardia keeping a tight watch over his boat. On December 27th, the wind shifted to the east—it was the perfect direction. McNally unloaded two bags of surplus equipment onto the dock, asked the Guardia to keep an eye on it, and announced he was taking a trial sail. He was off...

McNally soon found himself crossing a busy shipping lane at night and he watched in horror as a huge freighter approached on a collision course. He signaled with his flashlight but was unable to use his radio as the batteries were flat. As the ship approached, its bow wave tossed *Vera Hugh* to one side, only for the passing hull to suck him back. Memories of his previous encounter with the Russian trawler flashed through his mind as his tiny boat bounced down the side of the ship while McNally tried to push himself away with a paddle. As the vessel sailed on, his boat was left holed and half full of water. Shivering and shaking from delayed shock, McNally pumped all night to stay afloat.

Once clear of the shipping lanes, he spent the next day checking for damage, but found he could not repair his boat at sea. He laid a course for the nearest land, Tenerife in the Canary Islands. It took him two weeks to sail there (still pumping) but as he approached the harbor, a violent storm blew him offshore to the north. It took another six days sailing in rough conditions to make it to Funchal in Madeira, 270 NM miles (500 km) away. He had been at sea for 38 days but had sailed less than a fifth of the way across the Atlantic.

McNally repaired the damage and laid a course back to the Canaries, but now a second storm pushed him south, this time towards the Cape Verde Islands. He was now well off his planned route for Puerto Rico, and he struggled to claw his way back to his intended course. Later, his water-maker failed, and he was forced to drink saltwater. He finally arrived in San Juan, 113 days out of Sagres, 25 lbs (11 kg) lighter and with his kidneys failing. McNally rested for two weeks before continuing on to Ft. Lauderdale in Florida to complete his Atlantic crossing; he arrived on June 30, 1993, and had beaten the record set by Hugo Vihlen and *April Fool* by 10 in (25 cm).

The next year Hugo Vihlen shipped *Father's Day* back to Newfoundland, now 2 in (51 mm) shorter—and critically ½ in (12.7 mm) shorter than McNally's boat. Within a couple of hours of his departure, blustery winds spun his boat around and damaged the mounting for his two booms—he was not even out of sight of land. He returned to make quick repairs but was concerned that he was already two weeks behind schedule. He finally left St. John's the following day on June 14, 1993, heading for Falmouth, England.

For the next 115 days, Vihlen experienced the usual problems all single-handed sailors face in small boats, including busy shipping lanes and the fear of collision. By day five he was in dense fog over the Grand Banks, formed when warm air blowing from the south-west meets the Labrador Current bringing icy cold water down from the Arctic north; the moist air cools and condenses to form the infamous fog banks to the east of Newfoundland.

Hugo Vihlen after his transatlantic crossing in Father's Day, just 5 ft 6 in (1.68 m) long.

Father's Day was gliding almost silently like a ghost ship through a pea-soup mist, with visibility down to just a few feet.

In contrast to Tom McNally's label-less cans of food, Hugo Vihlen had carefully calculated his food rations for the voyage. Cooking was too risky on a boat the size of *Father's Day*, and he had no room for a cooker and fuel. Each day he ate a pre-planned menu of ready-to-eat military rations and high-energy drinks, giving a high nutritional diet, low in salt. After 41 days at sea, Vihlen realized the voyage was taking longer than expected and he went on half-rations. Water was even more of a concern, and he limited himself to a 1 qt (0.95 liter) a day, or just four cups. He had enough for three months (90 days), after which he would have to make fresh water by reverse osmosis with his water-maker.

For the first time in history, Tom McNally and Hugo Vihlen were sailing in boats that were shorter than the crew was tall. All sailing boats heel with the wind, so Vihlen had to adjust his sitting position so that he could keep the boat more-or-less upright. There was not enough room to sleep stretched out horizontally, so both men slept with their knees bent. The constant dampness also took its toll; saltwater sores on their buttocks would not heal despite using antibacterial cream, and toenails and fingernails receded in the damp conditions.

On July 28th, 46 days into Vihlen's voyage, strong winds built up waves 20-25 ft (6.1-7.6 m) high, the worst he had encountered. He battened down the hatch to ride out the brutal conditions; each time a wave broke over

Father's Day, the boat was buried under solid water that seeped into the boat. Three days later he was visited by whales. They were most likely just being inquisitive, but there have been instances where whales have attacked boats—probably a mother believing her young calf was being threatened. Vihlen was worried about being surrounded by cetaceans six times longer than his boat, so he started his outboard motor, and the high-pitched whine from the engine seemed to do the trick and the pod lazily swam off.

On September 13th, day 92, and with less than 260 NM (481 km) to go, Vihlen spotted wispy clouds high in the morning sky, commonly known as mare's tails; every sailor knows what they predict—strong winds, this time from the tail-end of Hurricane Floyd. Hurricanes lose their tropical power as they blow over the cooler waters of the North Atlantic and become re-classified as extra-tropical storms. Even so, they can still pack a punch; when the remnants of Floyd reached Brittany in France that summer, the coast was hammered by sustained winds of 70 knots (128 km/h)— hurricane-force winds.

At sea, all that Vihlen could do was lower and lash the sails, lock the hatches, tighten his safety strap, and brace himself for the roller-coaster ride that was coming. As he peered out of the porthole, he could see 30 ft (9.1 m) waves with breaking crests rolling towards his boat, the air filled with foam, spray blowing off the tops of waves, and visibility down to practically zero. There was nothing more he could do, other than put his faith in his boat.

As sure as night follows day, storms are followed by gentle winds, although it still took Vihlen another two weeks to complete his voyage. Having passed the Bishops Rock Lighthouse on September 26th, he had officially crossed the Atlantic, west to east, in the smallest boat. On arrival in Falmouth, he found he had lost 34 lbs (15.4 kg) and could barely walk, having been unable to stretch out properly during the voyage. His arrival in Falmouth was very low key—a waiting journalist bought him a Cornish pasty to eat while his boat was towed around to a local yacht club. When everyone arrived at the club for a celebration tea, they found it had closed. Vihlen was phlegmatic—at least he had regained his record.

Father's Day was donated to the National Maritime Museum in Falmouth and is now on public display.

≈≈≈≈≈≈≈

Having held the record for less than three months, it should be no surprise that McNally would try again. In 2002, he made the 650 NM (1,204 km) crossing from Gibraltar to Gran Canaria in the Canary Islands in his new 3 ft 10½ in (1.18 m) *Vera Hugh–Cancer Research*; it was the size of a small

Tom McNally sailing Vera Hugh–Cancer Research off Gibraltar in 2002.

coffee table. During his stop-over at Mogán, his boat and all his equipment were stolen.

McNally built a new boat and could not resist the temptation to make it just a little smaller, this time built with foam-sandwich and GRP, making it stronger and lighter than any of his previous boats. He now planned a double-crossing of the Atlantic in 2009 in the 3 ft 10 in (1.2 m) *Big C*, to raise money for the charity Sail 4 Cancer. His planned route took him from Cadiz in Spain to the Canary Islands, and then on to Puerto Rico; he then intended to sail north up the eastern seaboard to Newfoundland, before heading back to his home port of Liverpool.

Sadly, illness thwarted his plans. After battling cancer for more than eight years, he died on June 12, 2017, at the age of 77.

Tom McNally's attitude epitomized the irrational, outlandish, and determined resolve of the many people who took on the Atlantic in ever-smaller boats. "Of course I'm afraid at times—only fools and liars are never afraid," he once wrote. "Dying is about the only absolute certainty in life; I'm just more afraid of not living."

Steam Across the Atlantic

On August 17, 1807, people living along the banks of the Hudson River just north of New York City witnessed a terrifying spectacle. Coming upriver at the respectable speed of 4 knots (7.4 km/h) was a long, narrow riverboat unlike anything they had seen; a floating, fire-monster spewing out smoke and flames like a mobile, aquatic pyrotechnic. To everyone's amazement, the vessel was propelled not with sails, but by steam; it soon became known as "Mr. Fulton's Folly." Most people expected the vessel would explode—either that, or it would roll over like a log and sink like a brick.

How wrong they were.

The "Mr. Fulton" in question was Robert Fulton of Pennsylvania, a man of extraordinary talents and vision. As a schoolboy, he designed a hand-operated paddle wheel for a rowing boat, made lead pencils and household utensils for his mother, and created fireworks for his town's celebration. As an adult, he was an artist, an inventor, and a mechanical engineer. He became a pioneer in dredging canals and building locks, and he invented a device for making rope and spinning flax. In 1801, he even built the world's first working submarine called the *Nautilus*. The vessel could dive to a depth of 25 ft (7.6 m) and it caught the attention of both the British Admiralty and Napoleon Bonaparte, the Emperor of France. Fulton was nothing short of an engineering genius.

At the age of 42, Fulton found himself steaming up the Hudson River in the summer of 1807 on his latest creation, a 150 ft (46 m) river steamboat called the *North River Steamboat of Clermont* later known simply as the *Clermont*. The steamboat made the 150-mile (240 km) trip from New York City to Albany in 32 hours, including one overnight stop. This was a dramatic improvement over sailing boats that took several days to make the same journey. Although Albany had a population of only 10,000 people, it was still one of North America's largest towns and an important transportation hub, giving access to the Great Lakes and the continental interior beyond.

Within a month, Fulton was running a scheduled service up and down the Hudson River, with the *Clermont* sometimes carrying 100 passengers; she made the round trip every four days until floating ice heralded the beginning of winter. The vessel was not the first river steamboat to be built in North America, but it was the first to become a commercial success.

The age of marine steam power had arrived.

In the years following the Hudson River service, steamboats began operating on rivers, lakes, and coastal bays and they became part of modern life along North America's rapidly industrializing East Coast; but taking such a vessel on a voyage across the ocean was a very different proposition. Experienced mariners did not think it could be done, for these early steamboats, they declared, were simply too flimsy and unwieldy to withstand the dangers of the deep.

The North River Steamboat later named the Clermont.

One man who thought otherwise was a sea captain from Connecticut named Moses Rogers. He had been on one of the first runs up the Hudson River with Fulton, and Rogers began to understand the potential of putting a steam engine in a large vessel; his interest lay not in river steamboats, but in operating ocean-going steamships.

Rogers took command of his steamboat, the *Phoenix*, and it became one of the *Clermont's* first rivals. However, Fulton held the monopoly to operate a steamboat on the Hudson River, so in 1809 the owners of the *Phoenix* risked an open sea passage from New York to the Delaware River, where the boat began operating a regular 32-mile (51.5 km) ferry service between Philadelphia and Trenton, New Jersey. Here, Moses Rogers not only

Moses Rogers (1779-1821)
(Left)

Robert Fulton (1765-1815)
(Right)

learned about the technical demands of running a steam-powered vessel, but he also began to understand the needs of the traveling public who were only just beginning to accept this new-fangled transport.

By 1817, Rogers was operating a regular coastal steamboat service from Charleston to Savannah and was beginning to develop ideas to run a fully steam-powered service across the Atlantic. The original 13 American colonies had gained independence from Britain barely 30 years previously, and the North Atlantic route was now attracting more and more shipping as the United States improved links with European countries.

During the early nineteenth century, the North American continent was generally seen as a vast wilderness to be opened up and settled by newcomers (albeit with little regard for the original residents). These pioneers came from all over Europe, and with them were shipped the tools they needed to build a new country. As a

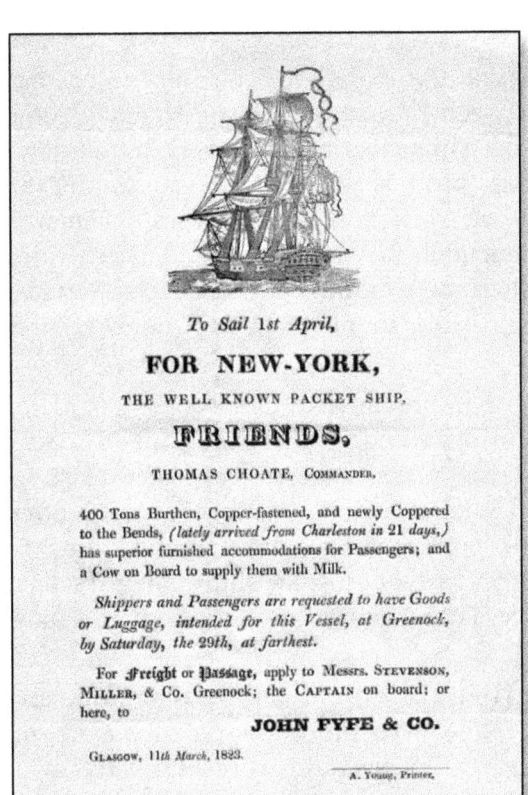

A packet boat announcement from 1823. The Atlantic route was highly competitive and shipping companies were constantly making new offers to attract passengers, whether it was a fast ocean passage or fresh milk.

result, transatlantic shipping became the lifeblood of the budding American nation.

Most immigrants sailed from Europe in packet boats, the workhorse of the North Atlantic route. These sailing ships were typically 100-130 ft (30-40 m) long and were contracted by the U.S. and European governments to carry urgent cargo, including mail, small packages, and newspapers. The bulk of their cargo, however, was passengers. Ships sailed from Britain and Ireland as well as continental ports to the East Coast harbors of the United States and Canada.

Packet boats provided reasonable accommodation for a privileged few and unreasonable accommodation for hundreds more who were squeezed below decks. Conditions were usually crowded, dark, and damp; rats, insects, and disease were endemic, and poor sanitation and stormy weather made life even more intolerable.

This was a lucrative business and there was intense rivalry to become the biggest and fastest service between Europe and North America. Soon, the competition between shipping companies became every bit as fierce as the rivalry between commercial airlines today. However, running an Atlantic packet boat service faced two main problems, as Moses Rogers well understood: slowness and unpredictability. A crossing could take five or six weeks, or it could last more than three months during adverse weather conditions. It was therefore impossible to maintain a regular, reliable schedule under sail.

When crossings took longer than anticipated, conditions aboard for steerage passengers changed from appalling to something much worse. Supplies of food and water ran low, and passengers were forced to pay a premium for more—even then, it was barely edible. One shipowner admitted that the food aboard was "adequate to prevent death or starvation but not to survive and thrive." It was little wonder that on some ships, one passenger in every ten died during the voyage. Those who survived the passage almost always arrived undernourished.

There was clearly money to be made from the Atlantic run, and potentially lots of it. Moses Rogers believed the way forward was to run steamships, creating an ocean service that would match the success of Robert Fulton's river steamboat service on the Hudson. He now needed three things: a suitable boat, a reliable engine, and a very wealthy benefactor who was prepared to take a risk.

These were early days in the development of steam engines and the technical challenge to put this machinery into wooden-hulled, ocean-going ships tested engineers and builders alike. But Rogers was convinced this was the future and if successful, it would be the first service of its kind. He found the perfect vessel under construction at the Fickett & Crockett shipyard in New York—a standard packet boat no larger than a big sailing yacht by today's standards: her 320-ton hull measured 100 ft (30 m) overall, with a beam of 26 ft 3 in (8 m). Like all packet boats of the day, she was lean with an easily driven hull.

Rogers set about persuading William Scarborough, a successful shipping merchant and part-owner of Scarborough & Isaacs of Savannah, Georgia, to purchase the vessel and convert her into a steamship by adding an auxiliary engine. By doing so, Rogers argued, they would gain the prestige of inaugurating the world's first trans-ocean steamship service. Scarborough took the bait, and on May 7, 1818, he became the principal investor and president of the newly formed Savannah Steamship Company.

The mechanics were all made locally: the engine was supplied by the Allaire Iron Works of New York, and the rest of the mechanical components and running gear were manufactured by the Speedwell Ironworks of New Jersey. Back in New York's East River, Moses Rogers supervised the installation of the machinery, while his brother-in-law, Steven Rogers (not a blood relation) was contracted to oversee the completion of the hull and rigging.

Rogers' low-pressure steam engine had a huge single 40 in diameter (101 cm) cylinder and a 5 ft (1.5 m) stroke; despite its size, it was only rated at 90 hp. The mechanical equipment was unusually large for the period and Rogers had problems finding a suitable boiler. He eventually settled on a copper cylinder that had a secret design to prevent salt from caking the sides of the boiler when the water produced steam. The boiler was laid horizontally to distribute the weight more evenly.

The engine powered two wrought-iron paddle-wheels, each 16 ft (4.9 m) in diameter, with eight "buckets" per wheel. When sailing, the paddles could be folded like a fan and lifted up and secured on deck. This procedure took only 15 minutes, and the *SS Savannah* is thought to be the only ship ever to be fitted with such an innovative system.

The smokestack and paddle wheels looked ungainly to many eyes, but the interior of the ship received universal praise. The vessel was intended to appeal to wealthy passengers who wanted to travel in comfort, so no expense was spared in fitting out 16 staterooms, each with two bunks. There were three well-furnished saloons featuring imported carpets and curtains; full-length mirrors were placed carefully to create an illusion of space and to reflect the elegant polished mahogany, rosewood, and brass

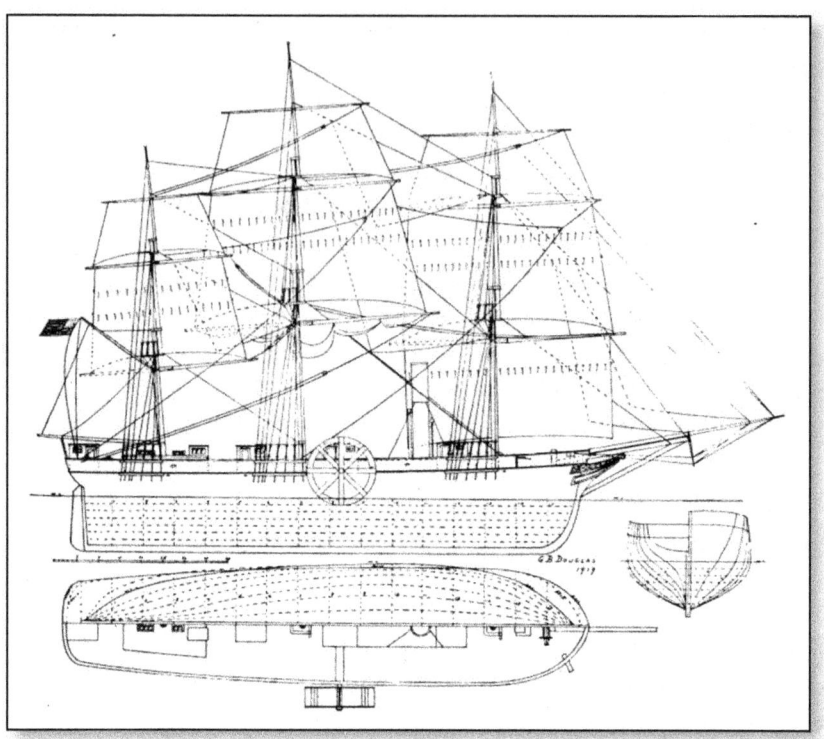

The revolutionary SS Savannah: note how little of the paddle wheels are submerged.

ornamentations. Of course, the downside of all this accommodation meant there was little capacity for the bunker coal—something which became a serious problem.

Essentially, the *SS Savannah* was fully rigged like a normal packet boat except for the absence of royal-masts and royals—these are small sails set at the very top of the masts on a square-rigger; it was the 90 hp steam engine that made the *SS Savannah* unique.

Rogers now faced some immediate problems: once it became known the vessel was intended for the transatlantic run, the ship was quickly dubbed the "steam coffin" and no New York crew would agree to sail in this smoking hybrid. Instead, Rogers went north to New London in Connecticut, where he had a good reputation as a competent ship's captain, and he had no trouble raising a crew who had few worries about the seaworthiness of the new-fangled vessel.

On March 22, 1819, the captain ran an engine and machinery trial in New York harbor for a couple of hours. A week later, owner William Scarborough took the helm on her maiden voyage, sailing south to Savannah, Georgia.

On the first morning at sea, the crew raised steam for the first time on the open ocean, but they only ran the engine for half an hour before rough weather persuaded Rogers to stow the paddle wheels and revert to sail. The ship reached her destination on April 6th, with the engine running for a respectable 41½ hours during the 207-hour voyage.

On May 11, 1819, William Scarborough reaped the benefits of building his radical new ship when President James Monroe visited the *SS Savannah* prior to her departure for England. The President dined aboard and talked enthusiastically about the possibility that a vessel—designed and built in North America—would establish the world's first transatlantic steamship service. Monroe was impressed and invited Scarborough to bring the *SS Savannah* to Washington D.C. on her return from Europe so that Congress might see the ship and possibly acquire her to tackle troublesome Cuban pirates—piracy being a constant menace to North American merchant shipping, both at home and abroad.

The euphoria did not last as the company was not able to find passengers willing to risk traveling by steam power on the open ocean, despite the opulence of the accommodations. The company also realized they could not carry enough coal to power the *SS Savannah* all the way across, even without passengers.

It would have been fascinating to be a fly on the wall of the boardroom when the owner and directors of the Savannah Steamship Company were informed about this limitation. Fearing they had a floating white elephant on their hands, they came up with the inspired idea to sell the ship off to the U.S. Navy, but the Secretary of War was not interested in buying an unproven steamship. Even before leaving on her maiden voyage, there were rumors of a possible sale to Russia, but nothing came of that idea either. In one last desperate attempt to find passengers, Scarborough postponed the departure, but patrons were still not forthcoming. In the end, the departure was delayed again when an unfortunate crew member returned to the ship drunk, fell off the gangplank, and drowned.

On May 24, 1819, the ship finally cast off on her passenger-free maiden voyage to Europe, just 12 years after the *Clermont* made her historic journey up the Hudson River. Apart from her crew, the *SS Savannah* carried 75 tons of coal and 25 cords of wood to fuel the boilers. This took up nearly 5,300 cu ft (150 cu m) of space, equivalent to four large single garages—a lot of space to find on a 100 ft (30 m) vessel. With limited fuel, the ship sailed whenever possible and only proceeded under power for a relatively short time—just 90 hours in 29½ days at sea.

The SS Savannah under sail and power.

On June 17th, the ship was sighted off the Irish coast with so much smoke and steam billowing from the single-cylinder engine that onlookers feared the ship was on fire, and a British naval cutter was dispatched to investigate. The *HMS Kite* gave chase and followed the steamship for several hours, believing the vessel to be ablaze. Unable to catch the *SS Savannah*, the naval captain fired warning shots across her bow; Rogers took the hint and brought the steamship to a halt. By then, the fire under the steamship's boilers was almost out, as the ship had run out of coal. Rogers put into Kinsale, Ireland and filled the vessel's bunkers before heading to Liverpool, where they arrived on June 20, 1819.

During her layover in Liverpool, the ship was visited by thousands of people, including officers of the British Army and the British Royal Navy. Britain and the U.S. had been at war only a few years previously and suspicion remained about the steamship's true mission. Some even suspected that the vessel might be used to rescue Napoleon Bonaparte from prison on the island of St. Helena in the South Atlantic. Nevertheless, the ship remained in Liverpool for 25 days, giving the crew time to repaint the vessel, service the engine, and replenish fuel and supplies. She then sailed for Denmark, Sweden, and Russia.

The voyage proved that a steam-powered vessel could cross the Atlantic, albeit largely by sail on this occasion. Rogers visited royalty and heads of state in England, France, and Russia, and the King of Sweden even offered to buy the ship for $100,000, to be paid for in hemp and iron. Rogers turned the offer down—a decision he would later regret.

Despite the accolades, the *SS Savannah* was not a commercial success. Scarborough was ruined after a fire swept through the city of Savannah in 1820, destroying his elegant home. The company converted the ship back to a sailing packet, and the ship ran the Savannah to New York route under sail only; the ship's engine was later sold for $1,600. On November 5, 1821, the vessel ran aground off Long Island and broke up. It would be another 20 years before steamships made regular crossings of the Atlantic, and almost 30 years before an American ship duplicated the achievement.

≈≈≈≈≈≈≈

A couple of years before the *SS Savannah* embarked on her maiden voyage, the Black Ball Line of New York established a packet service across the Atlantic that attempted to run something close to a regular, scheduled service under sail. Until 1817, dates were never advertised. A vessel's arrival depended on the wind and the ship returned when fully loaded; often the packet boat stopped off at other ports to top up the cargo or take on more passengers before finally crossing the ocean.

A group of New York Quaker merchants changed all this by establishing the Black Ball Line and committed ships to leave New York on a specific day each month, irrespective of the amount of cargo or number of passengers. Their service had teething problems and it was several years before it became fully established, but it became a success. In 1822, sailings were increased to twice a month and the company cut the price of tickets to 35 guineas. The Black Ball packets were famous for keeping to rigid schedules, but this often entailed the harsh treatment of seamen, earning the ships the nickname "blood boats."

It was a significant undertaking by the company and their success attracted competitors. Typically, passage times from New York to Liverpool were 23 days, and 40 days for the return, knocking a week or more off previous times. When the sailing conditions were good there were some very fast passages, and a record of 15 days 16 hours on the easterly route was set in 1823. Westward crossings against the prevailing winds were usually slower, but in 1830, the Black Ball Line's *Columbia* set a remarkable record of 15 days 23 hours during an unusually long period of easterly winds.

Leaving on schedule was a good start to running a reliable service, but the packet companies still could never guarantee when their ships would arrive. In 1832, an American lawyer, Junius Smith, became stuck on a voyage from London to New York that lasted 54 days—but he managed to turn his

The 924-ton Montezuma, with the company's black ball on its foresail.

frustration into inspiration. Smith had been a merchant in London for 30 years and he saw a lucrative commercial opportunity: he proposed a four-ship London to New York steamship service with fortnightly departures in each direction, where two ships would be owned by an American company, and the other two by a British affiliate.

Smith received little interest at first, but his proposal began to gain traction when the Scottish shipbuilder, Macgregor Laird, became an investor. This was just the sort of expertise (and funding) that Smith needed. A prospectus seeking like-minded investors was published in THE TIMES of London in November 1835, proposing the creation of the British and American Steam Navigation Company. The intention was to run a regular transatlantic steamship service offering passengers something new—scheduled departure times and reliable arrival times.

This was a time of rapid technological progress in Great Britain and investors were keen on new initiatives that could make their fortunes, so it was inevitable that good ideas would soon produce competitors. In this case, the rivalry came from a group of investors based in Bristol in the west of England, who were inspired by their local hero, Isambard Kingdom Brunel.

Brunel was an English engineer who literally changed the face of Britain during the Industrial Revolution with ingenious, ground-breaking engineering schemes. He built whole dockyards, railways, innovative steamships, and numerous important bridges and tunnels. His designs

Isambard Kingdom Brunel, taken in Bristol in 1857.

transformed public transport and revolutionized Victorian Britain.

A year after Junius Smith's prospectus was published, Brunel and his group of investors formed the Great Western Steamship Company. They intended to build a fleet of steamships to run from Bristol to New York. This brought them into direct competition with Smith's British and American Steam Navigation Company.

There was just one small problem: neither company had any ships.

The race was now on to run the biggest, the fastest, and the most reliable steamships across the Atlantic. This became a story of boardroom arguments across Europe and North America, of clashes between naval architects and shipbuilders, of battles waged above decks between ship's captains, and in the engine rooms below where stokers slaved away in hellish conditions of intense heat and fumes. The prize for the winner was wealth and prestige; the losers paid the price with lost ships and bankruptcy.

The British and American Steam Navigation Company outlined their plans in a prospectus to build four steamships, each with a gross registered tonnage (grt) of 1,200; (grt was a measure of a ship's internal volume expressed in "register tons," each equal to 100 cu ft (2.83 cu m). In other words, grt is a simple measure of the carrying capacity of a vessel).

The Bristol-based Great Western Steamship Company soon announced plans for a ship with a capacity of 1,340 grt (later increased to 1,700 grt). This was going to be the biggest vessel ever built, and Brunel's design was criticized for being too big to be safe. But what Brunel understood better than most was that a vessel's carrying capacity increased by the cube of its dimensions, while the hull's water resistance only increased by the square of its size. This meant that bigger ships were more fuel-efficient, an important factor in long voyages across the Atlantic. His new ship was to be called the *SS Great Western*, and her keel was laid in William Patterson's shipyard in Bristol on June 26, 1836.

The enormous size of the new steamship from Bristol threw the Scottish owners of the British and American Steam Navigation Company into something of a panic—their design was now outclassed by their southern rivals. The designer, Macgregor Laird, went back to his drawing board and

The 245 ft (75 m), 1,850 grt SS British Queen (above).
The 236 ft (72 m), 1,350 grt SS Great Western (below).

enlarged their new ship to 1,850 grt. This dramatic increase meant their ship, to be named the *SS British Queen*, could now carry 207 passengers compared with the *SS Great Western's* 128 passengers (plus 20 servants). The passenger saloon of the *SS British Queen* was also 30 ft (9 m) wide, compared to 21 ft (6.4 m) wide in *SS Great Western*. Clearly, size mattered on the North Atlantic run.

It was now a race to complete the ships and become the first across the Atlantic. This was Victorian cutting-edge technology and both ships were bigger than anything ever built before; each was more than twice as long as the *SS Savannah* and with carrying capacities that dwarfed the 320 grt of the earlier steamship. These new vessels also needed large steam boilers to power them across the Atlantic; this too pushed Victorian engineering to its limits.

The two ships were surprisingly similar. The *SS Great Western* had a traditional oak hull, iron-strapped for strength, with four masts carrying auxiliary sails. (The *SS British Queen* had three masts). Twin steam engines powered side paddle wheels, and the sails were used in rough conditions to stop the ship from rolling and to keep the paddle wheels in the water. The *SS Great Western* was launched on July 19, 1837. She sailed for London where she was fitted with two side-lever steam engines built by Maudslay, Sons & Field, producing 750 hp between them—more than eight times the power of the *SS Savannah*.

Meanwhile, the British and American Co. contracted Curling and Young of London to build the hull of the *SS British Queen*. They originally intended to use the experienced Scottish engineer, Robert Napier, to design and build the engine. However, Napier's bid of £20,000 (nearly £2 million in today's prices) was considered too high, and the company went for a lower quote from Claude Girdwood, another Scottish engine maker.

Claude Girdwood & Co. went bankrupt in 1837 before finishing the engine, so the British and American Steam Company returned to Napier to build their engine. This delayed the completion of the *SS British Queen* by a critical 18 months. Junius Smith was furious and accused Napier of delaying the construction while he completed other contracts for the British and Russian Governments. The two men fell out, and Napier went on to become an important early backer of another competitor, the Cunard Line.

With the *SS Great Western* nearing completion and the *SS British Queen* still months away from being ready, it looked as if Brunel and his Bristol investors would reap the prestige of being the first across the Atlantic with paying passengers. But the directors of the British and American Steam Navigation Company had other ideas and they were working on an audacious plan: to charter another steamship and beat the *SS Great Western* to New York.

The company had its eyes on the *SS Sirius,* 178 ft (54 m) long with a capacity of 703 grt, or about half that of Brunel's flagship. The *SS Sirius* only carried 40 passengers and was designed for use on the London to Cork ferry service, so she was not a particularly good choice for an Atlantic crossing (especially on the challenging east to west route). However, the Scottish company was determined, and on March 28, 1838, the ship left London under the flag of the British and American Steam Navigation Company, heading for Cork and then New York.

The 177-foot (54 m), 703 grt SS Sirius, built in 1837.

Three days later, the *SS Great Western* left London for Avonmouth (Bristol), where she was scheduled to embark passengers for her maiden voyage to New York. As the ship sailed down the Thames Estuary, a fire broke out in the engine room. The flames were extinguished quickly and there was little damage, but Brunel fell 20 ft (6 m), injuring himself. Word soon spread of the fire—one of the most terrifying emergencies that can happen at sea. As a result, more than 50 passengers canceled their bookings for the voyage.

Meanwhile, the *SS Sirius* arrived in Cork and refueled for the crossing. Being a coastal vessel, she had a range of under 3,000 NM (5,556 km); the route to New York was 2,708 NM (5,015 km), so there was little reserve in the event of headwinds. The ship left Cork on April 4th, with 45 passengers and overloaded with coal. It was still early in the year and they had a stormy crossing, but the ship arrived in New York after 18 days, 4 hours, and 22 minutes, averaging 8.03 knots (14.9 km/h); the normal westbound passage by sailing packet was 40 days.

Journalists in New York reported that the vessel ran out of coal and claimed the captain ordered cabin furniture, spare yards, and a mast to be burned to keep the boilers going. The story even inspired a similar sequence in Jules Verne's travel book, *Around the World in Eighty Days*. It was a good news story, but it was not true. The crew worked hard to conserve their coal stocks and burned five barrels of resin instead; the ship still had 15 tons of coal left on arrival. It was a remarkable achievement, but their triumph was short-lived.

Within a few hours, a great smoking behemoth was seen approaching New York harbor at speed: it was the *SS Great Western*. The ship had left Avonmouth with only seven passengers, four days after the *SS Sirius* had cast off from Cork. The bigger ship had averaged 8.66 knots (16 km/h) and made up the lost time.

For a few hours only, the *SS Sirius* claimed to be the fastest ship across the Atlantic, but she was clearly too small for an ocean crossing and passengers swarmed to the bigger and faster Bristol ship. The *SS Sirius* completed one last round trip before returning to her owners, the St George Steam Packet Company of Cork. After one voyage to St Petersburg in Russia, the steamship was put on the Cork to Glasgow route. On January 16, 1847, she struck rocks off Ballycotton in Ireland in dense fog. The ship was re-floated but leaked so badly that the captain ran the crippled vessel into shallow water in Ballycotton Bay. The ship struck rocks again; although most passengers and crew were saved, 20 people drowned.

The *SS Great Western* fared a little better. For the next two years, the ship ran a regular transatlantic service, averaging 16 days (7.95 knots) westwards to New York and 13 days and 9 hours (9.55 knots) on the return trip. In 1838, the Great Western Steamship Company paid a handsome dividend to its shareholders, but that was to be its one and only disbursement because of the runaway cost of building Brunel's next ship. By 1845, the *SS Great Western* had made 45 Atlantic crossings in eight years before her service was suspended. She was sold to the Royal Mail Steam Packet Company in 1847 and used on the West Indies run, before serving as a troopship during the Crimean War. In 1856, she was taken back to the Thames where she was broken up.

Meanwhile, the British and American Steam Navigation Company continued work on the *SS British Queen,* and she eventually sailed on her maiden voyage on July 12, 1839—15 months after the *SS Great Western*. For a year, she was the biggest passenger ship in the world and certainly roomier and more comfortable than anything else afloat ... at least for a while. Before the *SS British Queen* had even sailed, the company laid the keel of another steamship, the *SS President,* this time with a capacity of 2,350 grt. The ship was 25 percent bigger than the *SS British Queen* and easily the largest and most luxurious ship afloat. She sailed on her maiden voyage on August 1, 1840, but was underpowered and top-heavy; after just two round-trips she needed a refit after heavy seas weakened and twisted her wooden hull. In March 1841, the *SS President* became the first steamship to founder on the transatlantic run, and all 136 souls aboard were lost.

The *SS British Queen* continued to ply the Atlantic route but only made nine round trips before the company collapsed due to the loss of the *SS President*. The *SS British Queen* was sold to the Belgian Government to establish an Antwerp Cowes New York service. This was not a success, and the ship was laid up after just three return voyages. Like the *SS President*, the *SS British Queen* was built too lightly for the tough North Atlantic route, and she was scrapped in 1844, after just five years of service.

The SS President struggling in an Atlantic storm.

Despite the loss of the *SS President* and the collapse of the British and American Steam Navigation Company, side-paddle wheel steamship services flourished on North Atlantic routes for several decades. By 1877, 15 steamship companies were operating between Britain and North America in what became a regular ferry service. French and German services also operated from continental ports.

One of the great success stories of the period was a new company created by Samuel Cunard (a shipowner from Prince Edward Island in Canada), and the Scottish engineer Robert Napier (who so memorably fell out with Junius Smith over building the engine for the *SS British Queen*.) In 1839, Cunard and Napier were awarded the first British transatlantic mail contract, and they established the British and North American Royal Mail Steam-Packet Company (later called the Cunard Line). The company ran four paddle steamships between Liverpool and Halifax/Boston, and for most of the next 30 years they held the record for the fastest crossing of the North Atlantic.

Cunard's success was, in part, due to their investment in bigger vessels. In 1861, the company launched the last paddle steamship built for international service, the *SS Scotia*. This giant was 400 ft (122 m) long and had a capacity of 3,871 grt—more than twice that of the *SS British Queen*. The *SS Scotia* was specifically designed to win back the company's preeminence on the Atlantic route, and during her sea trials she achieved a remarkable speed of 17 knots (31.5 km/h). Economical passage making, however, was crucial, and even at her normal cruising speed of 13 knots (24 km/h) the vessel burned an excessive 145 tons of coal a day.

The paddle wheel steamship had reached the end of the line for ocean routes for several practical reasons. Inland, paddle wheel steamboats were ideal for use in the shallow water of rivers and lakes, where the vessel operated in smooth water. Problems arose when paddle wheels were used at sea—ideally, the paddles should operate near the surface where they sweep down into the water, then backward, thrusting the boat forward. However, ships left for a transatlantic voyage heavily laden with coal and sat low in the water. This pushed the axle of the paddle wheel lower in the water and the initial stroke of the paddle slapped vertically down into the water, before sweeping backward; as it rotated, it lifted water up before the paddle broke the surface; this resulted in poor efficiency.

Problems become worse when a paddle wheel steamship rolled and pitched in rough seas. Under these circumstances, one wheel went deep in the water while the other was lifted high, sweeping ineffectively across the surface of the water, or even becoming completely airborne. This caused the vessel to lurch in one direction before suddenly turning the other way. Not only was this very inefficient, it was also very uncomfortable for the passengers, and the snatching created heavy loads and destructive stresses on the machinery.

≈≈≈≈≈≈≈

By the early part of the nineteenth century, Britain was importing most of its timber for shipbuilding and economic necessity began to favor riveted iron for building steamships. The practical limit for a wooden hull was about 300 ft (91 m); anything longer than this and the hull flexed as waves passed under the ship (an effect called hogging). Iron offered much greater structural integrity and suffered less from hogging. By end of the 1830s, rolling mills in Britain could produce metal plates big enough to make iron-hulled ocean-going ships a practical and economic alternative. A new age in shipbuilding had arrived.

The directors of the Great Western Steamship Company decided to build the first ocean-going iron ship; it was to be named the *SS Great Britain*. At first Brunel and the other engineers were cautious about changing from timber to iron, but they became bolder with each new version of the design, and their plans became ever larger. By the fifth draft, the ship had grown to 3,400 tons—more than 1,000 tons bigger than any ship ever built.

The problems with paddle wheel vessels on the Atlantic run were now well understood, so Brunel decided his new ship would have a different system and he took an interest in a revolutionary screw-propeller that he had seen on the relatively small 125 ft (38 m) *SS Archimedes*. The advantages were obvious: propellers were lighter and more efficient, they were mounted low in the hull which improved stability, saved space, and unlike paddle wheels the propellers remained submerged at all times. The company agreed to make the changes, but it delayed the completion of the new ship by nine months.

Brunel's new design was 322 ft (98 m) long with a gross registered tonnage of 3,443 tons or more than 2½ times the capacity of her sister ship. The new vessel was designed to carry 360 passengers (later increased to

The SS Great Britain in Bristol, April 1844, with her original five masts. This is believed to be the first photograph ever taken of a ship.

730)—a significant improvement over the 128 passengers carried on the *SS Great Western*. When the *SS Great Britain* was launched by Prince Albert on July 19, 1843, she was not only the biggest and most technologically advanced ship of her day but also the first ocean-going, iron-hulled, propeller-driven ship ever built. It was a remarkable achievement, but it came at a price.

The ship was too big to be launched, so she was floated out of her dry dock. The builders had originally intended to tow the vessel around to the River Thames to be fitted out. However, the ship had been widened to accommodate the new propellers and a late decision was made to fit the engines before launching. Now the ship was too wide and too deep to fit through the lock gates in Bristol harbor.

Negotiations with the harbor authorities dragged on for months before the locks were modified. When the *SS Great Britain* eventually left a year late, she stuck fast in the second set of locks; this would have resulted in very serious structural damage if the ship had not been quickly hauled back into the harbor. Brunel took advantage of a slightly higher tide the next day, and after removing coping stones and platforms around the lock gates, a tugboat appropriately named the *Samson* hauled the monster steamship down the River Avon and into the safety of deep water at Avonmouth.

The *SS Great Britain* eventually went into transatlantic service on July 26, 1845; she was five years overdue and 67 percent over budget, but she was also a magnificent technological achievement. Everything was on a scale never seen before: the cylinders of the two 500 hp engines each had a diameter of 7 ft 4 in (2.2 m) driving a propeller shaft 68 ft (21 m) long and 28 in (0.71 m) in diameter; the original six-bladed "windmill" propeller was 16 ft (4.9 m) in diameter.

Brunel was anxious to prevent the hull from hogging, so he designed it to be massively strong. The iron keel plates were 1 in (2.5 cm) thick, overlapped, and double-riveted, and the ribs of the hull were 6 x 3 in (15 x 7.6 cm) of solid iron. The designer also incorporated a double hull and five watertight bulkheads for strength and safety. In total, 1,500 tons of iron (including the machinery) went into building the ship.

The inside of the vessel continued to break records. There were two upper decks for passengers, with cargo stowed on the lower deck. In the aft section, the upper passenger deck contained the principal saloon that was twice the area of a tennis court, 110 ft (34 m) long, and 48 ft (15 m) wide. Below was the slightly smaller dining saloon, 98 ft 6 in (30 m) by 30 ft (9.1 m), but still with room to accommodate 360 people at a single sitting.

This latest generation of transatlantic steamships catered to a new traveler—decadent, wealthy tourists. Passengers expected the very highest level of service equivalent to the top hotels they visited when in New York or London. Vintage wines and the finest food were served on linen tablecloths by attentive waiters.

Two decks below, life was very different for the men who fueled the vast furnaces to drive the engines. A stoker usually worked a grueling four-hour shift shoveling coal in temperatures ranging from 120-160 deg F (49-71 deg C). He usually spent three minutes at a furnace, and when he had finished stoking, he would rush to an air pipe gasping, and wait for his next turn to shovel. The intense heat could render stokers temporarily insane and there were many incidents where men made their way up on deck and jumped overboard, rather than continue working in a transatlantic Hades.

The *SS Great Britain* made her maiden voyage in July 1845 from Liverpool to New York in a respectable 14 days and 21 hours, averaging 9.25 knots (17.1 km/h); her return voyage took 13½ days. None of these passages broke any speed records, but the ship pushed the boundaries for technical innovation, and it marked the beginning of a new era of luxurious voyaging across the Atlantic.

A revolutionary creation like the *SS Great Britain* inevitably brought engineering problems and failures. Brunel had to replace the propeller to improve efficiency, and the ship lost one of her five masts and three propeller blades in a storm. The ship also rolled badly even in calm weather, much to the discomfort of the passengers. In her second year, a navigational error resulted in the ship running aground in Dundrum Bay in Ireland; she was a huge vessel to move, and remained stuck for nearly a year before being re-floated at huge expense and towed back to Liverpool. The rescue mission exhausted the company's dwindling resources and the Great Western Steamship Company's balance sheet was enough to give any accountant heart palpitations. The original estimate to build the ship was £70,000, only to rise to £117,000; the vessel was out of service for a year when aground, and it cost £34,000 to be re-floated; the ship was eventually sold to Gibbs, Bright, and Co. for the knock-down sum of £25,000.

After a substantial re-fit, the ship gave 30-years of service running migrants from England to Australia, including the first English cricket team to tour Australia. The vessel also served as a troopship during the Crimean War and the Indian Mutiny. In 1882, the *SS Great Britain* was converted to a sailing ship and used to transport bulk coal. On her final working voyage in 1886, she was damaged beyond economic salvage by fire and sold to the Falkland Islands Company as a storage hulk for bunker coal.

On April 24, 1970, after years of fundraising, the ship was towed back from the South Atlantic to Bristol and into the same dry dock where she was built. After substantial conservation work, the ship was opened as a visitor attraction in July 2005, 162 years after she was launched. Today, Brunel's *SS Great Britain* is visited by 200,000 people a year.

≈≈≈≈≈≈≈

Throughout the nineteenth century and into the twentieth, competition between steamship companies on the Atlantic run became fierce. Everyone vied to have the biggest and fastest vessel, with the most extravagant service and the most reliable schedule. The diesel engine replaced the steam engine, it required less supervision and maintenance, did not need large boilers or a water supply, and so allowed more space for passengers and cargo.

One enduring legacy of the battle between the *SS Sirius* and the *SS Great Western* was to recognize the fastest crossing of the North Atlantic. The prize has become an enduring legend on the transatlantic steamship route, but in reality, it has only ever been an unofficial and weakly regulated award. Even so, it created the prize of the "Blue Riband."

This accolade became an honor awarded to any passenger ship that recorded the fastest time on a regularly scheduled passenger crossing of the North Atlantic. The term was borrowed from horse racing, but it did not become widely used until after 1910. Even so, the award recognized the technological achievement of steamship companies, and after 1930 in particular, national prestige, military interests, and international politics all became important as taxpayer's money was spent on developing and building record-breaking steamships.

One problem was that nobody agreed to the terms of the competition. Vessels sailed from different ports in both Britain and continental Europe, and they arrived at different destinations in North America. Passage times varied depending on which direction the ship was heading; voyages from west to east benefited from the prevailing wind and the Gulf Stream, and were nearly always faster than the opposite direction. The Blue Riband had never been granted official status; however, that did not prevent certain ship captains who had a Blue Riband from hoisting it to make a point. Newspaper journalists (especially in New York) loved the idea of a speed competition across the Atlantic, and they monitored the claims and made sure that the shipping companies adhered fairly to the unwritten statutes.

These ill-defined rules eventually required the winner to cross the Atlantic faster than the current holder in a westerly direction, i.e. from Europe to North America. There is an important difference between "passage time" and "average speed." Average speed can be calculated to within a fraction of a knot which is why this criterion was adopted, rather than the actual duration of the voyage. Anybody who has been on a cruise knows that leaving and arriving at a destination can take many hours, depending on the efficiency of the harbor authorities and the movements of other shipping. The duration of a crossing (and thus the average speed) was therefore calculated between fixed points outside the confines of a harbor; these included the Mole in Cherbourg, the Ambrose Lightship off New York, and the Bishops Rock Lighthouse off the Isles of Scilly in the extreme south-west of Britain.

Nobody can argue the first holder was the *SS Sirius*, even though the prize had not been created when the ship arrived in New York in April 1838. The honor did not last long, as the *SS Great Western* steamed into the harbor just a few hours later. The Bristol ship held the record until June 15, 1841, when the upstart Cunard Line took the record with the *SS Columbia*; the company dominated the rankings for the fastest crossing to the end of the nineteenth century, by which time the record stood at an average speed of 21.81 knots (40.39 km/h), set by the *SS Lucania*.

The RMS Mauretania at full speed. The ship's steam turbine engines helped the ship set the transatlantic record that held for 20 years.

Germany entered the competition with a record-breaking speed set by the *SS Kaiser Wilhelm der Grosse* in 1898. But it was Cunard's 1909 record of 26.06 knots (48.26 km/h) set by the *RMS Mauretania* that held for 20 years. The ship's high speed resulted from her slim design combined with four newly-developed steam turbine engines. Inside the ship was luxurious, with swimming pools, Turkish baths, gymnasium, squash court, and spacious lounges. Like many transatlantic liners of the period, the ship was built with a government subsidy to allow her to be converted to a light merchant cruiser, although she was never used in war.

German ships held the record between 1929 and 1933 when the Italian *SS Rex* took the record. At this point, the 67-year-old Sir Harold Keates Hales entered the transatlantic history books. Known affectionately to his friends as H.K., TIME MAGAZINE once described him as "a nearly perfect example of a self-made middle-class Englishman."

Hales was, to say the least, eccentric. He made his fortune as a shipping magnate, but some of his more notorious deeds included flying an airship around St. Paul's Cathedral, and in 1910 he became one of the first people to survive an air crash. After spending World War I serving in Turkey, he traveled the world promoting British industry. His four years as Conservative Member of Parliament for Hanley in Staffordshire from 1931 to 1935 are best remembered when he intervened in a House of Commons debate on the herring industry and enlivened his speech by waving a fish in the air; fortunately, it was dead at the time.

Hales harbored a life-long ambition to donate an award to the fastest passenger liner to cross the Atlantic. In 1933, he approached a silversmith in Sheffield with a detailed design for an ornate, baroque-style, solid silver and heavy gilt trophy, comprising a large globe resting on two winged figures, decorated with miniature galleons, ocean liners, and figures of Neptune and Amphitrite—the god and goddess of the sea. This huge edifice would certainly not sit comfortably on your mantlepiece.

Harold Hales with his trophy in 1935. The cup stands more than 4 feet (1.2 m) high and weighs nearly 100 lbs (45 kg).

The Hales Trophy was specifically intended to be awarded for the fastest east to west Atlantic crossing; by the time it was completed in 1935, the Italian ocean liner *SS Rex* still held the record. H.K. decided the vessel should become the first holder, and he arranged for the Italian ambassador to collect the trophy at a lavish ceremony in London in August. Before the trophy could be awarded, the French liner *SS Normandie* (in what was almost certainly a spoiling tactic), completed her maiden voyage to New York on June 3rd in a faster time.

Hales was left in an embarrassing position having promised the trophy to the Italians, but now finding it was rightfully due to the French. The solution? He retrospectively changed the rules to prevent a new claim being lodged within three months of a ship establishing a new time, ostensibly to give the existing holder a chance to defend their record. All parties agreed to this diplomatic fudge and it was agreed the *SS Rex* would hold the trophy for three months, before passing it to the French. Unfortunately, even this did not work as the *SS Normandie* was scheduled for a refit when the trophy was due to be presented; another compromise was reached, and the Italians handed the Hales Trophy back a month early so the French could receive it when their ship was still on active service.

The following year the British (Royal Mail Ship) *RMS Queen Mary* established a new record for the fastest crossing, and the Hales Trophy was duly offered to the Cunard Line. The company's Chairman, Sir Percy Bates, announced testily that Cunard operated a regular, scheduled service for which a trophy would not be appropriate. The captain of the ship added: "We don't believe in racing on the Atlantic, Blue Ribands, or trophies and the like."

The RMS Queen Mary in Long Beach, California; 2011.

H.K. took offense and decided to change the rules again, this time to specifically exclude British vessels. The *SS Normandie* took the trophy again in 1937 with a new record of 30.31 knots (56.13 km/h). In the end, the Cunard Line had the last chuckle when the *RMS Queen Mary* set a new record in 1938, which she held for the next 14 years ... without ever qualifying for the trophy.

World War II brought a halt to the transatlantic passenger route, and ocean liners were requisitioned to serve as troopships; many did not survive the war. The *SS Normandie* was often considered to be the greatest ocean liner of the period. She was requisitioned by the U.S. military and renamed the *USS Lafayette*; she caught fire on the Hudson River in 1942 and capsized. In 1944, the *SS Rex* was attacked by the British Royal Air Force in the Mediterranean and burned for four days before sinking. The *RMS Queen Mary* survived as a troopship and returned to the Atlantic run; together with the newer *RMS Queen Elizabeth*, the Cunard Line dominated the route until the 1950s, when passenger jet aircraft began to operate a cheaper and quicker service across the Atlantic.

In 1987, after her transatlantic service, the *RMS Queen Mary* was moved to Long Beach, California, as a tourist attraction and is officially recognized as an Historic Hotel of America. The *RMS Queen Elizabeth* was sold to a Hong Kong businessman who spent £5 million converting the ship to a floating university. During refurbishment in 1972, a fire broke out under unexplained circumstances and the vessel capsized from the weight of the huge volume of water used to fight the fire. The wreck was deemed an obstruction to shipping and she was partially scrapped where she lay.

The SS United States in 2017 at Pier 82 in Philadelphia awaiting restoration.

Meanwhile, the indefatigable Harold Keates Hales drowned in 1942 in the River Thames at Shepperton, and his trophy was mislaid during the war years. It was found stored at the original silversmiths in Sheffield in 1952, just in time to be awarded to the new record holder; the *SS United States* had made a transatlantic crossing in 3½ days at an average speed of 34.5 knots (63.9 km/h). The ship maintained an uninterrupted schedule of transatlantic service until 1969, when she was sold several times, with each new owner trying unsuccessfully to make the liner profitable. Since 2009, a preservation group called the *SS United States* Conservancy has been soliciting funds to save the ship. If insufficient money is raised, alternate plans include turning the vessel into an artificial reef, rather than scrapping her.

≈≈≈≈≈≈≈

Controversy came back to haunt the Hales Trophy in 1985 when the British businessman, Richard Branson, built the 65 ft (19.8 m) twin-hulled *Virgin Atlantic Challenger* with the express purpose of beating the record set by the *SS United States*. His first attempt failed when the catamaran sank off Land's End, 86 NM (160 km) short of the finish line. He tried again the following year with the bigger 72 ft (22 m) *Virgin Atlantic Challenger II* and set a new average speed record of a little under 36 knots (66 km/h).

The Virgin Atlantic II, Richard Branson's "little toy boat."

However, the trustees of the Blue Riband denied Branson the award on the grounds that he had broken two competition rules: firstly, he had stopped to refuel, and secondly, the vessel was not on a genuine commercial voyage. The American Merchant Marine Museum (AMMM) also refused to surrender the Hales Trophy, claiming the *Virgin Atlantic Challenger II* was not a commercial passenger ship, and the voyage had been in the faster west to east direction. The AMMM went further and disparagingly referred to Branson's vessel as "a little toy boat." Ouch.

Branson's attempt on the record was little more than a publicity stunt to promote his new airline that had just begun commercial flights between London and New York. But the entrepreneur was undaunted, and he established a new trophy, announcing that "we are throwing down the gauntlet for anyone else to make a transatlantic challenge and beat it."

The First Atlantic Yacht Race

*L*ate October in New York City can be cold, and the autumn of 1866 was no exception. As office workers hurried home and lamplighters came out in their dozens to illuminate the city's streets, three young friends headed for their private club in downtown Manhattan. As dusk faded, they were grateful to get out of the wind chill and into the opulent entrance hall of the Union Club. They were soon settled into wing chairs, cigars in hand, sipping their first brandy cocktail of the evening. The latest graze was a "Razzle Dazzle" — their preferred mix being a lethal concoction of ginger ale, brandy, and absinthe.

The Union Club of the City of New York, to give it its full name, was then situated on the corner of Fifth Avenue and East 21st Street and was the oldest private members club in town. Founded in 1834—27 years before the civil war tore the country apart—the Union Club was considered to be the most exclusive social club in New York. The three hedonists that evening were very exclusive and very social, and despite their youth, they were also three of the richest and most influential men in America.

The undoubted leader of the pack was James Gordon Bennett Jr (25), heir to the NEW YORK HERALD, then the most successful and profitable newspaper in America. Bennett's real interest, however, lay not in journalism but in drinking, fast women, and later in life, even faster cars. Gordon Bennett has gone down in history as one of the first international playboys. Amongst his many social faux pas was the occasion when he arrived blind drunk at a New Year's Eve house party thrown by his fiancée's parents, only to relieve himself into the fireplace in front of their astonished guests. The engagement did not last, but the infamous exclamation "Gordon Bennett" most certainly has and is used as a euphemism for a four-letter word to explain extraordinary behavior.

Bennett's friend, George Archer Osgood (46) was a successful stockbroker who had amassed a fortune in shareholdings, including stocks in the new-fangled railroads. He also handled some of the trades made by his father-in-law, Cornelius Vanderbilt. Osgood had, as they say, married well. He was a keen yachtsman and had crossed the Atlantic some years previously on Vanderbilt's luxurious 252 ft (76.8 m) steam yacht, the *North Star*. The magnificent vessel had been built expressly for the Vanderbilt family's first Grand Tour of Europe, but the ship suffered the ignominy of running aground on at least two occasions.

The last member of this wealthy, reckless triumvirate was Pierre Lorillard IV (33), owner of the oldest tobacco company in the United States and a keen racehorse owner and yachtsman. He had a reputation for pomposity, no doubt further enhanced when he changed his name from Peter to Pierre to acknowledge his French Huguenot ancestry. Lorillard was extremely rich and became one of America's first millionaires. During the 1880s, he helped make Newport, Rhode Island, one of the biggest yachting centers in the world. He also owned a summer estate there called "Breakers," which he later sold to Cornelius Vanderbilt for $400,000 (then the biggest real estate deal in history).

These three fabulously wealthy young men were a mix just as potent as the copious amounts of Razzle Dazzle cocktails they consumed that night. As the evening wore on, their drunken disputes turned to offshore racing. They all owned fine twin-mast schooners, each over 100 ft (30.5 m) long, and inevitably each of them believed his yacht to be far superior to the others. That evening's drinking session resulted in one of the most audacious and foolhardy proposals in the history of yachting.

Gordon Bennett owned the fine-looking schooner, the *Henrietta*, 107 ft (32.6 m) long, and displacing 205 tons. Bennett was an experienced sailor who became the youngest member of the New York Yacht Club at the tender age of 16. When the *Henrietta* was launched in 1861, the American Civil War had just started and Bennett loaned his new vessel to the Union government to help with the war effort, offering himself as her 20-year-old captain. He enlisted as a third lieutenant on a monthly salary of $353 and was given command of a 12-man crew. The yacht patrolled the East Coast between South Carolina and Nantucket as a customs cutter. Bennett soon tired of his contribution to the war effort, and by April 1862 he withdrew himself and the *Henrietta* from active service. However, his year as a naval officer turned him into a competent sailor.

George Osgood was the equally proud owner of the schooner *Fleetwing*. Built just two years previously in 1864, she was narrower and deeper than the *Henrietta*; at 212 tons, she was also slightly heavier. The *Fleetwing* had a very similar length at 106 ft (32.3 m) overall, and both vessels were fine examples of traditional American racing yachts of the period.

Pierre Lorillard's new boat, *Vesta*, was altogether different. Although practically the same length as Osgood's *Fleetwing*, Lorillard's yacht was a light displacement schooner with a lifting centerboard instead of a deep keel. The *Vesta* gained some of her stability from her extra wide beam, and Lorillard argued his vessel was at the cutting edge of modern yacht design and far superior to either Bennett's *Henrietta* or Osgood's *Fleetwing*, that were heavy, narrow, and slower by comparison … or so he claimed.

James Gordon Bennett Jr. as a young naval officer.

As the effects of the Razzle Dazzle cocktails took effect, any scrap of common sense the young men might have had slipped away along with any vestiges of sobriety. The flames of their argument were further fanned by a recent article in Bennett's NEW YORK HERALD urging yachtsmen to be more adventurous, encouraging America's "smooth water gentry" to cruise further afield, perhaps to South America or even Europe. The article went on to claim such a voyage would "perpetuate your memory, reflect luster on your deeds, and resound to the honor of your country."

The three friends decided to settle their argument over who had the fastest boat by racing across the Atlantic—it had never been done before and they decided it was about time that it was. It was an audacious plan, but there was more to come. With money to burn, the three sailors each wagered $30,000 on the race, with the winner taking all. They were too impatient to wait until summer, so they decided they would race as soon as possible, and a start date of Tuesday, December 11th was agreed. Sailing in mid-winter was a senseless and rash proposal that risked life and limb, but the next morning—despite their thumping heads—they met up at the New York Yacht Club (where they were all members) to seal the deal.

The New York Yacht Club (NYYC) is a private social and yacht club founded in 1844, and it remains arguably the most exclusive sailing club in the world where members can only join by invitation. Since 1901, the Club has been housed in a fine six-story limestone building on West 44th

Street in mid-town Manhattan. Back in 1866, however, it was based in an altogether more modest clubhouse in Hoboken, New Jersey, on the west bank of the Hudson River. It was here that Gordon Bennett and his two friends presented themselves to formalize their $90,000 wager—worth nearly $1.5 million in today's money.

During the early decades of the club, racing for prize money was the main objective among most of the wealthy members, sometimes with several thousand dollars being placed on a single race. But this new wager to race across the Atlantic in the middle of winter was far beyond anything that had previously been proposed. The Commodore, William McVickar, patiently heard their proposal then rejected it out of hand. But Bennett and friends persevered and McVickar was finally persuaded to back the race, and the rules were finalized.

In this way the sport of offshore yacht racing was born, on the sozzled whim of three wealthy, arrogant, and egotistic young drunkards.

≈≈≈≈≈≈≈

Their luxury schooners were complex, sophisticated racing machines requiring a permanent crew of 20 or more experienced sailors, and the summer racing schedule of the NYYC produced fierce competition up and down the East Coast from New York to Cape Cod and Nantucket. But these yachts were designed for inshore summer sailing in light to moderate winds when you were never far from shelter, and they were massively over-canvassed to make the most of whatever breeze was available. They were never intended for sailing offshore, and certainly not to be raced across the Atlantic in the middle of winter.

The yachts were much the same length with similar schooner rigs. However, their performance during the 1866 summer racing season created a clear bookmaker's favorite. The *Henrietta* might have taken the prize as the most elegant of the three yachts with her tiger-skin rugs and deep mahogany paneling, but she was now four years old and outclassed in head-to-head racing with the other two. The *Henrietta* lacked a fine entry at the bow, and her narrower 22 ft (6.7 m) beam was thought to limit her ability to carry maximum sail when the wind increased.

The *Vesta* had a good summer's racing by comfortably winning against the *Henrietta* and narrowly beating the *Fleetwing* in a 180 NM (334 km) race in lively conditions. Bennett's heavier yacht also lost out to the others in lighter conditions. Despite the *Vesta's* success that year, there were still nagging doubts about the lightweight design and how the yacht would

Antonio Jacobsen's 1879 painting of the NYYC schooner fleet shows the remarkable similarity between the yachts.

cope with the full force of a North Atlantic storm—which the yachts would inevitably face.

The race caught the public's imagination and there was frenetic betting, with the *Fleetwing* becoming the bookies' favorite with odds of 2½ to 1, the *Henrietta* was offered at 3 to 1, and the *Vesta* was the outsider at 3½ to 1. One million dollars was staked on the race—a huge sum for a city with a population of only 900,000.

James Gordon Bennett was an astute yachtsman and he understood the limitations of his beloved *Henrietta*. His usual skipper, Martin Lyons, knew the boat well but he lacked experience in sailing offshore. In a stroke of ruthless brilliance, Bennett demoted Lyons to "sailing master" and sought a new skipper who was more familiar with the North Atlantic. There was probably nobody better to take race-command of the *Henrietta* than 41-year-old Captain Samuel Samuels, a seafarer with a formidable reputation.

Samuels was given his first command at the age of 21 and soon gained respect as a successful master of Red Cross Line packet boats sailing between Amsterdam and New York. By the 1850s, the lucrative Atlantic passenger trade was under pressure from the first steamships run by pioneers such as Samuel Cunard. The directors of the Red Cross Line, therefore, decided to build the ultimate, fast packet boat to take on the steamship challenge, and they persuaded Samuel Samuels to become its sailing master; he was asked to take partial responsibility for her design and full responsibility for her construction.

The result was launched in 1853, the 212 ft (64.6 m) *Dreadnought*, a tough transatlantic packet boat that could be pushed hard in the worst of weather, and it soon earned her the nickname "the wild boat of the Atlantic." Captain "Bully" Samuels ran a fast schedule averaging 19 days on the eastward route, with many voyages taking less than 16 days. Within a short time, the ship became the highest-earning packet boat on the Atlantic run, and private cabins for the wealthier passengers were fully booked a season in advance.

Samuels' legendary reputation only grew during a particularly violent storm in the mid-Atlantic. Five days out of Liverpool, his vessel was overwhelmed by a monstrous sea that carried away the ship's rudder and killed the carpenter. Samuels was thrown across the ship, shattering his right leg below the knee and puncturing an artery. The crew tried to reset his leg, and he wrote: "After an ineffectual attempt by three strong men to pull the limb into place, I became exhausted that they desisted ... then I decided on amputation."

Nobody was prepared to do the job and overcome with unbearable pain, he prepared a tourniquet and knife to remove his own leg. Fortunately, his second mate persuaded him to strap the limb and head for land. Without

The two-masted schooner Henrietta under full sail.

a rudder, the ship could not turn into the wind, and Samuels still wracked with pain, retained command, and sailed the *Dreadnought* backward for 52 hours to the Azores. His days as master of his ship, however, were over and he spent a year in physiotherapy to rehabilitate his crushed limb.

Having decided that Samuels was his man, Bennett had to persuade this sailing legend to take command of the *Henrietta*. It was an odd couple who met up to discuss the proposal—a 26-year-old wealthy wastrel with a penchant for Razzle Dazzle cocktails, and a 41-year-old grizzled seadog with 39 return Atlantic crossings to his credit, and a fearsome reputation for discipline. Bennett's approach was simple—he offered Samuels $10,000 to take command of the *Henrietta* ($150,000 in today's money). The money meant nothing to Bennett, but it was instantly acceptable to Samuels and the deal was struck. Such was Samuels' confidence in himself that he is said to have immediately gone to a bookmaker and placed $7,500 of his earnings on himself to win the race.

Samuels' first job as the new master was to look over the schooner, then lying to her mooring on the Hudson River. With only a few weeks to go, he had little time to spare. The *Henrietta* was well-built and came from the board of a good designer, but the yacht was set up for inshore summer racing along the East Coast, not for crossing the North Atlantic in mid-winter. This playboy's plaything could not have been more different from his tough, rugged *Dreadnought*—and even this tough packet boat had been bested by the worst of Atlantic storms, as the ache in his right leg constantly reminded him.

The skipper first looked over the rig. Like all NYYC racing schooners, the *Henrietta* was hugely over-canvassed and could carry over 9,000 sq ft (836 sq m) of sail, equivalent to the area of two basketball courts. The enormous boom was over 60 ft (18 m) long and weighed over a tonne, making it a dangerous spar to control in a storm. (The boom on the second mast was not much smaller). Samuels ordered that 6 ft (1.8 m) be cut from the main boom, and the other spars shortened proportionately. This also required the sails to be re-cut and reduced to fit.

The rest of the rig had to be managed in the usual way—with an experienced crew and lots of brawn. The mainsails were hoisted on heavy pine gaff spars running along the top of each sail, and these required several men to hoist and lower the sails, working carefully in unison. Even the "fisherman's topsail" set flying between the two masts had an area of 600 sq ft (56 sq m). The bowsprit was nearly 40 ft (12.2 m) long, and setting or taking in the flying jibs was another dangerous job—the bowsprit was often given the ominous nickname as "the widow-maker."

Samuels did not need reminding of the destructive power of waves and he ordered the large, open cockpit be covered over, and for larger freeing ports to be cut in the yacht's bulwarks to allow any water that found its way on deck to drain away quickly. The yacht's internal ballast had additional lashings to stop it from moving in the event of a knock-down at sea. Finally, the long tiller on *Henrietta* was replaced with wheel steering. A tiller was not often seen on sailing boats as big as these, but on the NYYC schooners, they allowed for delicate adjustment to the yacht's course during racing. In the open ocean with big following seas, a snatching tiller would be a liability, and at worst the yacht could become unmanageable.

George Osgood also chose a good skipper for the *Fleetwing*. Captain Dick Brown had been a Sandy Hook pilot for nearly 20 years and had a reputation for being one of the most skillful sailing masters in those waters. In 1851, he sailed the yacht *America* to England and trounced the cream of British yacht racing when he skippered the schooner in the Royal Yacht Squadron Regatta in Cowes that August. America was so far ahead of the rest of the competition that Queen Victoria—who was watching the race with great interest—allegedly turned to one of her aides and asked, "Who is second?" The reply came: "Ma'am, there is no second." A silver cup was awarded to the Americans who took it back to New York, where they contemplated melting it down to strike medals from its silver. Eventually, they donated the prize to the NYYC as "a challenge cup open to all foreign clubs." Today, the America's Cup is the oldest trophy in international sport.

Dick Brown took much the same approach to prepare the *Fleetwing* as Samuels had done with the *Henrietta*, by cutting down the booms and reducing the sail area. However, he chose not to cover the cockpit nor did he enlarge the bulwark ports to assist ridding the decks of surplus water. This was a decision he would later come to regret. However, his impressive reputation for sailing the *America* to victory contributed to the *Fleetwing* becoming the bookies' favorite to win.

Lorillard chose Captain George Dayton as *Vesta's* skipper. Dayton did not have the high profile of either Samuels or Brown, but he was a safe pair of hands with the reputation of being a conservative and careful seaman. This is exactly what was required with the lightweight *Vesta* and her controversial centerboard. The drop-down keel could be raised when the wind blew from behind, thereby decreasing the wetted surface area of the vessel and allowing the yacht to sail faster. However, the centerboard did not give *Vesta* the same stability as the other schooners with deep keels, and she was untested in offshore sailing.

Dayton understood the limitations of the *Vesta* in the deep ocean. If the weather turned nasty, then the yacht could not "lie a-hull" in the traditional manner with only a scrap of canvas to give the yacht steerage; this heavy-weather tactic allowed the waves to pass underneath with (relatively) little effect. Instead, *Vesta* would have to run downwind, towing a sea anchor to slow the boat down. However, with two masts and masses of rigging, the schooner had a lot of windage, and running down giant Atlantic rollers in storm conditions would be a hair-raising experience. These schooners also had wide sterns and were vulnerable to being "pooped," where large waves can break over the stern, with potentially disastrous consequences.

Preparing their vessels proved to be the easiest part of the preparations; finding the right crew was proving to be almost impossible. The best crews were the East Coast cod fishermen, well-experienced in working the treacherous Grand Banks. They fully understood the harsh realities of the North Atlantic in winter, but most were wary of signing on to this crazy, rich man's game. Bennett offered $100 a man to crew the *Henrietta*, but it was not enough. A few days before the start, most of her 23-man crew walked away, not willing to take the risk for the money. The NEW YORK HERALD reported the problem by diminishing the jeopardy, and instead blamed the setback on their womenfolk:

> "*Some difficulty was experienced in securing seamen to cross the Atlantic in such vessels and such weather. The men were willing enough to engage, but their mothers, wives, and sweethearts all interfered and persuaded them not to sign articles. Moved by such feminine solicitations, the crew of the Henrietta deserted her a few days before the start and their places had to be supplied by a lot of landlubbers, few of whom could climb a mast.*"

It must have come as a great relief to all concerned that the crewing problem on the *Henrietta* was caused by "feminine solicitations," and not because this was a dangerous, hare-brained scheme dreamed up by drunken playboys who knew enough about sailing to realize that lives could be lost. Given time, Samuel Samuels certainly had the experience to whip "a lot of landlubbers" into shape, but with only a few days before facing the fury of the winter Atlantic, it was asking a lot even of this legendary skipper. At least he could take some satisfaction from the fact that he was not alone in having crew problems.

In a bizarre, last-minute decision, Osgood replaced Dick Brown—the *America's* triumphant skipper—with Captain Albert Thomas, to take command of the *Fleetwing*. Brown was demoted to sailing master, and decided to quit on the spot; unfortunately for the new skipper, eight other crew members followed Brown off the vessel. They were replaced by eight hardened whalers who had seen more long winter nights on the high seas than any of them could recall.

In addition to the crew, each of the yachts was required to carry two judges appointed by the NYYC to guarantee the rules were followed to the letter—after all, there was nearly $1.5 million at stake in today's money. The judges brought the *Henrietta's* complement to 30 men, the *Fleetwing's* to 25, and the *Vesta's* to 26. One of the judges on the *Vesta* was George Lorillard—the owner's brother—who was hardly likely to be an impartial arbitrator.

As for the owners, Pierre Lorillard was happy to allow his 23-year-old brother to suffer the privations of the winter crossing and he sniffly announced that he would not sail himself, claiming: "I am altogether indifferent to the race." Presumably, he preferred to eat at the Union Club, where the dining table at least remained horizontal for the duration of the meal.

George Osgood did not even bother to announce he was not sailing, but perhaps he never had any intention to be aboard *Fleetwing*—even though it was favorite to win. It was not, however, unusual for owners not to be aboard their yachts during a race, as sailing these boats (especially in competitive racing), was a tough and brutish sport best left to professionals.

To his credit, Gordon Bennett chose to sail on his, and not surprisingly his reputation was boosted when his father's paper declared: "… people who do not intend to sail in yacht races ought not to decide whether other people shall cross the ocean in midwinter." Even the HERALD's rival, the NEW YORK TIMES was equally withering about Osgood and Lorillard's spinelessness:

> "We confess the race would have more interest and be a pluckier affair if [all] the owners boarded the yachts and personally took part in the race. They may plead, and doubtless with reason, the claims of business, the discomforts of such a voyage, and the chances of being drowned, as reasons they should not go: but all these hazards and hardships are incidental to the peculiar sport they have seen fit to patronize."

≈≈≈≈≈≈≈

There was feverish activity aboard the yachts in the days running up to the start. Each captain cast an experienced eye over his charge, tweaking rigging where necessary, renewing ropes that had frayed, and oiling the mechanical equipment that could not be allowed to fail or seize. Spare sailcloth, extra rope, canned food, and water for the crew were all brought aboard—and rather better food and dozens of bottles of vintage champagne for the judges.

At 7:00 a.m. on the bitterly cold Tuesday morning of December 11th, the yachts were towed down the Hudson River and anchored off Stapleton, on Staten Island. If any of the crew entertained doubts about the voyage, it was now too late for them to jump ship. New York harbor was alive with steamers, skiffs, and spectator boats, all wanting to get a close look at the schooners.

Aboard the steamer *River Queen*, Lorillard was celebrating in style by quaffing champagne at a dangerously early hour. Meanwhile, his challenger, Gordon Bennett, was demolishing a magnum of champagne aboard the *Schulz*. All three owners were determined to make the most of their big day, but only one of them would be watching the sunset that evening over the Atlantic's western horizon on his boat.

Meanwhile, one of the HERALD's staff journalists, Stephen Fiske, was hiding aboard the *Schulz* in the most bizarre circumstances. Several days previously, he had been called into the inner office of the formidable Bennett Sr, editor of the NEW YORK HERALD, and given strict instructions: "This race. Yachts. One of 'em's m'son's. Cover it. No fooling around. Fall in the sea for all I care but get the news. Properly. Understood?" Fiske was quaking in his shoes and he understood perfectly. He could allow nothing to stand in the way of getting his story. Unfortunately, he had witnessed a minor scuffle on the streets a few days previously, and he had just been subpoenaed to appear in court as a witness.

On the morning of the race, Fiske had been forewarned that court officials were down on the waterfront looking for him, intending to bring him to testify before the magistrate. Fiske (wisely) feared the wrath of the old man more than he did the U.S. Justice Department, and he boarded the *River Queen* by helping the overstretched porters carry cases of champagne up the gangplank. Once aboard, he hid, knowing the steamer would rendezvous with the *Schulz* at some time during the morning. As the two steamers came alongside, Fiske took his chance and literally jumped ships:

> "... I clambered over the rail of the River Queen and made a hazardous leap to the deck of the other vessel. Staggering about a little, I managed to convey to many cheering witnesses that my athletic feat had been of the charming kind always achieved by the drunken and I had no more than a fleeting impression— there was so much cheering, gallavanting and dancing going

on and the tension was so high, that the odd appeared perfectly ordinary."

Fiske was now safely aboard the *Schulz*, but not safe from the court officials. He decided to hide again and bribed a crewman with a $5-dollar bill to let him hide himself in the one thing that he knew would be carried aboard the *Henrietta*—a crate of champagne, although he did suffer "the greatest cricks and cramps as a result." The crate was swung aboard the schooner and as it landed on deck, Fiske "pushed up the lid of my temporary abode to come face to face with my master cum employer for the duration of this trifling journey across the Atlantic." Better that than the court officials.

It was now 11:30 a.m. and the *Henrietta* and her two competitors raised anchor and were towed towards the starting line. As the conditions became decidedly choppy away from the shoreline, the yachts raised sail and the tugs slipped their lines. The crew on the schooners were beginning to get a foretaste of what was to come—it was 23 deg. F (minus 5 deg. C), and colder still with the wind chill factor. Captain Samuels claimed it was "the rawest of days."

For the next hour, the three professional skippers were more concerned with avoiding a collision with one of the scores of pleasure boats that had come out to watch the start, than with what might lie ahead over the horizon. It seemed that most of the inhabitants of New York City were afloat that day, drinking, gambling, fighting, and cheering on the three schooners. There was, after all, a lot more money at stake than just the $150,000 wager between the owners.

By 12:30 p.m., the yachts had settled down under modest sail and were getting ready for the start, each tacking and jostling to gain the best position. The skippers did not want to carry too much canvas at first in case it limited their ability to maneuverer at close quarters. Just before 1:00 p.m., the starting official leaned over to light the touch paper of his brass cannon. The three schooners timed their start to the second, slowing down when necessary to make sure they were not over the line before the start, but still wanting to cross at maximum speed when the cannon sounded. The gun exploded with a sharp boom, and the skippers ordered sheets to be tightened and the helmsman to harden up for a course to England.

The reporter from the BROOKLYN DAILY EAGLE, pocket watch in hand, reported on a very exciting start:

"The Henrietta set her topsail and jib and went off with the lead, followed by the Vesta, which was rapidly crowding on all sail. At one o'clock and five minutes the Henrietta set her squaresail; one o'clock and eight minutes the Vesta set her fore and main gaff topsails; and at one o'clock and eleven minutes, the Fleetwing set her squaresail. At one o'clock and fifteen minutes they were going over the bar, with all canvas [sic] set, the Henrietta ahead, the Vesta second, and the Fleetwing last."

The yachts at the start of the race; the Fleetwing is left, the Henrietta is in a commanding position upwind, and the Vesta is to the right. All three yachts have hoisted their huge square sails from the foremast.

The three black-hulled thoroughbreds were neck and neck and quickly left the New Jersey skyline behind as they stormed east at 12 knots—close to their maximum theoretical hull speed. The steamships carrying spectators did their best to keep up, but could only do so by piling on full power. Within 30 minutes the yachts were alongside the Ambrose Lightship, six miles from the start; the *Vesta* was slightly ahead of the *Henrietta*, then the *Fleetwing*, but it was almost too close to call. As the steamships turned back, they sounded a cacophony of bells, whistles, and guns. The three schooners were now on their own.

≈≈≈≈≈≈≈

Once the skippers had settled "into the groove," their thoughts turned to tactics. Ahead were over 2,645 NM (4,900 km) of open ocean during one of the coldest winters in living memory, and they had to decide on the most favorable route.

On the long crossing to England, the shortest route involved staying close to the coast of Newfoundland, taking the vessel over the Grand Banks where the notorious fog banks, steep waves, and adverse currents coming south from Greenland slow a yacht—these same currents also bring icebergs into the area.

The alternative route was to sail a longer distance by going further offshore to avoid the Grand Banks; this also puts the vessel into the favorable Gulf Stream. This huge ocean current has lost much of its energy this far north, but it can still boost a vessel's speed by 10-20 NM a day (18.5-37 km).

Trying to predict the weather was another challenge. Go too far north and you risk sailing into the polar high-pressure system that brings light easterly winds. Staying further south you are more likely to pick up strong westerly winds and the air temperature is warmer, but the sailing distance is longer. These were just some of the many tactical decisions that the three skippers had to make.

According to Captain Samuels, the *Fleetwing* and the *Vesta* adopted different tactics at the start of the race:

> "We had known before the start that the captains of the other two had orders not to let us out of sight... We trimmed and hauled off to south'ard; they trimmed and hauled offshore to south'ard. Night set in and we put out our lights and hauled inshore. This time, they did not observe us."

Sailing at night without lights is potentially dangerous and risks a collision at sea, but it had the desired effect and the *Henrietta* was able to lose the other two yachts on that first night. Samuels certainly knew the North Atlantic better than the others, and this probably explains their instructions. As far as he could tell, the *Fleetwing* seemed to have taken a slightly northerly course, and the *Vesta* more to the south. That night, Samuels had to decide on his own tactics: should he follow the shortest route and risk sailing over the Grand Banks? Or sail further south and hope to pick up a free ride from the Gulf Stream?

Stephen Fiske, the HERALD's journalist aboard, explained Samuels' tactics:

> "[The] Henrietta was confessedly the slowest boat, and the Captain had decided to put her on the steamer track [a northerly route close to the great circle], and keep her there, regardless of wind or weather, because it was the shortest route."

It was a wise, tactical decision given the *Henrietta's* speed disadvantage. The yachts had now separated and none of the skippers knew what the others were planning. In fact, Samuels' earlier assessment that the *Fleetwing* had gone north and the *Vesta* to the south was incorrect—the *Fleetwing* stayed south and it was the *Vesta* that was going north over the Grand Banks, on a similar course to the *Henrietta*.

By midday on the first full day at sea, the schooners were well out to sea and experiencing exhilarating sailing. Despite losing each other during the night, they had actually followed similar courses in the first 24 hours. The *Vesta* was in the lead having sailed 240 NM (444 km), averaging 10 knots. Two miles to the south and three miles behind was the *Henrietta*, with the *Fleetwing* still further south, having sailed 230 NM (426 km). The conditions were moderate and suited the lightweight *Vesta*; the *Fleetwing* had done well to stay close and could expect to perform even better when the inevitable gale arrived.

Fiske was impressed with Samuels and wrote that he "... jockeyed [the] *Henrietta* as if she were a racing mare." As the winds changed, so the skipper had his novice crew out on deck day and night, hoisting, lowering, and constantly trimming the sails for maximum effect: "... giving the yacht all she could bear, and relieving her by reefing the instant that she was overstrained." If the wind freed and began to blow from behind, Samuels would order the huge square sail to be set from the foremast. There was not only his reputation at stake, but $7,500 of his own earnings were sitting in a bookmaker's safe back in New York.

Making a judgment about how much sail to carry was a finely balanced assessment for all the skippers to make. They needed to keep the boat sailing as fast as possible without being overpowered or breaking equipment. The *Fleetwing* too was sailing well, although there were grumblings below deck over how Captain Brown had been treated—but that was hardly the new captain's fault, as the decision to replace Brown was made by the owner (who was notable by his absence).

Progress was not quite so smooth aboard the *Vesta*. Captain Dayton was a very different skipper from the man pushing the *Henrietta* to her limits. Samuels was so full of confidence in his abilities that he had wagered most of his racing fee on the *Henrietta* to win; by comparison, the older, careful skipper of the *Vesta* had weighed the risks of the race he had taken on and had even drafted his will before he left, to provide for his wife and 17 children should anything go amiss. Nor did the cautious captain appeal to George Lorillard, the owner's brother. George was a keen and

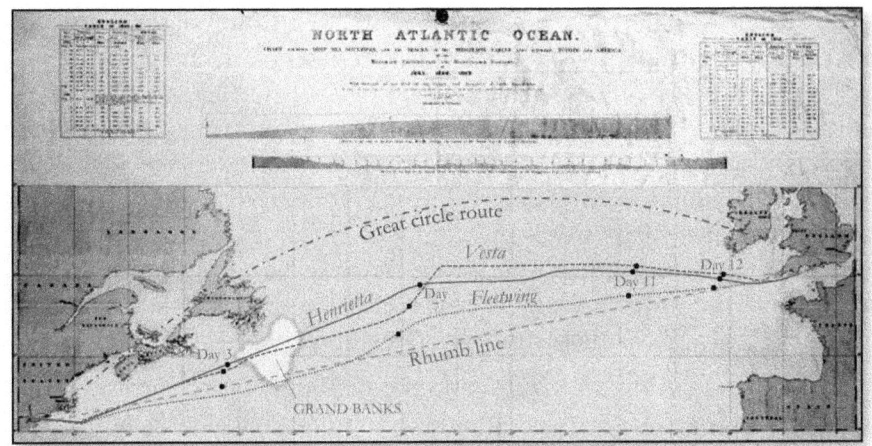

A plotting chart from 1869, superimposed with the course of the three yachts sailing from New York to the Needles.

experienced yachtsman, but he found Captain Dayton to be polite but dull, and complained that he had: "No order, no drive, no discipline."

On the morning of the second day, the first breakages occurred. The *Fleetwing* had taken a more southerly route than the other two schooners and was experiencing stronger winds and bigger seas. Captain Thomas was pushing the schooner hard and made the mistake of going over that unseen line between sailing flat out and catastrophe. She was carrying too much sail, and with her lee rail dipping into the ocean and taking solid water on deck, the *Fleetwing* buried her bow.

The strain was too much on the rig, and with a loud crack, the heavy wooden jib-boom shattered; one of the judges, Ernest Staples, recalled that it "might have been no more than a matchstick." With the jib-boom gone and the headsail torn, the schooner's steering was heavy and the yacht became difficult to control. The damaged spar and sail were soon replaced, but the *Fleetwing* had lost valuable miles. The mishap was seen as a bad omen by some of the crew.

Meanwhile to the north, the *Henrietta* was experiencing excellent (albeit freezing cold) sailing, with clear skies and snow flurries. Captain Samuels understood his charge well, his tactics were sound, and the crew had every confidence that they were in capable hands.

Life was not quite so upbeat aboard the *Vesta*. By all accounts, Captain Dayton was not exerting the same discipline on the crew and the yacht was disorganized. To add to the general despair aboard, the decks of this lightly-built yacht began to leak, and that only added to the discomfort below.

By day three, the two northern yachts were approaching the Grand Banks off Newfoundland—a cluster of underwater plateaux where the ocean floor rises up from a depth of more than 6,500 ft (1,981 m) to sometimes as little as 50 ft (15 m) in places. This shallow water brings nutrients to the surface and creates one of the richest fishing grounds in the world where cod, haddock, and swordfish can be caught in abundance. But the shallow water also creates steep waves and confused seas, making this a treacherous place to be in bad weather—and even more so because of dense fog that forms where the warm waters of the Gulf Stream meet the cold water of the Labrador Current flowing south from Greenland.

The skippers of the *Henrietta* and the *Vesta* had taken this into account when deciding their racing strategy and factored in the risks of sailing over the Grand Banks in return for a shorter course. Of the two, it was the *Henrietta* that was better suited to the boisterous seas over the shallow seabed. As if to validate the skipper's decision, the schooner was experiencing strong winds from astern and covered 225 NM (417 km) on the third day. Fiske recalled that "the yacht sailed faster and faster, until as we looked over the side where the waves came cascading over the diminutive bulwarks we seemed to be fairly flying along."

The *Vesta* was experiencing similar conditions, although morale aboard had not improved. George Lorillard continued to be frustrated by the skipper's timid racing tactics, and "…recommended Captain Dayton to set the large squaresail as the weather was so fine, but no go as he is so careful with his crew…"

To the south, the *Fleetwing* did not benefit from the strong winds and slowly slipped behind the others. By the end of day four, the *Henrietta* had nudged a couple of miles ahead of the *Vesta* and was a good 20 NM (37 km) ahead of the *Fleetwing*. However, conditions were about to change. On December 16th—five days into the race—New York experienced freezing conditions, with a severe gale and a foot (30 cm) of snow. It would be only a couple of days before the deep depression overtook the three schooners, with disastrous consequences.

≈≈≈≈≈≈≈

Day six at sea was a Sunday and as the New York storm overhauled the three yachts, the temperature fell and the winds increased. Even though the schooners were carrying a substantial area of sail, the waves were affecting the motion of the boats through the water—sometimes stopping progress and putting huge stresses on the rig, or at other times the yachts swooped down the face of the waves, making it difficult for the helmsman to keep their charges under control. And all the time, freezing spray struck the crew on deck like shotgun pellets. Fiske described the conditions:

> *"The yacht was being driven at steamer speed by a succession of squalls and gales. Now and then a huge wave, like a white-crested monster of the deep, would crawl out of the darkness and fling itself upon the deck in a roaring rage."*

As the wind increased, so the *Henrietta* reveled in the bitterly cold conditions; Samuels pushed his vessel to the limit, and her lead continued to open. Six days and 14 hours into the race, the schooner reached the halfway point. The *Vesta* had fallen 61 NM (113 km) behind and the *Fleetwing* was struggling on the more southerly route, lying 119 miles (220 km) behind the leader. Samuels knew the prudent action would now be to "hove to" with only storm sails hoisted; this slowed the vessel down and allowed the *Henrietta* to safely ride the waves, with only storm canvas hoisted. Instead, he dropped the mainsail but kept two reefed foresails hoisted to keep the yacht sailing fast downwind—but it took two men on the ship's wheel to keep the unbridled schooner on course.

As darkness fell, the wind was recorded at 64 knots (119 km/h), now officially hurricane-force speeds. Captain Samuels wrote in the ship's log that a huge wave broke on deck and "boarded us abreast of the fore rig, burying everything forward—bow clean underwater and stern in the air." Another monstrous wave swept over the deck, "burying her almost completely" and ripping the foresail. Minutes later, yet another wave broke on deck, hurling the schooner on her side as if a bath toy and "carelessly smashed her lifeboat to smithereens." Below decks, Fiske wrote: "The groaning of timbers was like the fearsome shrieks of some demented soul in the depths of the ocean."

The *Henrietta* had, by now, also taken on a substantial amount of water and she could not continue to sail in these conditions without sustaining serious damage, or even foundering. Samuels went below to find the owner: "We must heave to Mr. Bennett," he announced, "she can stand the strain no longer." The owner agreed and Samuels ordered the helmsman to turn beam onto the wind and lie-a hull, with only a small trysail set to give her steerageway.

The *Vesta* was experiencing similar conditions, but Captain Dayton did not have the option of heaving-to in his lightweight centerboard schooner. The lack of a deep keel meant that if the yacht lay with the wind on her beam, she risked sliding down the side of the waves too quickly and possibly overturning. Dayton's only practical option was to raise a small storm sail and run before the storm at a hair-raising speed, down dark valleys of water and over moving mountains of white foam. Under these conditions and at this speed, the *Vesta* became almost uncontrollable. The *Vesta's* speed, however, was not an advantage because the yacht was being blown off course to the north-west, adding significantly to the distance sailed. During that roller-coaster of a night, the *Vesta* passed unseen just a few miles astern of the *Henrietta*, then snuggly bunkered down and hove-to in (relative) comfort. The *Vesta* survived the night but by morning, she had sailed far off-course to the north, with each mile taking the yacht into ever colder conditions.

Of the three yachts, the *Fleetwing* was in the most serious predicament. She was further to the south and was experiencing the same ferocious storm. Not only had she shattered her jib-boom, but her open helmsman's cockpit was leaking water and the ship's pumps had to be manned constantly to cope with the ingress of water. Despite the leaks, Captain Thomas decided to adopt the same tactics used on the *Vesta*—he lowered all sail except for two reefed foresails and sped down the mountainous Atlantic rollers. After all, the favorite was no longer in the lead and Thomas wanted to gain on his rivals.

Darkness comes early in late December. In some ways, this is a blessing, for you can no longer see the mountainous waves approaching from astern—but you can always hear their thunderous roar. Darkness also drains what little warmth there might be during daylight hours. That evening, the two helmsmen were clinging desperately to the ship's wheel trying to keep the *Fleetwing* on course. Meanwhile, six other deckhands were huddled together in the yacht's shallow, open cockpit, trying to stay out of the wind, and sharing as much human warmth as possible. The storm had now reached its apogee.

At 9:00 p.m., a thunderous roar from behind gave only a brief warning of the approaching wave. The men instinctively turned to see a monstrous wall of water towering over them. They stood no chance cowering in the shallow cockpit of this rich man's summer plaything. The low coaming of the *Fleetwing's* cockpit offered no protection against the breaking wave that dumped hundreds of tons of freezing Atlantic water on deck.

Back in 1866, deck crews had no safety lines attached to the yacht. The men stood no chance as solid water swept over the yacht, taking with it all eight crewmen. The fortunate ones would have been knocked senseless immediately; those aware of what had happened would mercifully only remain conscious for a few minutes in the freezing Atlantic water before hypothermia brought a compassionate end—or their heavy oilskins and seaboots would soon drag them to a watery grave.

One of the two judges, Ernest Staples, went on deck immediately after the event: "The cockpit which, but a few minutes before we had seen filled with the watch was now clean-swept of every living soul and the deck and cockpit, from the main rigging aft, was completely covered with water."

Without a helmsman to keep her course, the *Fleetwing* skidded sideways and lay beam-on to the full force of the storm. A water-heavy vessel in those conditions was vulnerable to becoming completely overwhelmed. Captain Thomas was quickly on deck, and hove-to in the forlorn hope of finding survivors. As the crew fought to get the schooner under control, they heard sporadic cries over the high-pitched screaming of the storm. Two men had been swept the full length of the vessel before grabbing a foresail that had torn free from the rigging and was now dragging alongside the hull. It was nothing short of miraculous, and no mean accomplishment to recover the two survivors, dragged exhausted, coughing, spluttering, and shivering, onto the deck of the *Fleetwing*.

To his credit, Thomas did his best to search for the other men. The ship's company scoured the storm-tossed Atlantic with lanterns for five hours, hoping to catch sight of more survivors. It was a hopeless task. As the storm began to abate in the early hours of the morning, the skipper called for more sail to be set as he squared away for England. The race was still on. In the next 24 hours, they made an impressive run of 260 NM (481 km), an average of 10.8 knots.

Little is known of the six lost crew members, and no record of their names remains in the contemporary accounts. Life was cheap, and the lives of paid hands even cheaper. By the standards of the day, their loss was considered regrettable, but expendable.

≈≈≈≈≈≈≈

By December 19th, the schooners were eight days into the race and each had sailed more than 1,700 NM (3,148 km). Despite the atrocious conditions, the yachts were still remarkably close. The *Henrietta* was ahead but her lead had been cut. The *Vesta* was 10 NM astern—hardly an hour's sailing—although she was further north of the direct course to England. The crew of the *Fleetwing* had recovered from their tragic loss and the yacht was now 86 NM (159 km) behind the leader. Of course, none of the skippers knew the position of the other yachts, and nobody other than the crew of the *Fleetwing* yet knew of the loss of six men. As far as the skippers were concerned, the race was still on, and they all had everything to play for.

With the deep depression that had caused so much havoc now to the east and lashing the coastline of the British Isles, the wind dropped to a near calm and the sun came out. Captain Samuels tempted fate and according to Stephen Fiske, "ordered all hands to ... whistle for a wind." Whistling on a boat is usually considered to bring bad luck, and risks bringing a storm. Perhaps the crew's whistling lacked conviction and only a light breeze filled in, but it was enough for the *Henrietta* to pick up speed. Gordon Bennett made the most of the warmth and settled into a deckchair, sipping one of his fine clarets and nibbling on plover's eggs. This really was the way to sail the Atlantic.

Life was not quite so benign aboard the *Vesta*. The tension between the cautious Captain Dayton and the brash 23-year-old George Lorillard continued, with the youngster constantly berating the old sea-dog for not pushing his brother's schooner harder. After one tetchy discussion in Lorillard's cabin, he wrote that Dayton: "left for the deck remarking that the yacht might go to Hell when she got to Cowes." However, Lorillard had a point and the yacht was in a high-stakes race. When Dayton eventually raised more canvas, they recorded a 24-hour run of 277 NM (513 km), an average of 11.5 knots. This resulted in the *Vesta* actually pulling narrowly ahead of the *Henrietta* and taking the lead.

Meanwhile, the crew of the *Fleetwing* was suffering from low morale and reduced numbers. By December 22nd, day 11, she was trailing the other two schooners by 140 miles (259 km), or more than half a day's sailing. With only a few hundred miles to go to the finish, the race was now finely balanced between the *Henrietta* and the *Vesta*.

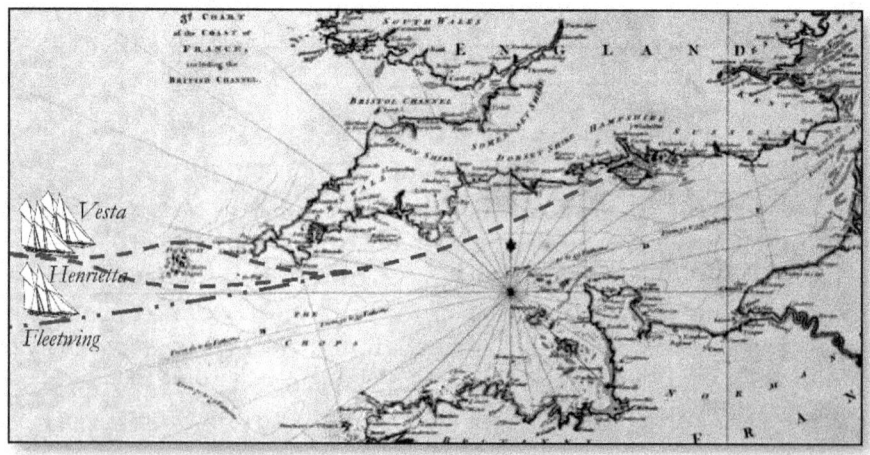

The options open to the skippers—to sail north or south of the Isles of Scilly.

By December 23rd, the three yachts were sailing flat out and approaching the Isles of Scilly—that archipelago of rocky islands lying 24 NM (45 km) west of Cornwall. The Scillies have a formidable reputation for wrecking ships and its first lighthouse was still under construction and would not be commissioned until the following year. The wind had also swung round to the south-east and was beginning to "head" the yachts, forcing the crew to sail close to the wind. This made the Isles of Scilly a potentially dangerous lee shore. The skippers were fully aware of the consequences of misjudging their position as they fast approached the islands.

The *Vesta* and the *Henrietta* were bearing down from the north-west and their skippers now had an important strategic decision to make. With the wind from the south-east, they could take the safe option and sail north of the Isles of Scilly but they would then run the risk of not being able to weather the Lizard peninsular—the most southerly point of mainland Britain. Alternatively, they could harden up into the wind and try to sail south of the islands, but if they misjudged the tactic, they risked being driven on to a rocky lee shore. To compound matters, the overcast weather prevented a position being taken by sextant, as Fiske recalled: "It was a murky, damp disagreeable morning and even at noon it was impossible to take a solar observation."

Both skippers decided to take the risk and took the southerly route. The *Vesta* was still slightly ahead, but she was the most northerly of the yachts and had to sail closer to the wind to weather the islands, and this slowed the boat down. The *Henrietta* was close on her heels and a little further south; this gave her a more favorable angle of sailing and she slowly overhauled the *Vesta*. The *Fleetwing* was about 100 NM (185 km) behind, but further south. This allowed Captain Dick Brown to capitalize on his position and ease the sails—the schooner reveled in the conditions.

Dawn on Christmas Eve saw the *Henrietta* in the lead and safely past the Lizard peninsula, before heading nor'-nor'-east up the English Channel. A few miles behind but still out of sight was the *Vesta*, and further astern still was the *Fleetwing*, but sailing fast and catching up. After 13 days at sea, it was a remarkably close finish. The wind veered to the south-west and increased as another gale began to roll in from the Atlantic, and the yachts had a fine sail up the English Channel in the freshening breeze.

As the *Henrietta* approached the Needles at the western end of the Isle of Wight, nobody ashore was expecting her. As Stephen Fiske later wrote: "A Cowes pilot was dragged aboard so quickly that he could not speak. But his eyes and the grip of his hand spoke for him. At last, he put his good news into words: "No other boat ahead of you! What yacht is this?" The *Henrietta* was first across the finishing line after 13 days, 22 hours, and 43 minutes—a remarkably fast passage.

The *Vesta* could not recover from losing her lead as she rounded the Scillies, even though the schooner was sailing fast in the freshening breeze. Darkness fell before they approached the finish line, and the pilot they had taken aboard earlier missed the loom of the lighthouse on the Needles, and mistakenly sailed past the finish line and continued south of the island. They only realized their error when they identified the light further along the coast at St. Catherine's Point. They had no option but to turn about and beat back to the finish line, before turning north into the Needles channel; they finished at 12:45 a.m. on Christmas morning.

As the *Vesta* crept up to her mooring off the Royal Yacht Squadron in Cowes, the crew not only saw the *Henrietta* at anchor but the *Fleetwing* as well. As the crew of the *Vesta* was laboriously beating back from St. Catherine's Point, the *Fleetwing* had snatched second place and crossed the finish line just 40 minutes ahead of the *Vesta*, as one of her judges recalled: "All hands were wretched. Faint yet unmistakable shouts of laughter came to us across the water from where our rivals were floating."

Christmas Day in Cowes that year was like no other, and the visiting sailors partied long and hard. Their achievement in crossing the North Atlantic at such speed in late December had certainly been (mostly) an impressive display of seamanship. Even THE TIMES of London was generous in its praise:

> *"We would not say that Englishmen could not have accomplished such a race, but the idea would perhaps hardly have occurred to them. Its novelty and boldness are eminently characteristic of Americans."*

≈≈≈≈≈≈≈

Inevitably, the race postmortems began, as they do after every yacht race. The crew of the *Vesta* argued that if they had not been forced to sail so far to the north in the mid-Atlantic gale, they would have been better placed when approaching the English coast, and could have won the race. The crew of the *Fleetwing* claimed they lost time looking for survivors after being overwhelmed, and could also have won the race. In the end, the winner of any yacht race not only makes the most of the right decisions, but also makes fewer mistakes, and the *Henrietta* was the deserving winner. Captain Samuels had sailed an impeccable race in what was the slowest yacht. Credit should also go to James Gordon Bennett Jr, who made the crucially important choice of a skipper and retained a good rapport with his captain that undoubtedly improved crew morale. The *Henrietta* was certainly a happy ship.

Never again would the three schooners compete in a race with such audacity and daring as the 1866 Atlantic yacht race. Gordon Bennett's sailing affections turned to a newer and faster schooner, the *Dauntless*, that he raced in the summer of 1870 from southern Ireland to New York against an English yacht, the *Cambria*. Once again, Bennett won convincingly. Pierre Lorillard was disheartened over the performance of the *Vesta* and always claimed he wanted to sell the boat in England, rather than bring her back to New York. The *Fleetwing* had a more transcendental retirement and ended her days as a sailor's mission.

The *Fleetwing's* owner, George Archer Osgood, continued to make money on the New York Stock Exchange, no doubt benefiting from his connections with the Vanderbilt family. He died in 1882 at the age of 60 after a long illness. Pierre Lorillard developed Newport as a major yachting center in the 1880s and continued with his other great passion—horseracing. He spent time living in France and England where, in 1881, his horse *Iroquois* became the first American-owned and trained horse to win a European classic race.

James Gordon Bennett returned to New York, where he became the youngest commodore of the New York Yacht Club. He also took control of the NEW YORK HERALD from his father and increased circulation with attention-grabbing stunts such as sending Henry Morton Stanley to East Africa in search of the Scottish missionary, David Livingstone. He also continued his debauched lifestyle of drinking and womanizing, and took up motor racing and flying later in life. He fathered an illegitimate child with an ex-showgirl, Camille Clermont, who claimed he "turned his back on all sorrow and suffering and merely lived for the pleasure of the day."

After the scandal of urinating into the fireplace of his fiancée's parents, Bennett left New York in 1877 and spent the rest of his life in Europe, mainly on his 301 ft (92 m) yacht, the *Lysistrata*, from where he ran the NEW YORK HERALD from a distance. This vast triple-decked steam yacht had a crew of 100 and boasted such facilities as Turkish baths, a theatre, and a padded stall for an Alderney cow that ensured a good supply of fresh milk while at sea.

Despite his hell-raising, Bennett eventually settled down and married—at the ripe old age of 73. His wife was Maud Potter, 25 years his junior and the widow of George de Reuter (of the Reuters news agency).

Meanwhile, Bennett became obsessed that he would die at the same age as his 77-year-old father. When he was 76, he visited a clairvoyant who told him that his two Pekingese dogs had only weeks to live and their deaths would quickly be followed by a member of his household. Shortly afterward, the two dogs passed away and Bennett, who had developed pneumonia, sat in his villa in the South of France, forlornly waiting for the end.

He died on May 10, 1918—on his 77th birthday.

The Arms Race

The southern tip of Manhattan has been called "The Battery" since the early seventeenth century when artillery protected the city from attack from the sea. Since then it has witnessed countless arrivals and departures across the Atlantic, but few were as daring or as dangerous as on the late afternoon of June 6, 1896, when two Norwegian-born fishermen headed off through the grimy waters of New York harbor in their rowing dory, with little more than two months of supplies and a couple spare sets of oars.

The leader of the expedition was George Harbo (32); born in southern Norway, he studied at nautical school and qualified as a navigation officer. Like many young, ambitious men from the poorer parts of Europe, Harbo went in search of a better life abroad. On arrival in New York in 1883, he joined the lines of predominantly Irish and German immigrants at the Castle Garden Immigration Depot in Lower Manhattan (the infamous Ellis Island did not open until 1892). This was the gilded age in America, where a few became rich, but the majority remained poor. The American Dream proved elusive, and Harbo could only find work as a dory man, fishing off Sandy Hook in New York; the wages were low and he was forced to live in a grim, waterside shantytown.

He eventually saved enough to bring his wife over from Norway. Anine was horrified by the squalor and violence in New York, where theft, extortion, corruption, prostitution, drug-taking, and murder were commonplace. But Harbo was confident that with hard work anything was possible, so he trained and qualified as a ship's pilot, bringing vessels in and out of New York harbor. The industry was poorly regulated, and although the swashbuckling era of harbor piloting produced plenty of work, it also created a lot of widows. During one savage storm in 1888, nine pilot boats foundered and seventeen men drowned.

Harbo now had two children and Anine decided she would rather be a poor fisherman's wife than a destitute pilot's widow. Harbo relented, and before their third child was born, they were back living in the squalor of a wooden shack where he started. Life became intolerable and despite her husband's protestations, Anine booked a steamer and headed home to Brevik with her three young children. Four days into the voyage, their youngest daughter died suddenly from pneumonia. During a short funeral ceremony, little Grace was wrapped in canvas weighed down with sand, and gently lowered over the ship's side, to quickly slip out of sight beneath the waves.

Harbo grieved alone back in New York, but he had at least found more lucrative work collecting soft shell clams along the tidal mudflats around Sandy Hook. During the long hours of back-breaking labor, he devised a grand plan to become rich and famous—after all, this was the great American Dream. He eventually made enough money to hire a fellow worker, Frank Samuelson, a tall, powerfully built Norwegian and several years younger. Samuelson (26) had spent six years at sea and was now a bosun's mate, and he too was looking for new opportunities in "the land of the free."

As they worked side by side, Harbo outlined his plan to row across the Atlantic Ocean. Why not do it together? The younger man wondered if his boss had taken leave of his senses—no one had attempted the crossing in an open rowing boat before. Was it even possible? They both knew the grim story of Howard Blackburn (see chapter *Big Ocean Little Boats*), whose Gloucester-based fishing schooner foundered over the Grand Banks a decade before. Blackburn rowed alone back to Newfoundland but lost all his fingers, a foot, and half the toes on his other foot to frostbite. (Blackburn went on to sail the Atlantic single-handed in 1903 and prospered as a

Frank Samuelson and George Harbo (above).
Afloat in the Fox (below).

result, but as far as Harbo and Samuelson were concerned this was still in the future).

Samuelson was persuaded and the two Norwegians invested their modest savings in a rowing dory from a respected local builder, William Seaman. The 18 ft (5.5 m) boat had a double-ended hull and was made from the best materials—white cedar clinker planks on oak frames; the boat was certainly strong, but also heavy. There was no cabin, so the builder added a canvas cover to stretch across the boat to prevent it from being swamped in rough seas. The boat had watertight metal lockers to keep equipment and documents dry, and these also provided buoyancy to prevent it from sinking if rolled over. The builder also installed grab rails along the bottom of the hull that allowed the crew to right the boat if it did capsize.

Only when their boat was nearly complete did Harbo have the courage to pick up a pen and write to his wife. He carefully explained to Anine how carefully William Seaman had built the boat, incorporating any number of safety features; he outlined the beneficial effects of the Gulf Stream, which he assured his wife would help carry them eastwards to Europe; and he reminded her of the publicity and financial rewards that awaited them after a successful crossing.

Anine thought her husband was certifiably insane, and everyone back in Brevik who knew anything about the ocean agreed his plan was suicidal. In an exchange of letters, Anine pleaded with her husband not to go, but Harbo was determined—this was, after all, his route to fame and fortune. There were, he argued, many East Coast sailors such as Alfred Johnson, Thomas Crapo, the Andrews brothers, and Frederick Norman, who had crossed the Atlantic and made themselves rich. If the Atlantic could be sailed, then why could it not be rowed?

What Harbo now needed was a publicist, and he found just the man in Richard Kyle Fox, then aged 40. Fox had immigrated to New York 20 years before from Dublin; he was a boxing journalist and promoter, although his real interest was in bare-knuckle fighting. Just three years after arriving in New York, Fox had raised enough money to buy a failing newspaper—the NATIONAL POLICE GAZETTE. This infamous tabloid covered mainly crime and criminals and was intended for a general readership—not as its name suggests, the police. Fox proved to be an astute editor with a keen nose for sniffing out salacious stories of debauchery and lurid murders, and it flourished on images of scantily clad strippers and burlesque dancers—often bordering on what was then considered to be legally obscene. When the news was light, he simply created stories by offering gold medals to people who broke weird or risky records, thus making Fox very wealthy.

The NATIONAL POLICE GAZETTE was an obvious choice, and the Norwegians headed for Fox's brand-new headquarters at 338-344 Pearl Street in Lower Manhattan. As they faced him in his palatial office, Harbo outlined their proposal to row across the Atlantic from New York to Le Havre in France. Fox was intrigued and listened carefully, then made them an offer: if they named their dory after him, his newspaper would promote their expedition and award them each a gold medal on their return. For the multimillionaire owner of the tabloid, it was a cheap deal—he got a great story and some valuable self-promotion, all for a couple of gilded decorations.

Fox stuck to his deal and the rowers received their promotion. Curious New Yorkers gathered on the waterfront at The Battery to watch the men load the *Fox* with equipment and supplies: 60 gallons of water (estimated at a gallon a day), 100 lbs of canned food, hardtack biscuits, jam, coffee, wine, and a wooden box of eggs carefully wrapped in seaweed.

Fox's tabloid publicity was effective, at least up to a point. More than a thousand people turned out on June 6, 1896, to watch the Norwegians leave—but not quite the 36,000 people who watched Frederick Norman and George Thomas sail from Gloucester, MA, 16 years previously (see chapter *Big Ocean, Little Boats*). If Harbo and Samuelson were expecting a similar send-off from a cheering New York crowd, then they were doubly disappointed. It took time for the two

The pugilistic Richard Kyle Fox (above), proprietor of the NATIONAL POLICE GAZETTE. The front page of the newspaper (below) from an October edition in 1919—a typically spicy image.

rowers to stow their stores and balance the boat properly for rowing, and this exceeded the boredom threshold of the spectators; soon the crowd began to let their disappointment be known. This was not the grand departure the readers of the NATIONAL POLICE GAZETTE had been promised. The impatient onlookers heckled from the quayside as Harbo tried (ineffectually) to explain to the crowd what horrendous conditions they were about to face; the increasingly unsympathetic crowd were having none of the Norwegian's pleas for compassion and understanding.

By the time the tide turned just before 5:00 p.m., the two men were ready. With a compass, sextant, Nautical Almanac, a set of oilskins for each of them, and three sets of oars lashed carefully in place. The rowers were towed out as far as the narrow entrance to New York harbor; after that, they were on their own. They only rowed a few miles that evening, but it was enough to be free from the dockside barracking. As night fell, they anchored off the promenade at Coney Island in a heavy mist, safely away from the main shipping channel. Ahead lay more than 2,800 NM (5,185 km) of open ocean, including crossing the notorious Grand Banks.

The next morning dawned with visibility less than 20 yards (18 m); the dory men wrote in their log:

> *"Sunday, June 7th. Lifted anchor 4:00 a.m. Wind north-east moderate with rain and fog. Started to row out to sea. Passed Sandy Hook lightship 11:00 a.m., bearing west, distance 5 miles. This is the last bearing."*

From now on they would have to depend on their sextant and an unreliable clock to calculate their position, or ask a passing ship in the time-honored tradition of small boat sailors who had gone before them. The conditions were not ideal at first and they found themselves rowing almost directly into a stiff north-easterly breeze. They had no option but to keep to their alternating three-hour shifts, with a chance to doze briefly when off-watch. Later, the wind swung around to the south and that helped their progress.

The two rowers faced a different challenge from the likes of Alfred Johnson, Thomas Crapo, and the Andrews brothers who sailed the Atlantic in previous decades. Apart from the obvious fact that you work harder physically in a rowing boat, the craft behaves differently at sea. In a sailing boat, a headwind requires you to sail off at an angle to the wind, but you still make progress in generally the right direction. With a headwind in a rowing boat, you have no choice but to keep rowing into the wind—if you stop, you go backward, and rowing sideways to the wind gains no advantage.

The boats also behave differently in storm conditions. On a sailing boat, you can raise especially strong, small "storm sails"; these allow you either to sail slowly or to "heave-to" in strong winds. Either way, the motion is more comfortable than in a rowing boat, that is viciously tossed around in confused seas. In extreme conditions, a sea anchor towed from the stern will keep any boat lying relatively safely to wind and waves.

By day five, Harbo and Samuelson found themselves in exactly this situation. The wind had swung around to a more favorable westerly direction but had increased in strength. As the sky darkened and spume flew off the crests of the waves, the Norwegians struggled to keep the stern of the *Fox* to the onslaught; if the dory turned broadside, it could be rolled over in an instant. And all the time, they had to bail, row, cook, eat, and sleep.

What Harbo and Samuelson had in common with their sailing predecessors was incredible toughness, resilience, and a stoic attitude towards the unexpected. Take, for example, their logbook entry for their sixth day at sea:

> *"Friday, June 12th. Both of us rowed all night. This morning the oil stove set fire to its house. Looked like danger for a few minutes but was soon put out."*

Any sailor will tell you that a fire at sea is one of the most terrifying things that can happen, especially in a small boat. Yet the two Norwegians made light of the event, even though the kerosene stove had literally exploded into flames.

A couple of weeks into the crossing found them somewhere south of Newfoundland in the vicinity of the Grand Banks. They were able to determine their latitude north of the equator with a noon sun sight using their sextant, but without an accurate chronometer they could not calculate their west-east position and had to rely on "dead reckoning"; this is an intelligent estimate of your position based on boat speed, currents, and any effects of the wind. There were also fishing boats and transatlantic steamers around who passed on their position; however, the two men had agreed before the voyage that they would accept no other outside support, and they refused all offers of supplies.

When the German steamer, the *SS Fürst Bismarck* sighted them, the ship hove to and offered assistance. They were short on kerosene but Harbo refused any offers, preferring to stick to their self-imposed rule of self-sufficiency. The skipper of the steamship could not fail to notice the effect the conditions were having on the two rowers, whose skin was blistered and peeling from exposure. Harbo and Samuelson continued, but with little kerosene to spare, they resorted to eating their eggs raw and only cooked a hot meal on alternate days.

They were now within range of icebergs drifting south down the coast of Labrador. One dark night they could hear the sound of breaking waves, yet they still had another 1,730 NM (3,204 km) before they expected to sight land. Soon, a monstrous white cliff loomed out of the darkness—it was the eerie sight of an iceberg towering over them.

It was not long before bad weather returned and they found themselves again battling for survival, this time in hurricane-force winds exceeding 70 knots (130 km/h). As the waves grew to the height of a four-story building, all they could do was deploy the sea anchor to keep the boat's stern pointing into the waves, hang on, and hope. It was not enough. A huge rogue wave approached from the side and lifted up their tiny boat before the breaking crest rolled the *Fox* over. The men were tied on with ropes but were tossed into the icy waters of the Atlantic like rag dolls.

The men had practiced their capsize drill, but trying to recover the boat in storm conditions was very different. They blessed their builder for adding handholds to the bottom of the hull, and with a monumental effort, they hauled the boat upright and struggled to get aboard. Despite their exhaustion, they bailed frantically to lighten the boat before another wave capsized them. Only then could they assess the situation: they had lost most of their supplies together with their sea anchor, making it virtually impossible now to keep the boat stern to the waves. Their very survival hung in the balance, yet their logbook entry for that day was typically laconic:

> "Friday, July 10th. It has been blowing a gale for two days, and the sea is bigger than we have ever seen it on this trip. At about 8:00 p.m. a big sea struck us partly sideways, upsetting the boat and us into the water. In a few minutes; however, we got into the boat again. We lost many things this time: floating anchor and cable, dishes, frying pan, cookpot, and one rattan seat. Everything we have in the boat is soaked with water except the bread. This is the third night up without sleep."

The next few days brought light winds and they could rest and recover, but with only six days of food and little kerosene left, they could not survive much longer. Five days after the capsize they sighted a Norwegian cargo ship, the *Cito*, on passage from Canada to England. Captain Clausen invited the rowers aboard and they were given a hot meal and enough supplies to continue. Their position showed they were two-thirds of the way across, and they were determined to complete the voyage.

In the early hours of August 1, 1896, Samuelson spotted a light to the north and he woke Harbo. It was the Bishops Rock lighthouse and they were less than 20 NM from the Isles of Scilly. By late morning they entered Hugh Town harbor on the main island, St. Mary's, and ran the *Fox* onto the sandy beach—much to the bewilderment of local fishermen. They had been at sea for 55 days and 13 hours. Making the most of the five-hour time difference, THE NEW YORK TIMES ran a pithy report that afternoon:

> *"London, August 1st. – A dispatch from the signal station on the Scilly Islands [sic] states that the rowboat Fox passed there at 11:00 this morning after a passage of fifty-five days from New York. The two occupants of the boat were well but somewhat exhausted from the effects of their long row."*

For Harbo and Samuelson, the voyage was still not over and they continued on to Le Havre in France, as planned. By the time they arrived, word had spread and they were greeted with great excitement. With fame and fortune now within their grasp, Harbo imagined himself returning to a comfortable life in New York with his wife and children. After a brief stopover they rowed up the River Seine to Paris, but their reception there was more muted. Still determined to raise their profile, they put the *Fox* on public display, but people showed little interest in two crazy Norwegians who had rowed the Atlantic. They moved on to London where their show ran for two months, but ticket sales barely covered their costs. They went on to more European cities, but the reception was much the same and they decided to cut their losses and return home.

Disappointed, the two partners loaded the *Fox* onto a steamer and headed back to New York. Off Cape Cod and with only 260 NM (481 km) to go, the ship ran out of coal and the captain ordered all wooden objects aboard to be broken up and burned in the boilers. Harbo and Samuelson chose instead to lower the *Fox* over the side, and they completed the voyage under their own steam. On arrival, they performed one final show, and Richard Fox presented them with their gold medals.

The two men returned to the mudflats harvesting mollusks, and Harbo took occasional jobs as a pilot to supplement his income. Anine agreed to return with their children and the family moved into a comfortable house in Brooklyn, just across the bridge from the grand offices of the NATIONAL POLICE GAZETTE. Samuelson married, and he too stayed in New York for a while.

George Harbo died in 1909, aged 45, and Frank Samuelson eventually returned to farm in Norway, where he survived the Nazi occupation and died in 1946, aged 76.

Their transatlantic rowing record remained unbroken for 114 years.

≈≈≈≈≈≈≈

Unlike transatlantic records with sailboats, nothing more happened with attempts to row the Atlantic for 70 years. This was partly because of two World Wars, but it surely must also be because the idea of rowing across thousands of miles of open ocean was a daunting task. Then in 1966, a challenge came from the most unlikely source—a 33-year-old overweight British journalist with a restless spirit and a determination to make the most of life. It could have been his epitaph.

David Johnstone loved fast cars, travel, and adventure; he stood 6 ft 3 in tall and weighed 250 lbs (113 kg)—a testament to his other love in life, food. His signature dish involved removing the parson's nose from 46 chickens— also called the pope's nose or the sultan's nose. These are colloquial terms for the fleshy uropygium at the rear end of a bird that contains the gland that produces oil used by birds for preening. In Johnstone's dish, the chickens were discarded and the parson's noses then stewed for hours in an earthenware casserole with thick slices of ham, brandy, apricots, and mushrooms, and then served in a silver bowl piping hot. His friends claimed the result was delicious.

In August 1965, Robert Manry had sailed the ocean in the 13½ ft long *Tinkerbelle*, making this the smallest sailboat to cross the Atlantic (see chapter *The Great Space Race*). David Johnstone was inspired and that month he placed an advertisement in THE TIMES, that read: "Will five fortuitous oarsmen over 28 join me and engage in the second-ever transatlantic rowing voyage?" Johnstone was an experienced coastal sailor, but he was not a rower. Even so, he received over 100 replies, including one from a fellow journalist, John Hoare.

Hoare was a few years younger than Johnstone and was not an oarsman either. He was, however, fit and reveled in the outdoors; he was also a reservist in the British Army's Parachute Regiment and shared Johnstone's love of fast cars and adventure. The two men got on well from the beginning, but they were still four short for the voyage.

Another likely reply to the advertisement came from a Captain Ridgway, another soldier from the Parachute Regiment. On paper at least, John Ridgway was the perfect recruit; once they met, however, Johnstone was convinced they would never get along in a small boat—his concern was that Ridgway's assertiveness would bring about a clash of personalities. So Johnstone turned Ridgway down.

Meanwhile, Hoare and Johnstone made preparations for the voyage, carefully researching nutrition, clothing, equipment, ocean currents, and meteorology—about which they knew very little. The logistics were also complex; for example, a six-man crew rowing for 50 days required more than 13 cu ft of dehydrated food and 48 cu ft of drinking water—weighing well over a ton. Johnstone also realized that it was also overly ambitious to find a suitable crew of six compatible people. The two friends also realized that they needed to start in spring once the unsettled winter weather had passed, and time was now running out. Most urgently, they needed a boat.

Johnstone approached Colin Mudie (see chapters *The Great Space Race* and *The History Men*) to design their vessel. Mudie understood the challenge of the Atlantic, having sailed to America himself in 1952 in the 19 ft 1 in (5.8 m) *Sopranino*. Mudie promised to have a basic drawing within a week that would be adequate for a builder to give a quotation. Johnstone had successfully persuaded the British tabloid newspaper, THE PEOPLE, to sponsor the voyage, and this helped him raise the £2,000 needed to build the boat (£45,000 in today's prices). Now work could begin on Mudie's design, the 15 ft 6 in (4.6 m) *Puffin*.

Meanwhile, John Ridgway had been assigned a desk job at the British Army base in Aldershot in southern England. He had not forgotten Johnstone's plans—nor his rejection. So, Ridgway decided to have his own crack at an Atlantic crossing and announced a challenge to race Johnstone and Hoare. However, his problems seemed insurmountable, for he had no money, no boat, no crew, and even less time.

It was now mid-January 1966 and things began to move fast. A boatbuilder in Yorkshire who specialized in fishing dories had one boat left after showing them at the London Boat Show. With an overdraft advanced from his bank, Ridgway wrote out a check for £185 to the Bradford Boat Services in Yorkshire for his transatlantic craft.

A couple of weeks later Ridgway's old platoon sergeant, Chay Blyth, strolled into his office and made Ridgway a proposal he could not refuse. The two soldiers had previously rowed together in the Parachute Brigade Reading-to-Westminster overnight canoe race down the River Thames. They capsized early in the race and lost 30 minutes righting their canoe; undeterred, they continued and won the race by 11 minutes. They were a formidable team, and they now joined forces to take on the Atlantic together.

The sudden appearance of two new kids on the block took David Johnstone by surprise and he was panicked into cutting corners. He rushed completion of the *Puffin* and did not fit the exterior buoyancy bags, he canceled the sea trials, and he shipped the boat across the Atlantic as quickly

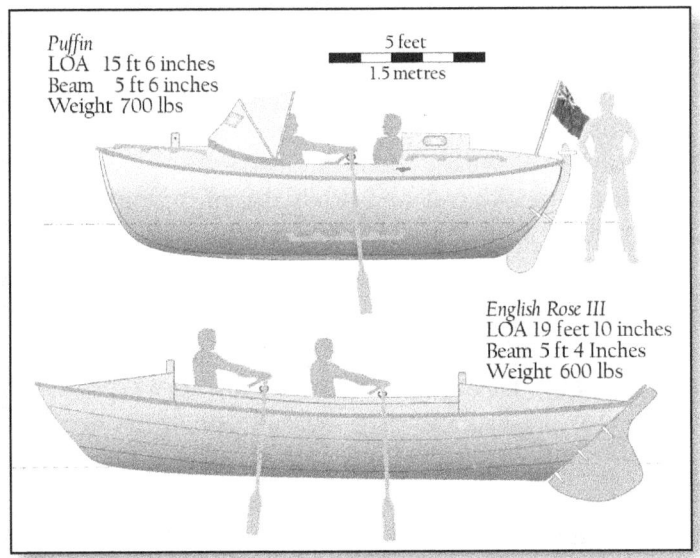

The two transatlantic rowing boats showing the significant differences in length, draft, and weight.

as possible. The two men boarded the *USS United States* in late April, and on arrival they made preparations for a quick departure from North Carolina in mid-May, hoping to steal a march on the two paras.

Exactly why they chose to leave from Cape Hatteras is difficult to understand, for it added several hundred miles to their journey and involved a long row through the busy coastal waters of the eastern seaboard. By contrast, Ridgway and Blyth made the more sensible decision to leave from Cape Cod in Massachusetts, making their rowing distance to Britain 600 NM (1,110 km) shorter.

The boats were as different as the two men. Johnstone's *Puffin* was specifically designed for the crossing and built by Souters on the Isle of Wight that was a top-quality boatyard in its day. The boat was an advanced design with a strong, molded plywood hull; with its deep keel, it resembled a sailboat more than a rowing boat. Aft was a small cabin where a crewman could sleep, and forward was a canvas cover that gave the oarsman protection. Johnstone also took five different lengths of oars, including a special pair 12 ft (3.7 m) long that folded in half to fit more easily in the boat. The *Puffin* was cleverly designed and well-thought-through, but it was short and quite heavy for its overall size.

Ridgway's boat was longer and lighter, making it faster and easier to row. Its dimensions were similar to Harbo and Samuelson's *Fox*, although probably half the weight. Ridgway was tempted to add a keel to the *English Rose III* for stability, but the Cape Cod fishermen talked him out of the idea, pointing out that even a shallow keel could "trip" the boat up and capsize it in heavy seas. His new-found friends also persuaded the rowers to reinforce the light plywood hull with solid oak planks—something that Ridgway willingly agreed to do. Ridgway and Blyth also picked up half a dozen pairs of oars from the local boat chandlers, hoping they were a suitable length.

What both boats had in common was a similar beam, even though the *Rosie* (as she came to be known) was significantly longer than the *Puffin*. Typically, a sailing boat is three times its beam, so a 20 ft (6.1 m) boat like *Rosie* would typically have a 7 ft (2.1 m) beam. However, this is too wide to row easily, so rowing boats tend to have a beam of no more than 5 ft 6 in (1.7 m). This inevitably restricts the carrying capacity of any rowing boat.

Johnstone had carefully researched his food requirements and took expert advice about nutrition. He loaded a variety of freeze-dried meals, plus "wet" meals for those days when they could not boil water. By comparison, Ridgway and Blyth seemed happy with ten days of fresh food and a 60-day supply of basic dehydrated army rations—all of it the same beef curry. In contrast to their undoubted professionalism as British soldiers from an elite parachute regiment, their transatlantic plans seemed to be rushed, almost casual.

Once the *Puffin* was ready for sea, Johnstone began to doubt the wisdom of leaving from Cape Hatteras and at the last minute he moved up to Virginia Beach, near the entrance to the Chesapeake Bay. It was not a good idea—the currents off the entrance to the Bay are complex and extend up to 50 NM (92.6 km) offshore. As a result, Johnstone and Hoare spent their first week at sea drifting up and down the coast, never out of sight of the unfailing loom of the Chesapeake lighthouse. At least it gave the two men time to settle into a shipboard routine, for their only time spent aboard previously was an afternoon's rowing in the Solent off the builder's yard in Cowes. In their haste to get away ahead of their competitors, their external buoyancy bags remained unfitted; these were designed to right the *Puffin* in the event of a capsize, and this was a serious omission.

Johnstone and Hoare left on May 21, 1966, and their first couple of days at sea were spent sorting out the gremlins that sea trials are designed to resolve. Their stove would not light and Hoare spent three hours dismantling and rebuilding it; they even considered returning to pick up a replacement. They also had a speed and distance recorder called a "Harrier"—a relatively new development in marine electronics that had only been commercially available for a couple of years. The unit was expensive, but did not work;

Johnstone took it apart and reassembled it, and it eventually sprang into life—but only sporadically. If you rely on dead reckoning, then you ideally need a continuous and reliable record of your distance covered. Johnstone doubted its accuracy and eventually slipped it over the side.

On June 4th, Ridgway and Blyth left Orleans harbor on Cape Cod; although they departed two weeks after their competitors, they were already several hundred miles closer to Britain. That same day, Hurricane Alma developed over Central America and began to move north. Alma was a rare June hurricane and the earliest continental hurricane for 141 years. After coming ashore in the Florida panhandle, the weather system weakened to a tropical storm, but then intensified as it moved into the Atlantic. By June 10th, it was classified again as a hurricane and traveling up the eastern seaboard.

Ridgway and Blyth had faced their first storm on day three at sea, but Alma was altogether different; it struck on June 14th, bringing 40 ft (12 m) waves. During daylight hours the men made good use of the conditions by rowing hard and surfing down the face of the giant waves. The night was very different, and they huddled in their little dory with the canvas covers pulled over to shed water, worried they could capsize at any time.

Johnstone and Hoare also had their share of bad weather and chose not to row in these conditions. On June 7th, they were resupplied by a passing ship and enjoyed the day drinking beer and smoking. With a strong Gulf Stream now carrying them towards Europe, they reasoned there was little point in spending too much time rowing and they limited themselves to eight hours a day each, leaving plenty of time to fish and chat. It was now a month into their voyage and the two men were enjoying themselves; they ate well, slept well, and were physically in good shape.

The two paras had a very different attitude and were pushing themselves hard by rowing 16 hours a day, leaving little time for anything else. They had agreed to be independent and not accept support from passing ships. However, they began to realize that the voyage would take longer than their estimate of 60 days, so they cut their rations to 2,000 calories a day; when they discovered that some of their supplies were spoiled by seawater after Hurricane Alma, they reduced their intake to just 1,250 calories. They had originally estimated they needed 6,000 calories a day to sustain their physical efforts, and they soon became weak from hunger, unable to think clearly, or even sustain a coherent conversation. Neither of the two men were sleeping well, huddled as best they could under a thin foil survival blanket.

Aboard the *Puffin*, Johnstone's easy-going tactics seemed to be paying off, and by their fourth week at sea they were briefly ahead of the *Rosie*, with the boats just 130 NM apart. From now, both crews would face more or less similar weather in the North Atlantic. However, the *Puffin* was further south and inside the main shipping lane, so the two men looked forward to picking up more supplies en route.

The mental state of the two crews was as different as their rowing schedule. Johnstone became moody and constantly feared failure. Hoare was more self-confident and optimistic and did his best to lighten the mood—but the psychological condition of the two men was not encouraging. Despite their poor physical state, Ridgway and Blyth were trained to cope with challenging conditions and they were in a stronger mental state, always confident that they would complete the voyage.

On July 26th, Ridgway and Blyth were spotted by a cargo ship that came alongside and offered them supplies. Ridgway was determined to cross without outside support and turned down their offer, despite knowing they could not complete the voyage with their remaining rations. They soon regretted their decision, and when a tanker came into view three weeks later, the two paras willingly climbed aboard for a meal of scrambled eggs, toast, and coffee. They were told the England soccer team had just won the World Cup and that Johnstone and Hoare were still in the competition. The captain of the tanker *Haustellum* loaded them up with two weeks of supplies and cast them off. That night, both men were violently ill from eating such rich food.

The best of the summer was now coming to an end. The winds seemed to blow from any direction except the west, and the only option was to stream a sea anchor to limit their drift back to North America. Both crews had been at sea for over 10 weeks, and the saltwater sores and sunburn made sitting and rowing painful. On August 24th, another storm struck the *Rosie*—this one even worse than Alma, and the two paras spent the whole night bailing out their dory.

Aboard the *Puffin*, the mood of depression had improved—no doubt fueled by fresh supplies every week or so from passing ships. The two men were well-fed, and even Johnstone began to believe they would make it. However, they were not making good progress and their logbook showed that during the six weeks in late July and August, their daily average had dropped from 43 NM (79.6 km) a day to just 13 NM (24 km), and they were over a thousand miles behind the *Rosie*. At that rate, it would take them many more weeks to complete the voyage.

The cause was not necessarily lethargy, but quite possibly the contrary currents in the Gulf Stream. Although Atlantic routing charts show a westerly current flowing from North America to Europe, the Gulf Stream (called the North Atlantic Drift as it approaches Europe), often has huge swirls and gyres that create surface currents that flow in anything but a westerly direction, and these could have slowed their progress.

Despite the general optimism aboard the *Puffin*, the men were not well-placed; they were much further south than the route taken by the *Rosie* and their competitors were now 1,000 NM (1,850 km) ahead. Johnstone considered taking a more southerly route and perhaps making landfall in Portugal; they had now been at sea for more than three months and were still only two-thirds of the way across. Early on the morning of September 3rd, Johnstone and Hoare sighted a passenger ship through a rainstorm, but it was too far away to get their attention and they were content to drink coffee and watch birds flying overhead.

As the two men watched the cruise ship disappear into the rain that morning, they could not have known that Ridgway and Blyth were approaching the rocky coastline of Ireland, with strong winds pushing them dangerously towards the rocks of Inishmore Island in Co Galway. By early afternoon, the two paras were gazing up at vertical sea cliffs and wondering

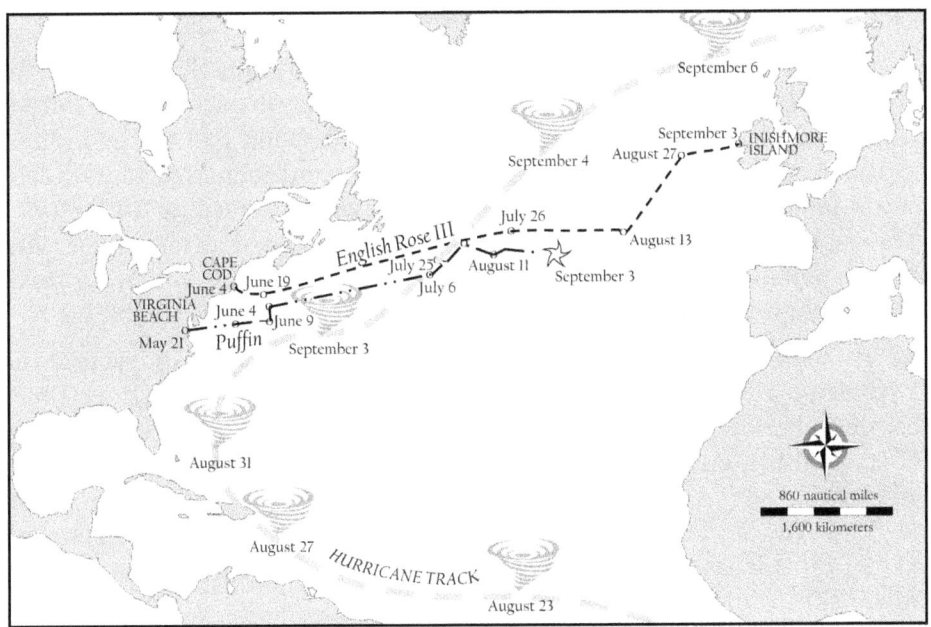

The routes of the Puffin and English Rose III, and showing the track of Hurricane Faith.

how they could make landfall in an onshore gale. The local lifeboat was launched and came to their assistance, but Ridgway insisted on arriving without help, and the two men rowed into the relatively calm waters in the lee of the island. Only then would they accept a rope and allow themselves to be towed into the harbor at Kilronan. The voyage had taken them 92 days.

Five weeks later, on October 14th, the Canadian destroyer HMCS *Chaudière* sighted the upturned hull of a small plywood rowing dinghy. Divers reported no signs of life, but they retrieved the wreck; aboard was Johnstone's journal with his last entry dated September 3rd, the same day that Ridgway and Blyth had completed their passage. Johnstone had noted the weather on that day was rainy with light winds, so what could have happened?

The *Puffin* was intact, so the two rowers had not been run-down—the boat must have capsized; yet Johnstone's very last line in his journal read: "No rowing because of force 2 NNW wind," so it seems unlikely anything happened on that day. However, for the previous couple of weeks, a hurricane had been developing to the south of them. Hurricane Faith stayed offshore in the Atlantic, but on August 31st it turned east. On September 3rd, it was still more than 900 NM (1,666 km) west of the *Puffin*, but it was accelerating quickly. By the following day, it was about 548 miles (833 km) to the north-west—close enough to bring very strong winds.

Weather observations from ships in the vicinity show that by 6:00 a.m. on September 4th, the *Puffin* was encountering a south-easterly gale force 8 (in excess of 34 knots); however, by midday, the wind had swung around to the WNW—almost the opposite direction—and increased to a violent storm force 11 (in excess of 56 knots), with waves exceeding 30 ft (9 m). This rapid change in wind direction would have created a vicious sea, with huge, short-lived pyramidal waves; these were conditions which no small craft could ever expect to survive unscathed.

In 2004, Graham Walters, a carpenter from Leicester, came across the *Puffin* in a Dorset boathouse. Walters had rowed the Atlantic three times before and he decided to restore the boat and complete the voyage in memory of David Johnstone and John Hoare. On February 3, 2007—at the age of 60 and rowing solo—he left La Gomera in the Canary Islands and arrived in St. Jean Bay, St. Barths, 99 days later. Shortly before leaving, he claimed; "The *Puffin* is an old boat, it weighs 2.5 tonnes, so it's a bit like trying to row a skip [dumpster] filled with concrete." His successful crossing won him a place in the 2007 *Guinness Book of World Records* for crossing the Atlantic in the smallest ocean rowing boat.

The *Puffin* is now on public display at the River and Rowing Museum in Henley-on-Thames, England.

≈≈≈≈≈≈≈

Ridgway and Blyth quickly published an account of their crossing, *A Fighting Chance*, and their book re-ignited the challenge of rowing across the Atlantic. John Fairfax was a young adventurer born in 1937 to an English father and a Bulgarian mother and brought up in Italy and Argentina. He was inspired by Ridgway and Blyth's achievement and it took him two years to prepare his own attempt—but solo. Fairfax raised modest sponsorship from a businessman and approached the celebrated Uffa Fox to design his boat. The *Britannia* was 25 ft (7.5 m) long and weighed 860 lbs (390 kg)—considerably larger even than the two-man *Rosie*. Uffa Fox's novel design could self-right after a capsize and had a self-draining system that would empty the boat in a matter of seconds. However, the boat was heavy when fully loaded and difficult to row.

Fairfax left Gran Canaria in the Canary Islands on January 20, 1969, and landed on Hollywood Beach, Florida, on July 19th; the crossing took 180 days. Although he chose the relatively easier southern route across the Atlantic, rowing for nearly six months alone across the ocean was a remarkable achievement. (In April 1971, Fairfax and his partner, Sylvia Cook, became the first people to row across the Pacific Ocean—7,000 NM (11,265 km) and took 361 days.)

Another veteran of the British Parachute Regiment and survival expert, Tom McClean, was also inspired by Ridgway and Blyth's crossing. McClean left Newfoundland in Canada, also rowing alone; he landed in Blacksod Bay in Ireland on July 27, 1969. Despite leaving almost four months after Fairfax, McClean came within eight days of beating him to the title as the first solo rower across any ocean. On June 9, 1982, McClean again departed from Newfoundland, this time in his 9 ft 9 in (2.97 m) sailing boat *Giltspur*. He arrived in Oporto, Portugal, on August 10 after 62 days, to claim the record for crossing the Atlantic in the smallest sailing boat (see chapter *The Great Space Race*) and the first to cross the Atlantic solo in both a sailing and a rowing boat.

After Fairfax and McClean's successful crossings, others followed and records tumbled. The Englishman Don Allum became the first to row the Atlantic in both directions. His first crossing was from Las Palmas in Gran Canaria to Barbados in 1971 in the *QE3* with his cousin, Geoff Allum; their crossing took 73 days, during which time they lost a quarter of their water supply from punctured storage bags. Their entire food supply was depleted, so they had to drastically cut down their consumption of both water and food. When they arrived at Harrison Point in Barbados on March 26, 1971, they had only 3.7 U.S. gallons (14 liters) of water remaining.

The following year the two cousins attempted a return crossing from Newfoundland, but Geoff Allum had to be rescued by a passing oil tanker after three days, suffering from hypothermia and severe seasickness. Don Allum continued, but on day 75 his boat was swamped by a large wave and he lost his oars, spare clothes, and most of his food. Luckily, he was picked up the following day by a passing ship.

Geoff Allum decided not to try again, and Don waited 14 years before making another attempt. At the age of 49, he made a solo crossing from Gran Canaria to Nevis in the Caribbean in 114 days but ran short of water. When he landed, he had lost half of his body weight and his eyesight and hearing were failing. This had a long-term effect on his health and eventually led to multiple kidney failures. Undeterred and still rowing his *QE3*, Allum left Newfoundland again on June 21, 1987, and rowed solo to Achill Island in Co Mayo, Ireland, in 77 days. He was now 50 years old, yet survived a severe gash to his head and several capsizes. He refused treatment for his kidney condition, claiming that: "I have done everything I want to do." He died on November 2, 1992, from a heart attack.

On December 3, 1999, the 36-year-old American Tori Murden became the first woman to row any ocean solo. She left Tenerife in the Canary Islands in her 23 ft (7 m) *Pearl* and arrived in Guadeloupe 81 days later. In March 2006, Julie Wafaei of Canada became the first woman to row across the Atlantic from mainland to mainland; she left Lisbon, Portugal with her partner Colin Angus, and made landfall in Costa Rica. They married a year later and have two sons.

In 1997, Chay Blyth organized the first rowing race across the Atlantic. On October 12th, 30 teams lined up for the start, each with two rowers in identical "one-design" rowing boats. Within 48 hours of leaving Los Gigantes in Tenerife, six teams had given up, exhausted by seasickness, exertion, and food poisoning; however, 24 teams made the crossing, including two boats that finished with a single competitor. The race was won by the *Kiwi Challenge*, rowed by Rob Hamill and Phil Stubbs after 41 days at sea. Second place went to the French team of the *Atlantic Challenge*, crewed by Joseph Le Guen and his rowing partner, Pascal Blond—who had only just been released from prison after serving 14 years as a convicted double murderer.

Since Chay Blyth's 1997 Port St. Charles Rowing Race, there have been ten more transatlantic races, making you wonder if crossing the ocean in a rowing boat has now become almost commonplace—an extraordinary thought.

And that original Atlantic record set in 1896 by Harbo and Samuelson from New York to the Bishops Rock lighthouse? Well, that lasted exactly 114 years until a British-led four-man team in their 23 ft (7 m) *Artemis Investments* arrived off St. Mary's Harbor on July 31, 2010, after 43 days, 21½ hours at sea. They succeeded in knocking more than 11 days off the old record.

≈≈≈≈≈≈≈

All rowing boats are narrow, and it is always a struggle to find enough space for supplies to last a crossing of the Atlantic. But kayaks? Well, that becomes a real challenge.

The first crossing of the Atlantic by kayak probably goes back more than 400 years, and we have the Rev James Wallace—the minister at Kirkwall in the Orkney Islands, Scotland—to thank for his report. In 1682, Wallace came across a man rowing in a skin-covered canoe off the Island of Eday. These people had been seen before and Wallace called them "Finnmen"; in practice, they were Inuit who had most likely rowed across the North Atlantic from Greenland or possibly even from Labrador. Wallace's account suggests these kayakers appeared in the Orkney Islands on several occasions, and they had with them the implements needed for fishing (and therefore survival). Further sightings were reported in the Orkneys in 1701, and in Aberdeen, Scotland, in 1728.

It took nearly 400 years before there was a modern attempt at crossing the Atlantic in a kayak powered only with paddles. (Incidentally, a canoe has a single-bladed paddle whereas a kayak has a double-bladed paddle). The man who tried it was Peter Bray, a former Special Air Service (SAS) diver in the British army, and in 1996 he circumnavigated the British Isles in a two-man kayak. Four years later, he decided he would attempt the first Atlantic crossing in a kayak in modern times.

Bray launched from St. Johns, Newfoundland, in June 2000, and somehow squeezed 100 days of food inside his kayak. He made good progress on his first day, then bedded down for the night in his small cuddy. He awoke to find his kayak three-quarters full of water and his electronic pumping system no longer working due to a faulty outlet valve. He resorted to pumping by hand to stay afloat, but being unable to keep up with the incoming water he was washed out of his kayak and into open water, twice. He realized his situation was unsustainable and he inflated his emergency raft, but his sinking kayak punctured the rubber hull of the raft. His kayak then capsized and he lost everything except for an emergency flare and a pump. He survived without food or fresh water, constantly pumping to keep his life raft afloat, and sitting in near-freezing water. He was rescued by the Canadian Coast Guard after 37 hours adrift, but such was his punishing ordeal that he spent the next four months learning to walk again.

Undeterred, he tried again exactly one year later, leaving Newfoundland on June 23, 2001, solo and unsupported. He intended to raise £100,000 for two children's hospices. His new 24 ft (7.3 m) kayak was an improvement over his earlier design and it used an ingenious system of water tanks for ballast. Behind the sitting position in his narrow craft was a small sleeping compartment clad in flexible solar panels. These were used to power a variety of ultra-high-tech systems, including a satellite phone, tracking system, GPS, desalinization units to make fresh water, and an electric bilge pump.

Bray encountered more storms than he could recall, including one that pushed him 54 NM (100 km) off course; he also broke his rudder and deck hatch. His crossing took 76 days, during which time there was only one night when he could see the stars, and one day of sunshine—insufficient even to charge his batteries. On nearing the coast of Ireland, he had a close call with a killer whale (an orca) and the coastal current swept him so far north that he risked missing Ireland altogether—easily done when you can only paddle 39-51 NM (72-94 km) a day. He did not see a ship during his entire crossing until he was 260 NM (481 km) from Ireland when he was forced to dodge a scattered fishing fleet.

After a 2,982 mile (4,800 km) voyage, he lost radio contact with his reception team and made an unannounced landfall at the small, isolated harbor in Belderrig in Co Mayo, Ireland, on September 5, 2001. A local man found Bray after he had staggered ashore and asked if he was in trouble. "No," Bray replied, "I was just arriving from Canada."

Peter Bray returned for another Atlantic crossing in 2004 when he joined the four-man crew of the 33 ft (10 m) *Pink Lady*—this time a rowing boat. They left from St. John's and after 39 days at sea, rowing virtually non-stop in pairs for two hours at a time, they were set to establish a new Atlantic rowing record. Then on August 8th, they were caught by the tail of Hurricane Alex and they estimated they were subjected to force 10 or 11 winds, with seas over 30 ft (9 m) high.

They were (relatively) comfortably bunkered down for the night when just before 2:30 a.m. they heard a thunderous roar unlike anything they had experienced before. Outside, a rogue wave with a huge breaking crest dumped tons of water over the *Pink Lady*, snapping the boat in two and plunging the crew into the freezing ocean. As the four men struggled to the surface in the darkness, they realized there was little left of their boat. The four men were now swimming in the North Atlantic in the middle of the night, in hurricane-force winds, with no boat, and no means to communicate with the outside world.

Peter Bray took the initiative and dived down to retrieve their grab bag that contained the satellite phone; he then went down a second time to release the emergency life raft, which inflated at the pull of a cord. They struggled to get inside—no mean feat in storm conditions—then activated their emergency distress beacon ... and waited. The following morning, they were rescued by a Danish cargo ship; they were just 321 NM miles (595 km) from their destination—the Isles of Scilly. In June 2005, Bray was awarded a bronze medal by the Royal Humane Society in recognition of his bravery on the expedition.

≈≈≈≈≈≈≈

No account of crossings of the Atlantic Ocean using arm-power alone would be complete without including the story of the remarkable Aleksander Doba. He was born in Poland in 1946, shortly after World War II when the country was run by a Soviet Union-backed communist government. After studying mechanical engineering at university, he became a maintenance engineer at a large chemical complex; in his free time, he took up competitive white-water kayaking. After the Iron Curtain came down and Poland's borders opened, he was able to make long-distance voyages, including paddling around the Baltic Sea, and Lake Baikal in Russia. But Doba had a much more ambitious plan and his biggest challenges were yet to come.

At home in Police in north-western Poland, Doba sketched out plans for a new kayak. He knew it had to be unsinkable and self-righting, and in the event of it capsizing, all lockers needed to be watertight; he also wanted a cabin to sleep in. With sketches in hand, he approached a boatbuilder and by the spring of 2010, the *Olo* was finished—named after his nickname, "Olek." Only now did Doba explain to his wife that he intended to paddle across the Atlantic.

On October 26, 2010, Doba left Dakar in Senegal on the west coast of Africa in his 23 ft (7 m) kayak—he was now 64 years old. The boat weighed only 600 lbs (272 kg), but once loaded with supplies the *Olo* tipped the scales at 1,540 lbs (698 kg). Inevitably, he encountered his fair share of problems including 20 ft (6 m) swells, stifling heat, bad weather, contrary ocean currents, and a broken desalination unit. He tried to paddle during the day but got sunstroke, so he slept in his tiny cabin during the heat of the day and paddled mainly at night. His eyes developed conjunctivitis and the constant dampness caused his fingernails and toenails to peel off. Salt water spray also caused painful salt-induced skin rashes and he developed blisters in his armpits and groin. He could never get his salt-infused clothing to dry, so he paddled naked to ease his skin problems.

Doba survived on dehydrated food, any fish that he caught, and supplemented his supplies by collecting rainwater. He took three kinds of freeze-dried oatmeal for breakfast, four flavors of freeze-dried soup for lunch, and a variety of freeze-dried dinners. Solar panels powered his electrical equipment, including a desalinator and a satellite phone that he used to text his support base back home; in return, they sent him regular weather reports. He also called his wife, twice, but when she got a bill for $500—a big chunk of his monthly pension of $700—she told him not to call again.

Doba's biggest challenge (apart from paying his satellite phone bill) was boredom. Long-distance ocean kayaking is mystifyingly monotonous and Doba understood the primary challenge facing a long-distance solo voyager is mental, not physical. He recalls, "Hundreds, thousands, maybe millions of repetitions [and] the brain is removed from the process." The tedium, he believed, induced a form of suspended animation.

As he neared the coast of Brazil, offshore winds and adverse coastal currents forced an exhausted Doba north-west of his intended place of arrival, and he landed about 54 NM (100 km) further along the Brazilian coast at Acaraú. Despite his age, he averaged a remarkable 30 NM (55 km) a day. The voyage was 2,910 NM (5,389 km) long and he spent 99 days and 6 hours at sea—easily breaking Peter Bray's solo endurance record of 76 days. On arrival, Doba found he had lost 31 lbs (14 kg) in body weight.

Within days of returning from Brazil, Doba was planning his next trip. It took him three years, and he was 67 years old before he set off on his second Atlantic crossing, this time leaving Lisbon in Portugal on October 5, 2013. Aboard were spare paddles, an electric and two manual desalinators, seven bottles of sunscreen, three liters of homemade wine, and 175 chocolate bars. The voyage started well, and having learned his lesson from his first trip, he paddled naked again.

After 75 days at sea, his satellite phone stopped working and he was worried that people back home would be concerned, so he activated the emergency button on his personal tracker. A large Greek vessel soon hove into view and tried to rescue him. Doba explained in his poor English that he only wanted his satellite phone fixed. The crew did not understand and continued their rescue attempt. He waved them off. They returned a second and third time to rescue him. Only when he bellowed a Polish vulgarity—

clearly something that transcended any language barrier—did the captain understand and the ship continued on passage. 47 days later, his phone began working—somebody at home had forgotten to pay the bill.

Doba had intended to make a crossing direct to Florida, but his rudder was damaged in bad weather and he found it difficult to maintain his course. Reluctantly, he diverted to Bermuda for repairs. While there, he continued to live off the same dehydrated rations he had carried from Portugal. After a little over five weeks on the island, he left on March 23, 2015, and continued west. He claims the most difficult part of his trip was navigating through the choppy Gulf Stream waters off the Florida coast.

After more than six months at sea, Doba paddled his kayak into New Smyrna Beach on April 19, 2014, to the cheers of hundreds of well-wishers; the trip had taken him 196 days. It was, perhaps, inevitable that within days of completing his voyage, Doba was planning a third—this time across the stormy North Atlantic. Almost everyone who knew him tried to talk him out of the idea—after all, the northern route was a much greater challenge than the relatively calm, warm waters of the tropical zone. But Doba was determined. His wife's reaction? "To be honest," she said, "[I was] a little pissed."

On May 29, 2016, Aleksander Doba paddled away from the New Jersey shoreline to start his third crossing, accompanied by a fleet of fellow kayakers. Doba had slept poorly the night before and the stress of the preparations left him exhausted. The weather report was not good either, but Doba felt obliged to leave because journalists and many well-wishers had come to watch his departure.

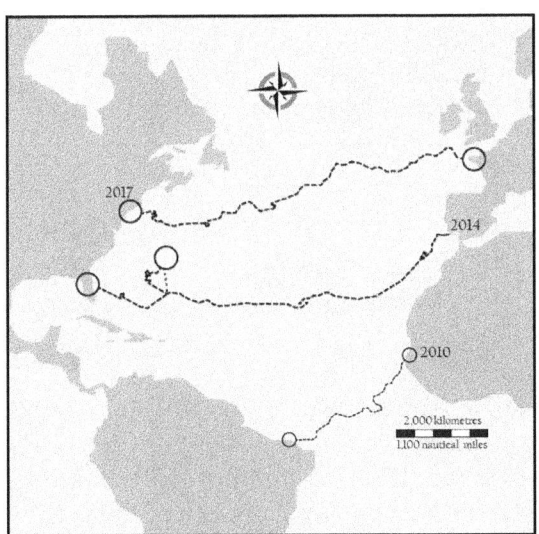

Aleksander "Olek" Doba's three routes across the Atlantic Ocean.

He fully understood the reality of what he was attempting—with a beam of a little over 3 ft (1 m), a kayak can easily be rolled over even in modest waves. Although the *Olo* was designed to be self-righting, recovering from a capsize is exhausting and Doba was no longer a young man. It took him four days even to clear Sandy Hook and the outer bay of New York harbor—a distance of no more than 18 NM (33 km)—during which time he capsized several times and both his GPS and electric desalinator failed. Onshore winds then blew him onto the beach; it was enough, and he called off his attempt.

Undeterred, he tried again the following year—he was now 70 years old. On May 8, 2017, he left New Jersey, but within three days he received his first storm warning. Wanting to avoid the exhaustion of the previous year, Doba returned to shore and landed at Barnegat Bay, calmly running his kayak onto the beach, ordered a steak supper, and checked into a hotel for a good night's sleep. The next day he was rested, afloat, and heading east again.

Aleksander" Olek" Doba in 2015, aged 68. Photo: Ralf Lotys
The Olo (below).
The GRP "horseshoe" spanning the kayak was added for the second and third crossings to assist in righting after a capsize.

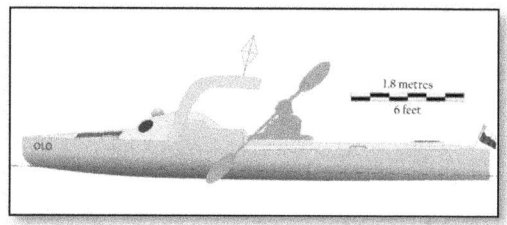

This time he managed three weeks before the first storm arrived, bringing with it winds over 55 knots (102 km/h) and huge waves that towered over his shallow-hulled kayak. Under these conditions, it is essential to deploy a sea anchor to keep the stern of the kayak facing the oncoming waves—if a wave strikes broadside, the kayak will roll. Doba's most serious moment came during a later storm that raged for two days and the rope on his sea anchor snapped. Wearing only his safety harness, he crawled out of the cockpit and across the bucking aft deck of the narrow kayak to deploy his spare sea anchor.

Again, the steering gear of the *Olo* proved to be a design weakness, and five weeks into the crossing his rudder was damaged. This time he had no means of steering and he drifted in the mid-Atlantic for a week before being picked up by a passing freighter, where the crew re-welded the steering gear. Once repaired, the captain of the bulk carrier, the *Baltic Light*, was reluctant to put the septuagenarian and his kayak back into the water, but Doba insisted and he was gently lowered over the side to continue his passage.

On August 29th, Doba had been at sea for 95 days and was literally a few hundred feet from the English coastline when he decided he would not go ashore. When he left New Jersey, he resolved that he would go from North America to the continent of Europe proper. As his family and friends nervously waited for his safe return, he continued on his way for another five days before paddling into the harbor in Le Conquet, France, on September 3, 2017. He was just a few days short of his 71st birthday.

≈≈≈≈≈≈≈

There are precious few "advantages" to rowing or kayaking across the Atlantic, but one of them has to be that you can at least sit down. Not so if you decide to take a paddleboard across, which is exactly what South African Chris Bertish decided to try.

Bertish was no stranger to extreme adventure sports. Born in Kommetjie near Cape Town in South Africa in 1974, he was a professional big-wave surfer with experience riding 40 ft (12 m) waves. As a paddleboarder he set a world record for a 12-hour open ocean voyage, covering 70 NM (130 km) in what he claimed were "great downwind conditions." Then in 2011, he began preparations to cross the Atlantic on a paddleboard; it took him five years to plan and build his unique craft.

Called the *ImpiFish*, his design cost $120,000 to build and it took design features from boats that had been built to row the Atlantic. The custom-built high-tech watertight craft was 20 ft (6 m) long and weighed 1,350 lbs (612 kg) unladen, but Bertish now believes it had a fundamental design problem: "The craft was probably too light," he claimed. "In the open ocean, you essentially get thrown around like a cork," and the jerky movement at sea made it difficult for him to stand and paddle effectively.

The *ImpiFish* was designed to right itself after a capsize, and inside the tiny cabin was room to sleep and a comprehensive navigation station that included a chart plotter, radar, radio and satellite phone, plus electric and manual bilge pumps, a water desalinator, navigation lights, and batteries—all powered by solar power. The craft was so low in the water that it was virtually impossible to be seen by radar among "sea clutter," so Bertish fitted an "EchoMax" system. This electronic device receives a radar signal from another vessel, amplifies it, and then re-transmits it—effectively making a vessel appear several times bigger when viewed on a ship's radar screen.

Every critical system on the boat had back-ups against failure, but even this was not enough. During his crossing, the batteries would not hold a charge, forcing him to cut down on his electrical use—including rationing use of his desalinator. He had to adapt to surviving on just 1.4 U.S. gallons (5.3 liters) of water a day, even though he should have been drinking over one liter an hour while paddling.

Despite careful planning and preparation, there was little he could do about the weather. He left Agadir in Morocco on December 6, 2016, and spent the first five days battling onshore winds and currents that threatened to push him back on the North African coast. Then his main steering failed—a problem that others had experienced with kayaks. "There were numerous times when I was worried about the craft handling the conditions well," Bertish claimed, "I was worried about it basically falling apart around me."

Another design problem unique to a paddleboard was the freeboard. Because you paddle standing up, the deck of the craft is low—only 4 in (10 cm) above sea level. For most of the trip, his feet and ankles were underwater and his "watertight" storage compartments also leaked. "I pretty much constantly felt like I was sinking," he recalled. Yet still, he continued heading westwards, paddling 12 to 15 hours a day. Like Aleksander Doba, he also found that paddling at night kept him out of the midday sun.

Bertish arrived in English Harbor, Antigua, on March 9, 2017, and became the first to cross the Atlantic on a stand-up paddleboard, unsupported and unassisted. The crossing took him 93 days, during which time he covered 3,520 NM (6,518 km) and made an estimated 2 million paddle strokes. He wanted to continue to Florida, but a poor weather forecast persuaded him to go no further. Bertish also set a paddleboard world record for traveling the furthest distance solo without support, across the open ocean in 24 hours—a distance of 62.56 NM (115.86 km).

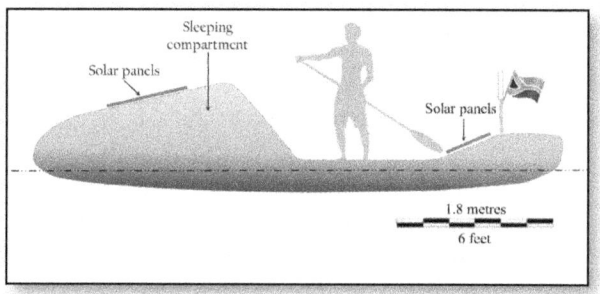

Impifish, the paddleboard taken across the Atlantic by Chris Bertish.

As a result of his achievement, Chris Bertish raised $412,000 in support of several South African charities that help feed, school, and provide medical support for children.

≈≈≈≈≈≈≈

If you have ever tried windsurfing, then you will know it is not easy, even on flat water. You have to clamber onto the sailboard and stand upright (no easy feat in itself). You are now balanced on a narrow, wet, rolling platform, and the sail is still in the water. You lean back to pull the mast vertical, hoping to stay upright as the wind catches the sail—and you are off. You also imagine that everyone on the beach is watching you with great interest and thinking that you are making a complete hash of things. Now try doing this 1,000 NM (1,852 km) from the nearest land in a rolling ocean swell. (At least you do not have to worry about people watching you mess it up).

A transatlantic crossing on a sailboard is a far cry from recreational windsurfing; you have to be prepared to endure gale-force winds and ocean swells the height of a two-story building for weeks at a time—and every minute of the day, you are wet and straining every muscle in your arms and back—much like rowing. Yet this is exactly what a French windsurfer first achieved in the early '80s.

Christian Marty had a passion for extreme sports, including water-skiing, downhill skiing, rock climbing, mountain biking, and windsurfing. He was also a commercial pilot with Air France, and his approach to his transatlantic crossing was as meticulously planned as any flight he made across the same ocean. Marty, then 35 years old, departed from Dakar in Senegal in February 1984 and sailed to French Guiana in 37 days—a distance of 2,084 NM (3,860 km), maintaining an average of 56 NM a day. He was accompanied by a support boat that supplied him with food and liquid, but he chose to sleep on his sailboard at night—a traditional, classic 1980s windsurfer. He was modest about the challenge: "I love to do battle with myself. Spending a month on the ocean is a form of retreat that holds appeal to the contemplative side of me."

Christian Marty sailed a traditional, classic sailboard from the 1980s, similar to the board pictured above.

Despite his careful planning, the crossing nearly cost him his life on more than one occasion. One night he rolled off his board while asleep, and nobody on the support boat knew what had happened. He woke up in the water to find his board drifting away. Fortunately, the flashlight aboard was still alight, so he was able to see where his board was in the pitch darkness. Even after this close-call, he still refused to have his board tethered to the mothercraft. "I didn't want to gain a single mile unless my wrists and arms felt it," he told a reporter after his arrival.

After his world-record crossing, Marty returned to Air France as one of their most senior pilots and qualified to fly Concorde. On July 25, 2000, Christian Marty was at the controls of Air France flight 4590, leaving Paris for New York. As the aircraft began to accelerate during take-off at Charles de Gaulle airport, it ran over debris on the runway and punctured a fuel tank, an engine failed, and the plane caught fire. Marty struggled at the controls to gain height, but it was fruitless. He was able to steer the aircraft away from a local hospital but crashed into a hotel. All 109 passengers and crew died instantly, together with four employees in the hotel. He left a wife and two children.

≈≈≈≈≈≈≈

It is so often the case that when somebody succeeds in achieving what seems to be impossible, it is not long before there is an attempt to out-do the impossible. In 1986, the French sailboarders Stéphane Peyron and Alain Pichavant defied the odds by taking on the Atlantic on a tandem sailboard—but making the crossing without outside support. This, of course, raises the obvious question of how you carry food and liquid for a month, and how do you sleep? Their purpose-built sailboard was 31 ft (9.4 m) long and 4 ft (1.2 m) wide, and this allowed space for watertight compartments inside the hull to store supplies, and even to squeeze into a coffin-size compartment to sleep.

Peyron and Pichavant, both 25 years old, left Dakar on February 27, 1986, intending to sail to Guadeloupe in the West Indies, a distance of 2,546 NM (4,715 km). However, things began to go wrong from the very beginning. On their second day at sea, the sailors encountered a storm with 44-knot winds (81 km/m, or severe gale force 9), with steep breaking waves. In these conditions, it is nearly impossible to even stay on the deck, and the waves swept everything overboard, including their fresh food and ship-to-shore radio.

Their sailing schedule was three hours on and three hours off, 24 hours a day when conditions allowed. When one was sailing, the other would sleep. They were sailing in the tropics with little protection from the sun, and they struggled with sunburn, fatigue, muscle cramps, skin fungi, seasickness, and boredom. They also attracted the attention of several sharks, which can approach very close when you are balancing on a sailboard only a few inches above the surface. Despite very obvious hardships, they completed the crossing in a very respectable 24 ½ days, averaging 104 NM (192 km) a day. From there, they sailed up the eastern seaboard of the United States in stages to New York, where they arrived to celebrate the centenary of the erection of the Statue of Liberty.

The following year, Stéphane Peyron decided that there was one more challenge left, and he sailed from New York on June 7th for Europe, again without assistance, but this time sailing solo. His specially designed sailboard was not dissimilar to the tandem board he used the previous year with Pichavant but was smaller: 24 ft (7.3 m) long, 4 ft (1.2 m) wide, and 2.5 ft (0.76 m) deep. The board was fitted with solar panels to power a light, a radio, and a satellite tracking system—although, after the previous crossing, he was prepared for the worst and claimed he was ready to go the whole trip without a radio.

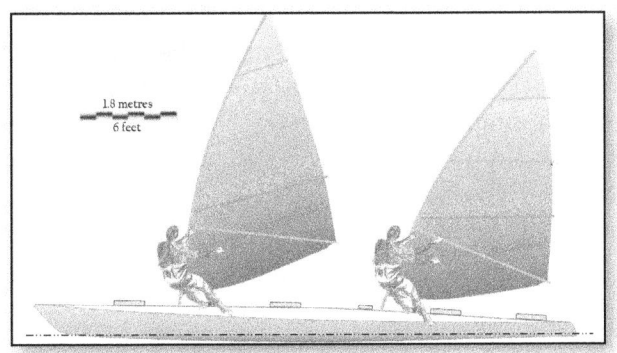

Peyron and Pichavant's purpose-built sailboard.

At night, he attached a kite to give the sailboard some direction, and to stop it wallowing in the swell. He then crawled into a virtually air-tight compartment, closed the deck hatch, and slept: "During the night," he claimed, "every 40 minutes I put my head out to check if there are any ships, to see if everything is in a good position, and get more air. There is never enough air!"

Conditions across the North Atlantic were much tougher than his previous Trade Wind route, and Peyron wore sunglasses and a wet suit for the whole voyage and survived on candy bars and dried fruit. He encountered his first storm just five days out that damaged his mast, and he cut his hand badly while making repairs. A week later his sailboard was overturned in the wake of a cargo ship, and shortly after he encountered another storm, this time accompanied by 20 ft (6 m) waves.

Peyron made landfall at La Baule on the west coast of France after 48 days at sea; he covered 2,851 NM (5,280 km) at an average of 59 NM (110 km) a day.

≈≈≈≈≈≈≈

In September 1998, four windsurfing teams assembled in St. John's, Newfoundland, for a race across the Atlantic to Weymouth in England, a distance of 1,944 NM (3,600 km). The Trans-Atlantic Windsurf Race (TAWR) pitched four crews from Britain, the United States, Sweden/France, and Greece, with each team comprising three sailors. The windsurfers took turns to sail their team board during the day, then in the evening, there was a formal race—in the middle of the Atlantic.

While team members raced, the remaining competitors stayed aboard the Russian support ship, with seasickness becoming a major issue. Meanwhile, the racing sailboards were accompanied by a fast RIB. This was seriously fast sailing and the race lasted just seven days, with the teams averaging about 390 NM (722 km) a day. During the crossing, the competitors encountered winds gusting to 35 knots (force 8) and 30 ft (9.1 m) waves. At times, the water temperature dropped to 39 degrees F (4 degrees C), and there was one case of mild hypothermia. At night, the sailors stayed aboard the mother ship.

All the competitors arrived safely in Weymouth on September 21st, and the race was won by the "Liberty" team, comprising two Swedes and a Frenchman.

The History Men

For thousands of years the Atlantic Ocean divided the Old World from the New, creating a barrier to trade and exploration. Then in August 1492, Christopher Columbus sailed to the West Indies and went ashore to claim the New World for Spain, and became the new poster boy for European colonization. At least this has always been the perceived wisdom, but the truth behind Columbus's fabled landing does not quite match the reality of what really happened.

Columbus made three Atlantic crossings, but he never actually set foot on the mainland of either North or South America, and the Spanish did not arrive in *La Florida* until 1513—nearly a generation after Columbus first arrived in the New World. Nor was his crossing quite the voyage into the unknown portrayed in the history books. A thousand years ago the Norsemen landed in Newfoundland and established a community there. More than 500 years ago and well before Columbus's voyage, the fishermen of Bristol and the Basque region of northern Spain were catching cod off Newfoundland, and they went ashore to smoke and salt their fish before returning home. These fishermen regularly sailed to North America in the summer months, but kept their destination a secret for commercial reasons, for salt cod was a lucrative commodity in Catholic Europe.

So, if Christopher Columbus was not the first European to sail across the Atlantic, who were the first to make this perilous crossing? Perhaps it is time to reconsider the history of the very earliest crossings of the North Atlantic Ocean.

≈≈≈≈≈≈≈

There is abundant evidence that North America was populated during the last Ice Age around 15,500 years ago. Sea level was lower then, and people from Asia walked across the land bridge that linked Siberia with Alaska, and migrated throughout the continent.

Then in the 1950s, the inspirational but controversial American archaeologist, Frank C. Hibben, suggested that North America was colonized long before this time by prehistoric Europeans. His ideas were discredited through the lack of any substantial archaeological evidence—at least until a few years ago. More recently, anthropologists from the Smithsonian Institute in Washington D.C. and the University of Exeter in England have analyzed all the evidence. They have concluded that crossing the North Atlantic in tiny, leather-skinned Ice Age boats would certainly have been an extraordinary undertaking, but would have been quite possible.

"These people," maintains Professor Dennis Stanford of the Smithsonian "would have been hunters as well as fishermen, and would have simply sailed around the southern edge of the packs of sea ice that covered the North Atlantic. If a storm arrived, they would have camped on an ice island until the weather got better. Eventually, they would have drifted west until they reach eastern America."

It was a remarkable claim, but with little hard evidence, Professor Stanford's ideas were likely to go the same way as Frank Hibben's. But if true, the journey across the North Atlantic would have been one of the most amazing migrations ever undertaken, for 20,000 years ago the northern and southern latitudes were desolate wastelands, blasted by storms and blizzards.

Then hard evidence of early European colonization of North America was found at six locations along the eastern seaboard of the United States, and several dozen European-style stone tools were discovered dating back to between 19,000 and 26,000 years ago. This is thousands of years before the migration of people from Siberia, yet there is no evidence of human settlement in the Alaskan region before 15,500 years ago. So, could these East Coast people have migrated from Europe, and not from Siberia?

These stone tools are similar to those used by the Solutrean people of Spain. If these Europeans did indeed arrive in North America 19,000 to 26,000 years ago, then they were later either absorbed by the Asian newcomers or died out through conflict or competition for resources. Although modern Native Americans possess mainly DNA of Asian origin, they also carry some variants found only in Europeans, further strengthening the case for early immigration from Europe.

These new discoveries are important archaeological and genetic breakthroughs. Not all archaeologists and anthropologists agree, but this new evidence suggests that early prehistoric peoples might have made long ocean voyages across the North Atlantic at least 20,000 years ago.

≈≈≈≈≈≈≈

The possibility of more recent transatlantic links between the peoples of Europe and the New World have also intrigued anthropologists. They have pointed out there are remarkable similarities between the cultures of pre-Columbian America—such as the Aztecs and the Incas—and those of the Mediterranean world. Then in 1992, Svetlana Balabanova, a German toxicologist, found traces of cocaine, hashish, and nicotine in the hair of Egyptian mummies. Her findings were immediately pronounced to be unlikely because two of the substances could only have come from American plants—and she was denounced as a fraud. However, many scientists found her work credible and they used her research as evidence of contact between the ancient Egyptians and pre-Columbian peoples.

More than 20 years before the mummy-hair discovery, Thor Heyerdahl had much the same idea. He was a Norwegian ethnologist and adventurer, and he wondered if the ancient Egyptians might have sailed across the Atlantic. Heyerdahl famously made a 3,725 NM (6,900 km) voyage in his *Kon-Tiki* balsa raft from Peru to the Polynesian Islands, to demonstrate that people from South America could have settled Polynesia in pre-Columbian times. Now Heyerdahl became interested in early contact between the peoples of Africa and the New World. He saw cultural similarities, such as pyramid building in ancient Egyptian and Mexican civilizations.

There were flaws in his theory; the Egyptian pyramids of Giza, for example, were built around 3500 B.C., whereas the American peoples built their pyramids from about 1000 B.C. until the time of the Spanish conquest in the early sixteenth century. Such problems did not seem to trouble Heyerdahl, and he was determined to sail the Atlantic in a replica ancient craft, modeled after boats displayed on ancient Egyptian artwork.

The ancient peoples of the Mediterranean certainly had a tradition of long sea voyages. Around 600 B.C., the Phoenicians sailed around Africa from the Red Sea and back via the Straits of Gibraltar. The Greeks were a great seafaring power and traded throughout the Mediterranean and as far as India and beyond. Later, Roman ships dominated trade throughout the region. However, all these ships had one thing in common—they were built of wood. Heyerdahl decided he would build his transatlantic vessel from papyrus, a material that was much less robust and used only by the Egyptians for river craft.

Heyerdahl chose reeds for the hull because only ancient reed boats were known to exist in both Egypt and the New World. If wooden boat building was introduced from the Mediterranean into Central America, he argued, then the early Americans would have built wooden boats. However, because they had only reed boats, any sea voyage from the Old World would most likely have been in a reed boat.

Ever the showman, Heyerdahl built his boat—named after the sun god Ra—at the foot of the pyramids in Cairo, even though it meant transporting the finished vessel nearly 3,000 miles (4,828 km) to Safi on the Atlantic coast of Morocco. Heyerdahl also brought craftsmen from Lake Chad in central Africa to build the boat. He had many detractors, but he argued that Egypt was the best place for the building site because the construction of papyrus boats was now a lost skill, and he needed the support and advice from Egyptologists based in Cairo.

As with his previous boat the *Kon-Tiki*, Heyerdahl found that many skeptics claimed his replica would never survive an ocean crossing. The head of the Cairo Museum thought the idea of a reed boat crossing the Atlantic was preposterous, and the President of the Papyrus Institute announced that the boat could never sail beyond the mouth of the River Nile because papyrus dissolves in seawater and breaks up in waves. It was not an encouraging start.

An Egyptian tomb painting from 1450 B.C.
Photo: NOAA

Reed boats certainly have a long history, and the earliest example was found in Kuwait dating back 7,000 years—and it was a sea-going vessel. Reed boats later became commonly used in Ancient Egypt, and a famous example is the ark of bulrushes in which the baby Moses was set adrift on the Nile. Reed boats were also built from early times in Peru and Bolivia, and boats with remarkably similar designs have been found on Easter Island in the Pacific Ocean. This was just the sort of link that Heyerdahl thrived on.

Heyerdahl settled on a 45 ft (13.7 m) design, 16 ft (4.9 m) wide, but the project had its logistical challenges. He calculated that he needed 5,000 cu ft (142 cu m) of reeds and decided the swamps surrounding Lake Tana in Ethiopia were the best site to harvest them. Once fully dry, they were divided into 500 large bundles and trucked 450 miles (724 km) to the coast, before being shipped 1,100 NM (2,000 km) up the Red Sea to Cairo. Three boat builders were recruited from the Lake Chad region of western Chad, and they needed medical certificates and travel documents before they could fly to Egypt. Everything involved mountains of paperwork in multiple languages.

Heyerdahl's technique was to bundle the reeds together in 2.5 ft (0.76 m) diameter tubes, 50 ft (15.2 m) long; they were strapped together with twine the thickness of a man's little finger. The cabin was woven by an old basket-maker in Cairo and was 12 ft (3.7 m) long and 8.6 ft (2.6 m) wide, and would become home to a crew of seven. Old Egyptian paintings showed a single mast on reed boats, supported by several stays that ran back to each side of the boat, thereby increasing the rigidity of the hull. A simple steering oar was mounted on each side.

The boatbuilding team faced unique challenges—midday temperatures in spring exceed 86 deg F (30 deg C), drying out both reeds and boatbuilders. Dust storms stopped work for days at a time, and once the word spread, tourists and journalists came from all over the world, and they proved to be just as much of a distraction.

Once completed, the *Ra* was shipped to Safi on the Moroccan Atlantic coast and the launch date set for May 27, 1969—Norway's national day. Without a keel, some expected the boat to immediately capsize, others thought that she would list to one side. The boat slipped down the slipway on a wooden cradle and floated off, looking for all the world like a fat goose (Heyerdahl's words, not mine). She floated perfectly upright.

In the hot, dry atmosphere of Cairo, the *Ra* weighed 12 tonnes, but after launching the papyrus bundles absorbed seawater, and tonnes more of spares and equipment were added. The heaviest piece was the huge wooden, ladder-mast that made the vessel top-heavy. Heyerdahl watched the waterline carefully, but the boat remained stable. Food for the voyage was kept strictly traditional: sheep's cheese in olive oil, fresh eggs in a lime solution, dried fish, nuts, mutton sausages in wicker baskets, plus live chickens.

Heyerdahl was famous as an internationalist, and he chose to sail under the flag of the United Nations; his seven-man crew came from seven different countries: the Soviet Union, the United States, Mexico, Egypt, Italy, Morocco, and of course Norway. May 25th was scheduled for departure and conditions were perfect, with a gentle offshore breeze. They were towed outside the harbor, then they hoisted the 450 sq ft (42 sq m) wine-colored square-sail for the first time. They were about to embark on a transatlantic voyage of 3,500 NM (6,482 km) in an archaic design made from papyrus reeds lashed together with rope—and the boat had never even been tested at sea.

There were the inevitable teething problems. The steering oars broke on the first day, but they found the boat sailed downwind perfectly fine without them. Of course, with only a few inches of the hull in the water, the

Ra was incapable of sailing across the wind and could only sail in the same direction—in this respect she was a raft rather than a boat.

Two things troubled Heyerdahl. First, they left Morocco one week before the start of the hurricane season in the Atlantic, generally taken as the beginning of June. The crew had no idea how fast the boat would sail, or how long it would take to arrive in the Caribbean, so they could not judge if they would be ashore before the hurricanes arrived. The second concern was losing a man overboard—the *Ra* had no guardrails and a crew member could easily slip over the side; with no keel and a following wind, there was no chance of turning around and picking somebody up. Rule number one (which applies to all boats) was to stay aboard.

Less than two days into the voyage the wind increased, becoming almost violent. Without steering oars, they had no control over their vessel, but the boats direction remained steady. When the wind swung around to the north-west, however, they had no choice but to sail south-east back towards the Moroccan coast. Six days into the voyage the wind increased to their first storm, and they were still dangerously close to shore. Heyerdahl ordered a double watch, hoping to avoid running aground off Cape Juby. With no control over their direction, there was little to do but hope, and they were lucky to skim past the headland, easily in sight of the little white houses on the clifftop.

By day nine they were clear of the coast and south of the Canary Islands. With a following breeze, they covered 60 NM (111 km) a day, averaging 2½ knots. They probably had at least ½ knot of favorable current, so the *Ra* was not going to break any sailing records. The crew used their time learning to get the most out of their ancient craft, and doing routine maintenance, cooking, fishing, and enjoying the occasional visit from pods of whales.

By June 11th, Heyerdahl was becoming nervous. The lashings that held the *Ra* together were coming loose and deteriorating. The stays on the 30 ft (9.1 m) mast had slackened and the top was swaying by as much as 2 ft (0.6 m). The mast stays also helped tension the bow and stern, and with slack stays, the stern began to sag. Another storm on June 17th, 24 days into the voyage, only hastened the boat's deterioration. They discussed abandoning the *Ra* but realized they had seven men aboard but a life raft for only six. It was not a serious idea anyway, as it is always better to stay with your boat—even one that is slowly sinking—than to take to a life raft.

Despite several gales, the crew kept the *Ra* together as an effective sailing vessel, albeit it a rather slow one. But the strong winds and constant flexing from passing waves took their toll. On July 14th they made radio contact with a motor yacht heading out from Barbados to rendezvous with them;

they reported that they were experiencing bad weather and 20 ft (6.1 m) waves. The following day the storm reached its climax and the crew on the *Ra* had to drop all sail. Their papyrus boat could not take much more battering.

The following day dawned fine, and the motor yacht came alongside. Heyerdahl now had a difficult decision to make. More bad weather was forecast, and the motor yacht was keen to return to Barbados. Should they continue and hope the *Ra* would stay together? Or abandon the reed boat and return with the motorboat? The crew was torn over what to do, and most wanted to continue. As skipper, Heyerdahl made the final decision; they had succeeded in sailing over 2,600 NM (4,815 km) and were only a few hundred miles from the West Indies. They had proved that a papyrus boat could cross oceans, and there was no point in risking lives. Heyerdahl ordered the crew to abandon the ship.

The *Ra* was an experiment in ancient shipbuilding and they had learned from the inherent weaknesses of the design and construction. Undaunted, Heyerdahl built a second papyrus craft, the *Ra II*, this time with the aid of Aymara Indian boatbuilders from Lake Titicaca in Bolivia. The *Ra II* was built stronger and bound together with lashings that went all around the hull. He also strengthened the steering oars. Again, he chose a multinational crew of seven, and the boat set sail from Safi on May 17, 1970. After a voyage of 57

The successful Ra II ashore, 39 ft (11.9 m) long and 16 ft (4.9 m) wide.
Photo: Pedro Ximenez

days and 3,456 NM (6,400 km), they made landfall in Barbados. On arrival, they were escorted by 50 vessels into Bridgetown harbor.

So, what did this all prove? Thor Heyerdahl was typically modest:

> "I still don't know. I have no theory but that a reed boat is seaworthy and the Atlantic is a conveyor. But I would hereafter consider it barely short of a miracle if the multitude of active maritime expeditions during the millennia of antiquity never happened to...be swept off course while struggling to avoid shipwreck in the dreaded currents around Cape Juby."

There is little doubt that Heyerdahl firmly believed that the "bearded white men" who some believe brought "civilization" to Central America originated from the Mediterranean region. Although he is not explicit, he implies they were probably of Egyptian and Phoenician origin and most likely made the crossing around 1000 B.C. Heyerdahl's grand experiment also showed that not all ocean voyages were necessarily taken in wooden boats. However, his controversial beliefs on human migration cut across the conventional wisdom of his day, and his ideas were heavily criticized by the scientific community. But there is no doubt that he was hugely popular with the public: he wrote several best-selling books about his voyages and won an Academy Award (Oscar) for Best Documentary Feature for the *Ra* expedition.

He died in his family home in northern Italy in 2002, at the age of 87.

≈≈≈≈≈≈≈

It might seem total madness to attempt to sail the Atlantic in a boat in which you have intentionally poked 30,000 holes, but that is exactly what Tim Severin and his crew did in 1976. The reason for this multitude of holes was because Severin built a hull made from ox hides stitched together with twine, and stretched over a light wooden frame.

Severin was an adventurer by nature. In 1961, he followed Marco Polo's route from Italy to China on a motorcycle, and six years later retraced the routes of early explorers down the Mississippi river. Now he was about to embark on his most audacious expedition yet—to cross the North Atlantic in a replica medieval sailing boat. His voyage was inspired by the Irish monk, St. Brendan (c. 486–578 A.D.), who allegedly crossed the Atlantic 900 years before Columbus and more than 400 years before the Norsemen set foot on the American continent.

The idea was inspired by Severin's American wife, Dorothy Sherman Severin, a specialist in medieval Spanish literature. She had just finished reading an account of Brendan's voyage called *The Navigatio*, or to give the text its full Latin title, *The Navigatio Sancti Brendani Abbatis*, or *The Voyage of St. Brendan the Abbot*. The story was first written down 300 years after Brendan's voyage, and there are more than 100 copies of the manuscript still in existence (including several translations), making it something of a medieval bestseller. Dorothy Severin thought the *Navigatio* was unlike anything she had read from the period. There was, for example, no mention of any miracles—unusual in manuscripts of this type. Instead, the text contained practical details about places visited, the times and distances of the voyage, and details of the boat that St. Brendan and his crew of monks were alleged to have sailed. It read like a travelogue.

Most academics thought the *Navigatio* was a fantastical fable, but Tim Severin wondered if there might not be more to Brendan's voyage and he spent several months researching in the British Library and pondering whether St. Brendan really did build a boat made of skins to cross the Atlantic. The more he read, the more intrigued he became.

St. Brendan was born in Ireland around 489 A.D. (about 10 years after the death of St. Patrick), probably near the lakes of Killarney in County Kerry in South-West Ireland. Christianity had only come to the country 50 years before he was born, and as an adult, Brendan went on to become one of Ireland's most important saints, with a profound influence on the early Celtic Church. He lived into his 80s and not only founded several monasteries but also traveled widely. Several medieval documents refer to his voyages to Scotland and Wales, with some crossings as far as Brittany, the Orkney and Shetland Islands, and even as far as the Faroes. Brendan really was the sailor's saint.

It was the *Navigatio* that established St. Brendan's reputation as a great traveler, and the manuscript described how he built a boat made with

St Brendan and the Whale, from a fifteenth century manuscript.

a wooden framework over which he stretched ox hides. He loaded food and supplies (as well as spare ox hides and fat to dress the leathers) and set sail westwards with a crew of 17 other monks. The *Navigatio* recounts extraordinary tales on their way to the "Promised Land," taken to be North America. They landed at one site where they found monks living under a vow of silence; they beached on the back of a whale, mistaking it for a small island; they encountered a huge crystal pillar floating in the ocean; and they sailed to an island where they were pelted with hot rocks. Brendan's voyage was said to have taken at least seven years. Was this remotely possible in a boat made from perishable ox skins?

Severin poured over his Atlantic routing charts and read the *Navigatio* carefully, and decided St. Brendan must have gone north to the Faroe Islands, then to Iceland, Greenland, Labrador, and Newfoundland. It looks a long way on a chart, but it is actually the shortest distance from Europe to North America because of the curvature of the earth. Even so, it crosses 1,750 NM (3,241 km) of stormy northern latitudes. It was an audacious plan and fraught with problems.

Severin was confident that Brendan's boat was similar to a currach (sometimes anglicized as "curragh,") and still used for fishing on the west coast of Ireland. The *Navigatio* describes how the ocean-going vessel was built: using iron tools, the monks constructed a wooden-framed boat *sicut mos est in illis partibus* (as the custom is in those parts), then stretched ox hides cured with oak bark over the frame to make the hull; wool grease sealed the gaps where the skins were overlapped. The boat could be sailed or rowed.

Severin's first problem was the ox hides that perish when permanently saturated. A breakthrough came when he found a traditional tannery in Cornwall that supplied oak bark tanned leather. The hides became proofed after being soaked for a year in a liquor made from ground-up oak bark and water—the mixture looked like thick beer with a creamy froth and smelled sickly sweet. As the hides absorbed the tannin they turned from a perishable skin into leather that Severin hoped would withstand being saturated in the Atlantic Ocean for weeks on end. Fortunately, the tannery had 57 of their finest oak-tanned hides available, and they were shipped to a wool mill in Yorkshire to be steeped in ¾ ton of wool grease. By any stretch of the imagination their unique aroma could never be considered pleasant—in fact, they smelled truly awful.

The next step was to find a naval architect and Severin approached none other than Colin Mudie, who had sailed the Atlantic with Patrick Ellam in the tiny *Sopranino* in the 1950s (see chapter *The Great Space Race*) and would later design the *Puffin* a transatlantic rowing boat (see chapter *The Arms Race*). Mudie listened carefully to Severin's brief, then declared: "There's nothing impossible either about a leather boat or the voyage you want to make." It was just what Severin needed to hear, but Mudie added a word of caution: "…what neither I nor anyone else can give you is the knowledge of how to handle this boat at sea."

Mudie's basic design was 36 ft (11 m) overall, with a relatively narrow beam of 8 ft (2.4 m). He thought the original vessel probably had twin sails that could be used to balance the boat and make it easier to handle. The bare hull weighed 2,400 lbs (1,089 kg), plus an additional 1,284 lbs (582 kg) for sails and rowing equipment, making the displacement 1.67 tons, but with storage, water, crew, and sea-water uptake into the leather, the full sailing displacement would be closer to 5 tons.

The flax sails were just 140 sq ft (13 sq m) for the mainsail and 60 sq ft (5.6 sq m) for the foresail, but both sails could be extended in light winds with a "bonnet" laced along the foot of the sails. The boat was steered with a large-bladed paddle over the starboard quarter and Mudie designed special slim oars, 12 ft (3.7 m) long, based on the style used by traditional currachs.

Severin was then living in the Republic of Ireland, so the obvious choice was to find a local boatbuilder and he settled on the traditional Crosshaven Boatyard in Co Cork. It was here that the Irish lifeboats were sent for overhaul, and their boatbuilding credentials were impeccable. The boatyard was responsible for the wooden frame, then Severin took over to cover the hull with the hides. The frame was made from Irish ash with the ribs tied with strips of leather thongs in the style of medieval boatbuilders—they found tying knots in the wet leather as easy as tethering two snakes. Severin's volunteers hand-lashed 1,600 joints using two miles of leather strips, then boiled buckets of wool grease and liberally painted the timber and leather for protection.

The wooden frame was then covered with the ox hides—tough ¼-in (6.35 mm) thick hides, each averaging 4 ft x 3.5 ft (1.22 x 1.06 m). Through trial and error, Severin found it best to overlap the skins by an inch. With one person working inside the hull and another outside, the stitchers poked an awl through two layers of hide then ran a blunt needle and flax twine through the hole before it closed; the hides were then pulled tightly together. It was painful work and the stitcher's fingers were soon bleeding from cuts, and it took a dozen volunteers several weeks to complete the hull. Severin anticipated extra wear at the bow and stern where he doubled-up the hides to ½ in (12.7 mm); at the very front he doubled the skins again, making the bow an 1 in thick (25 mm). More wool grease was liberally painted over the outside, soaking into the hides and flax stitching to give extra waterproofing and protection. On January 24, 1976, the Bishop of Kerry blessed the boat, a bottle of Irish whiskey was swung across her bow, and the *Brendan* slid gently into the cold waters of the Atlantic.

Any owner will tell you there is a lot of work still to be done fitting out a new boat after launching, but the south coast of Ireland was no place for test-sailing in winter, so the *Brendan* was trucked north to the River Shannon for rigging and trials. The boat lacked a keel and could sail no closer than at right-angles to the wind; even then, the boat made significant leeway and drifted sideways. It was also difficult to control with the side-mounted steering oar, and they kept running into the reed beds at the side of the river. Even with four men on the oars, the *Brendan* was also too unwieldy to row into the wind.

It was not an encouraging start, but Severin persisted and took the *Brendan* offshore for proper sea-trials. The capsize test proved the hull was more stable upside down than the right way up, so they could never re-float the boat in the event of a knock-down at sea; Severin prudently fitted blocks of foam buoyancy in the hull.

It had taken him three years of research, planning, and construction to get this far, and it was now time to prepare for the crossing. His boat was as authentic as he could reasonably make it, but he also made the most of modern equipment. Bright yellow tarpaulins were strapped over the bow and stern to give some protection for the crew and to make the boat more visible at sea. A life raft was carried backed up with distress flares. They

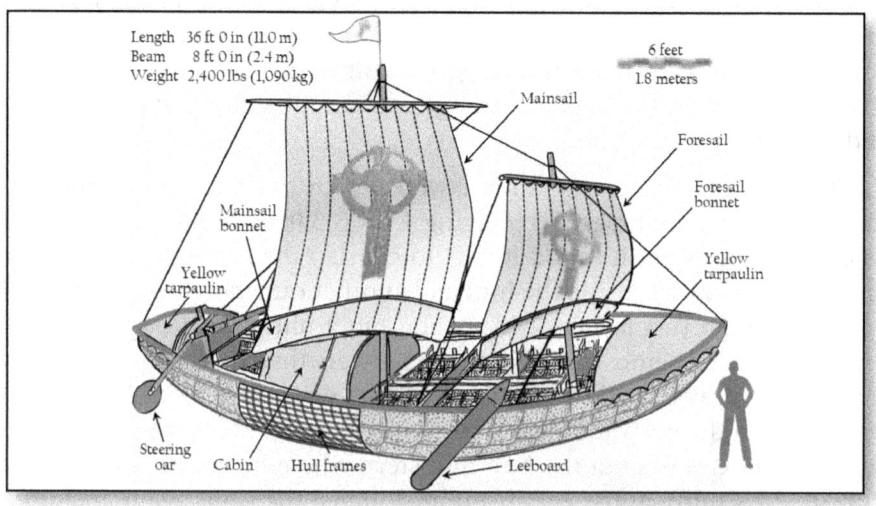

The Brendan, with side cutaway showing the ash frame for the hull.

had 12-volt battery radios, a sextant and charts for navigation, bilge pumps, heavy-duty oilskins, canned food, water in plastic bottles, and a paraffin stove.

Living conditions for St. Brendan's crew could not have been more different. The saint is thought to have taken 17 monks or more—a tight fit in a 36 ft boat. Their protection would have been heavy woolen, hooded gowns, and probably only leather sandals. Water was carried in heavy leather flasks, food was dried meat, cereals, and roots. They used wooden scoops to bail out the boat, and cooking was over a fire in an iron cauldron. But they also had two things in their favor: an almost unlimited amount of time and an unshakable faith in their Saviour.

Severin chose St. Brendan's feast day, May 16, 1976, as the day of departure but heavy rain and a westerly gale delayed them. Spectators gathered in the downpour, and one was heard to mutter: "They'll need a miracle if they hope to cross the Atlantic in that—more than St. Brendan ever did!" What mattered to Tim Severin, however, was not to test themselves but to test their boat.

The next day dawned fine with high cloud; as the tide began to ebb, the crew pushed away from the quayside and propelled the *Brendan* out of the creek with their thin, medieval-style oars. Severin claimed it was like trying to row a super-tanker with ballpoint pens. Once clear, they hoisted the sails and headed north with a favorable south-westerly breeze. The *Brendan* sailed like no other boat as she lifted to the Atlantic swell; the leather hull muffled the sound of the water, but the vessel flexed and creaked with each passing wave. They were heavily laden and had only 16 in (0.4 m) freeboard. A modest wave could swamp the boat, but she lifted gently as they passed underneath. But the movement was disconcerting, and soon two of the crew succumbed to seasickness.

The five-man crew settled into a routine with two-hour watches. The boat would not sail herself, so somebody had to steer at all times. When not on watch, they snuggled under the shelter that measured just 6 ft (1.8 m) square—no bigger than a king-size bed, and a lot less comfortable. Rain and seawater seeped into everything making sleeping difficult. Their sheepskins became sodden, and the rain-soaked flax sails doubled in weight when wet, making them difficult to handle and the boat top-heavy.

Hot food and drink were important, but lighting the recalcitrant stove was a challenge, and most meals comprised some type of stew with hot coffee. The food inevitably became flavored with wool grease and the cook always had to take care to prevent flare-ups with the cooker—after all, they were sitting in a highly combustible wooden-framed boat, impregnated with wool grease and carrying extra grease for repairs.

The wind soon veered west, at right angles to their course, but for every 10 NM (18.5 km) on course, they slipped sideways one mile. This excessive leeway was because the *Brendan* had no keel to stop her sliding through the water. Severin feared they would not round Slyne Head, a headland about 100 NM (185 km) north, so he wisely bore away and sheltered in the Aran Islands until the wind changed direction. The first Irish monastery was founded here by St. Enda sometime after 484 A.D., and St. Brendan is known to have visited the islands. The *Brendan* was following in the footsteps of her namesake.

Day five brought a fresh southerly breeze—a perfect direction. They easily cleared Slyne Head making a respectable 5 knots, but evening brought their first gale. This is always a big worry for a sailor with an untested boat. How would she handle? Would they take on heavy water? So many uncertainties, especially at night. Severin ordered ropes to be trailed to slow the boat, keeping her stern to the waves; the wind backed to the south-east and they were driven 100 NM (185 km) into the Atlantic. Eventually, the wind dropped (as it always does) and veered round to the west, allowing them to head back to Ireland, making landfall on Tory Island in Co Donegal in a flat calm. While rowing one of the crewmen injured his arm so badly that he was taken to hospital and was unable to complete the voyage.

On May 30th, they cast off with a new crewman and headed for the west coast of Scotland. Severin was beginning to understand the limitations of a medieval currach, and the margin for correcting course was limited. If the weather turned foul, he declared: "there was little one could do but hang on and hope." In ideal sailing conditions, however, with a strong following wind, they could reach 7 knots and exceed 12 knots surfing down waves, but these speeds were hard on the hull and rigging.

The third leg from Stornoway to the Faroes was an open water crossing of over 200 NM (370 km). Severin found the leather was now completely saturated with seawater, but the cold temperatures had a preservative effect and he could see no significant deterioration in the hides. The boat also changed shape as it flexed in the waves, and there was some leaking through the stitching, but nothing to cause concern. However, their modern equipment—saw blades, lamps, torches, and the radio, were more prone to deterioration in the salty conditions than anything "medieval." They also found their traditional clothing made from naturally oiled wool was better in the cold conditions than artificial fibers.

The crossing to the Faroe Islands took a week—again due to being blown off course. They easily identified the islands from 50 NM (92.6 km) away by the cloud formations hanging over the summits. The *Navigatio* told how St. Brendan and his monks landed on a remote island where they found rivers full of fish and great flocks of sheep. The medieval manuscript called the place the "Isle of Sheep," most likely taking the name from the Norse name for the Faroes, *Faer-Eyjaer*, meaning "Sheep Islands."

The description in the *Navigatio* of islands separated by narrow stretches of water fits the Faroes perfectly, and it was here that the *Brendan* was almost wrecked. In the open ocean, tidal currents are slight—usually less than half a knot—but closer inshore, the movement of water created by the tides creates much faster streams and the crew found themselves swept past tall cliffs and outlying rocks at 12 knots or more. In a boat sailing at five or six knots in a narrow channel, you have little control over your direction, and it was a hair-raising experience for Severin and his crew.

St. Brendan met Christian monks when they arrived—brethren who had earlier sought peace and solace in island isolation. The monks had previously introduced sheep to the Faroes where they flourished in the mild climate created by the warming Gulf Stream effect. Archaeologists believe the islands were settled as early as the sixth century, perhaps a generation before St. Brendan arrived. The monks, however, were celibate and new settlers had to join the community every few years if it was to survive. Presumably, they did, for in 825 A.D. the Irish chronicler and geographer, Dicuil, wrote:

> *"There are many other islands in the ocean to the north of Britain, which can be reached from the northern islands of Britain in a direct voyage of two days and nights with sails filled with a continuously favorable wind. There is another set of small islands, nearly all separated by narrow stretches of water; in these for nearly a hundred years hermits sailing from our country, Ireland, have lived."*

The Norseman later settled in the Faroes around the late eighth century and established farming communities there, wiping out any trace of the monastic Irish. The Faroes later became an important stepping stone on the long Viking voyages from Scandinavia to Iceland, and eventually to Greenland and Newfoundland.

After a short stay, the crew began the next leg of their journey. It is 430 NM (796 km) from Tórshavn in the Faroes to Reykjavík in Iceland, providing you are not blown off your intended course. This was their longest ocean crossing, but the 12-day trip was relatively fast due to easterly winds. Apart from a near-gale and some gear failures, the crossing was eventful mainly for whale sightings. They had their first glimpse of these giant cetaceans two days out from the Faroes when a large 60 ft (18 m) whale surfaced near the boat; it was probably eight or ten times the weight of the *Brendan*. The boat had the underwater profile of a large mammal, and the whale was most likely being inquisitive. After that, whales visited on most days.

The largest visitors were fin whales that grow up to 85 ft (26 m) and weigh 110 tons, second only in size to the blue whale. The fin whale or common rorqual is the greyhound of the seas and is faster through the water

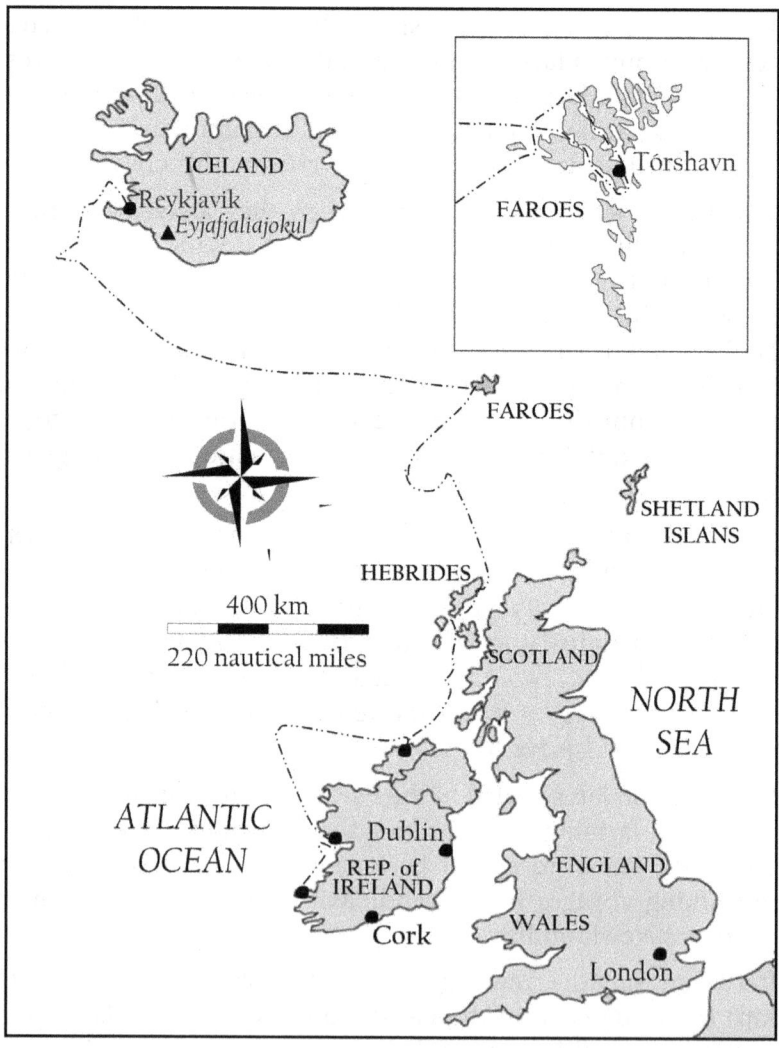

The Brendan's route from southern Ireland to Iceland in 1976.

than an ocean liner; its conservation status is classified as vulnerable. The humpback whale grows up to 60 ft (18 m) and migrates long distances in search of small fish, krill (tiny crustaceans), and plankton. Slightly smaller were the sperm whales—the species that featured in Herman Melville's "*Moby Dick*". Sperm whales feed on squid and possess the biggest brain of any creature on earth—typically four times bigger than the human brain.

The one visitor the crew feared most was the killer whale or orca. This medium-sized cetacean is an apex predator that feeds on fish, seals, and dolphins—the only marine mammal that devours other warm-blooded animals. These whales are often exhibited in marine parks, and although they are not considered dangerous to humans in the wild, the crew of the *Brendan* worried that a hunting pack of orcas could mistake their boat for a potential meal. Orcas have a huge appetite and massive teeth and could shred the leather hull of the *Brendan* in minutes. Pilot whales were also frequent visitors—another highly social cetacean that feeds on fish and squid. They are also displayed in marine parks, and hunted by the Faroese for their food and blubber.

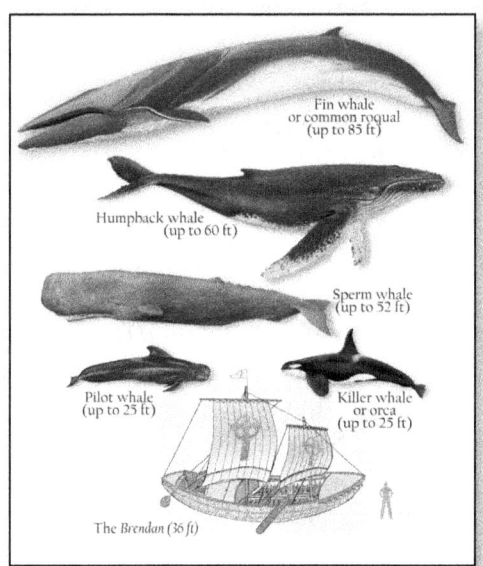

The Brendan and the whales encountered in the North Atlantic.

One of the more incredulous stories in the *Navigatio* involved a large marine "monster." As St. Brendan and his monks drifted from one island to the next, "following God's stepping stones," they stopped on an island to celebrate Easter Sunday Mass, happy to be on dry land. They lit a campfire, but the "island" turned out to be the back of a huge, slumbering beast that was woken by the searing heat on its back. The monster bucked and submerged as the monks beat a hasty retreat to their boat. Could the story relate to a large whale surfacing under their boat? The monks could not have mistaken the creature for an island, but the *Navigatio* was written 300 years after St. Brendan's voyage, so who knows what elaborations various scribes added to the original story?

The easterly gales pushed the *Brendan* further west than they intended, but on July 12th their luck changed and the wind swung around to the west. As the crew approached Iceland, the 4,700 ft (1,433 m) high Snæfellsjökull volcano could be seen from 70 NM (130 km) away, owing to the excellent visibility in the dry, polar air. This, and the near 24-hour daylight in mid-summer, could have helped St. Brendan if he found himself in a similar position, and it certainly helped the Norsemen who followed them 300 years later when navigating the "stepping stones" of the North Atlantic.

The *Navigatio* relates that St. Brendan and his monks found themselves blown by a southerly wind towards a large island that he called "The Isle of Smiths": "very rough, rocky, and full of slag, without trees or grass." Apparently, an irate inhabitant:

> "... came down to the shore near where they were, carrying in his hand tongs with a burning lump of slag of great size and heat. Immediately, he hurled the lump at the servants of Christ, but it did not harm them. It flew more than two hundred yards above them. The sea where it fell began to boil as if a volcano was burning, and smoke rose from the sea in a fiery furnace... The whole island appeared ablaze as if one great furnace. And the sea boiled like a cauldron full of meat boils when put on fire."

If St. Brendan had witnessed a volcanic eruption, he could not have understood what was happening. The most likely place for volcanic eruptions in the North Atlantic is Iceland, as the island is formed entirely from volcanoes—some still active. In 1963, an eruption created the new island of Surtsey; this rough, black, featureless island fitted perfectly St. Brendan's description of the "Isle of Smiths."

The *Navigatio* is not the only document to suggest that Irish monks might have sailed this far north. Dicuil, the learned monk of Charlemagne's court, wrote that Irish monks made regular visits to an island positioned so far north that in mid-summer: "the sun setting in the evening hides itself as though behind a small hill in such a way that there is no darkness in that very small space of time…" During the summer solstice in Iceland, the sun sets in Reykjavík just after midnight and rises by 3:00 a.m., and the sky never goes completely dark.

Severin planned to continue to Newfoundland that year, but the weeks passed with strong south-westerly winds, so he decided to lay-up for winter in Reykjavík. Everything was unloaded from the *Brendan* so they could check the condition of the hull. The boat had been afloat for eight weeks, and when it was lifted out of the water, they were relieved to find everything in good condition, with the wool grease still adhering to the hides. Only her shape had changed: on each side, two deep wrinkles had developed where the stern had begun to droop and this allowed the leather to slacken and pucker.

For the next nine months, the *Brendan* rested in an aircraft hangar, courtesy of the Icelandic Coast Guard.

The crew reassembled in Reykjavík in early May 1977 and began to prepare the *Brendan*. It took only five days to get everything ready, and the hull did not even need re-greasing. On the evening of May 8th, the *Brendan* was towed out of Reykjavík harbor and Severin laid a course west for Greenland. The first week brought light winds that allowed the crew to settle back into their medieval way of life. More whales and seals visited the boat, and they caught fish on hand-lines to supplement their diet.

It is about 220 NM (407 km) between Iceland and Greenland, and in the excellent polar visibility, the ancient navigators would take a back-bearing on the peak of the Snæfellsjökull volcano before waiting only a few days before the mountains of Greenland appeared ahead. One feature of the high latitudes that helped these early sailors was an effect called the Arctic Mirage, or the Hillingar effect. This is the polar equivalent of a desert mirage, where a stable air mass creates a temperature inversion that bends light as if through a giant lens, so objects far beyond the horizon appear to "float" above the horizon, sometimes upside down. For a sailor in a small

The Snæfellsjökull volcano in Iceland from offshore.
Photo: Tobias Kölling

boat, the horizon is only 3 NM (5.5 km) distant, but the Arctic Mirage can result in land being seen 80 NM (148 km) away or more.

Four days into the voyage, an exhausted bird landed aboard—it was on an ancient migration route from Europe to North America. The early navigators used signs like this to find their way across the ocean, but you need expert knowledge to make the most of these signs. In July, for example, puffins remain close to their eggs and feed inshore where food is plentiful; however, earlier in the year they forage much further from the coast, and so give a useful indication of the direction of land. The greatest migratory bird of all is the arctic tern; in spring they fly north to their breeding grounds in Iceland and coastal Greenland and fly south to the southern hemisphere in early autumn—a distance of 9,000 NM (16,668 km). Understanding the habits of different birds can make all the difference between a successful landfall, and disaster.

May 17th saw the weather change and life aboard became miserable. A force 9 south-westerly gale (winds in excess of 41 knots or 76 km/h) blew them northwards. During the night there was the ominous roar of a breaking wave followed by a crash, and solid water poured into their canvas cabin. It was icy-cold and everything was saturated—their sleeping bags, charts, notebooks, and radios—and they found themselves standing knee-deep in water. The *Brendan* was now vulnerable: the boat was half-full of water and lying heavy in the breaking seas, virtually dead in the water. Boats are unstable in this situation and can easily be overwhelmed by a second wave; that would be the end of their voyage, leaving no time even to get a mayday call out on the radio. Frantically they pumped with all their energy to lighten the boat in the freezing darkness. Minutes later, a loud hiss was

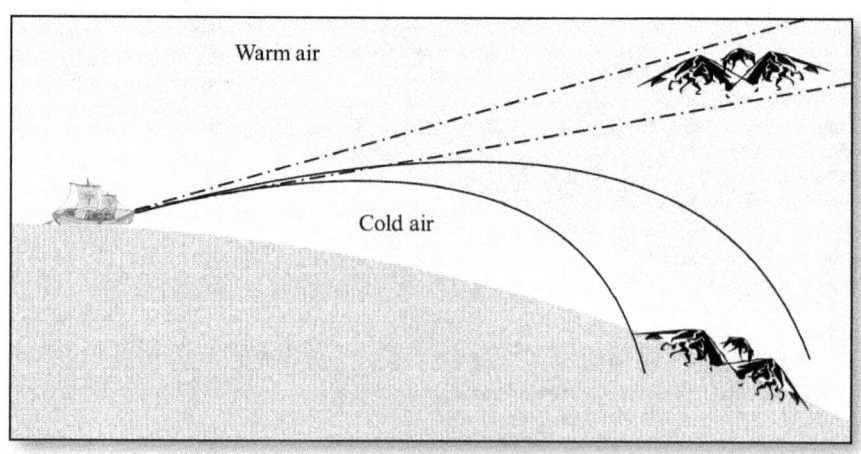

The Arctic Mirage or Hillingar effect.

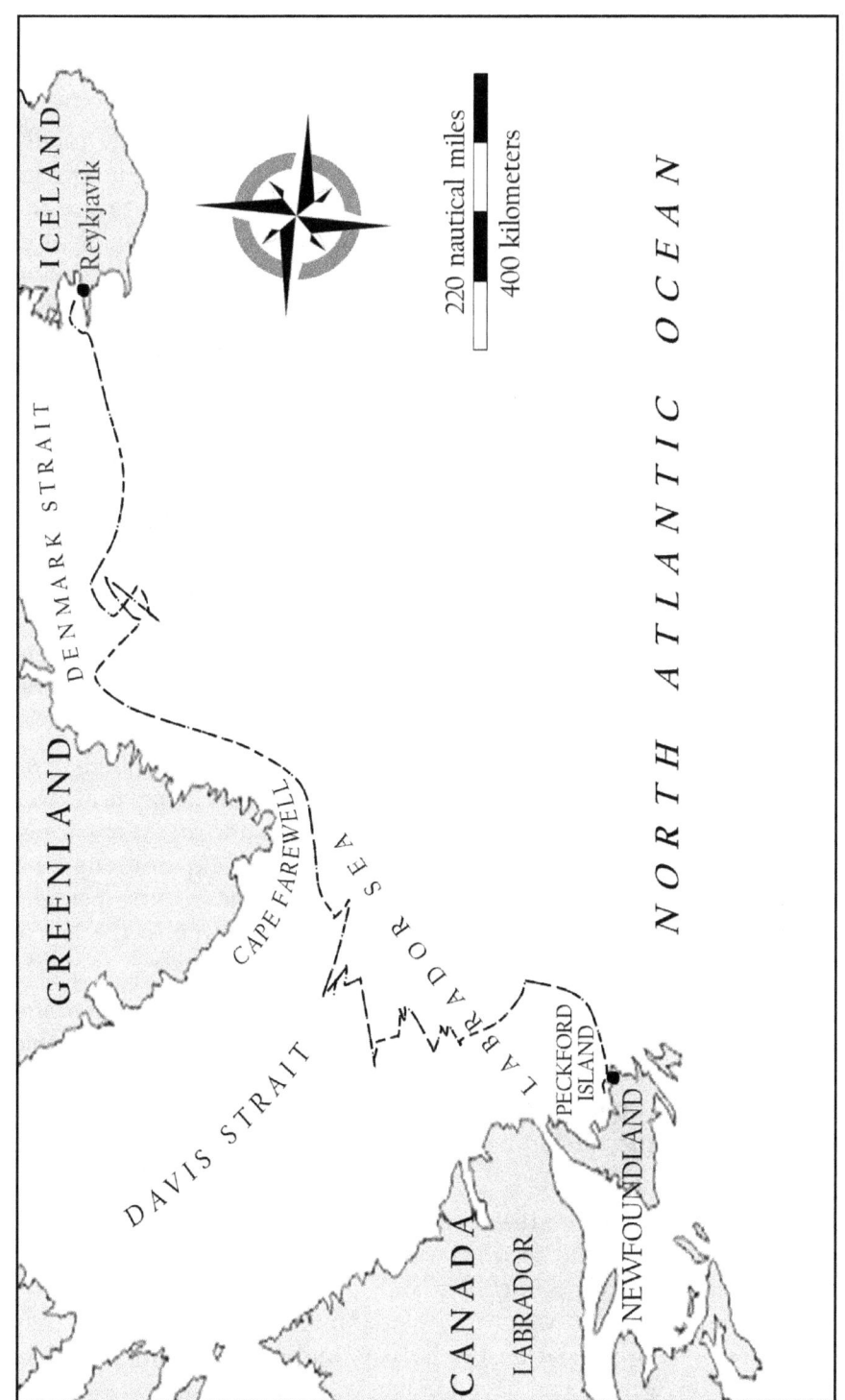

The Brendan's route from Iceland to Newfoundland in the summer of 1977.

followed by another boom and the same thing happened. The cabin was again awash and the crew went back to the pumps—this time laboring for an hour before the boat was empty.

The crew had now been awake for nearly 48-hours and were totally exhausted, but in a life-and-death situation, they tapped into unknown reserves of energy. They had to protect their boat and decided to use the spare ox hides to construct a tortoise-like cover over the boat. Within minutes of finishing there was another familiar roar as yet another breaking wave struck the boat—but this time the water poured back harmlessly where it belonged. The "leather tortoise" saved the *Brendan* that night, and they could, at last, get some sleep.

Since leaving Iceland, the favorable East Greenland current had carried the *Brendan* southwest. After three weeks they were south of Cape Farewell, the most southerly part of Greenland, and clear of the 70 NM (130 km)-wide pack ice that extends from the coastline, making landing impossible. The Norse sailors who arrived in Greenland around 1000 A.D. found fragments of skin boats and stone implements that archaeologists believe were left by Irish settlers, as there is no evidence of any Innuit (Eskimo) habitation there. So, perhaps the Irish monks landed here even before the Norsemen, but they would not have experienced the same conditions as Severin and his crew.

Climatologists have identified several periods in the last 2,000 years when the planet was warmer, for quite natural reasons. One peak was around 550 A.D. when St. Brendan made his voyages, and an even warmer period occurred around 1000 A.D. when Norse Atlantic explorations were at their peak. There were likely fewer storms during these warm periods, making voyages across the North Atlantic easier. According to the Norse sagas, their voyages were not unduly hindered by sea ice either.

As the *Brendan* crossed the Labrador Sea, the water temperature dropped to 28 deg. F (minus 2 deg. C); this low temperature is possible because the salt content lowers the freezing temperature of seawater. The current here flows at up to 1 knot, bringing icebergs south from Greenland into the North Atlantic, including the one that sank the *Titanic* in April 1912.

On June 19th, 42 days into the voyage, the *Brendan* sailed into pack ice. As they got close, they could see the swell lifting blocks of ice the size of a two-story building, then dropping them back, grinding and crushing the ice; this was no place for a light-weight leather-skinned boat. Fortunately, they sighted a Faroese fishing boat on the horizon and signaled with a mirror. Within hours, they were towed back to open water and safety.

A "Great Pillar of Crystal" surrounded by a net of marble fragments.
Photo: Michael Haferkamp

Their problems, however, were not over. They should have been 50 NM (93 km) clear of any danger, but that year a strong north-westerly wind had blown sea ice into the Labrador Sea, and now the *Brendan* was surrounded again—and this time it was more serious. As they sailed toward open water, they were caught between two large ice floes. As the gap between them closed, they feared their boat would be pulverized. With a huge combined effort, they pushed the boat free, only to find water rising inside the hull— the leather skin of the *Brendan* was punctured below the waterline.

Their first priority was to get safely to open water, while pumping continuously. Only then could they fix the leak—but they had no idea where the hull was holed, or if the ash frames had been fractured. They were only a few days from their landfall, but now they faced their severest test of the voyage. After hours of searching, the leak was eventually found amidships. The ice had made a dent the size of a grapefruit in the hull; the leather was split but the wooden frames were intact. When the boat rolled in the swell, they could see freezing water spurting into the bilge. Fortunately, the damage was in a position where it could be mended, albeit with some difficulty.

One crewman donned an immersion suit and eased himself over the side, his face only a few inches above the surface of the icy water. Meanwhile, a second man on the inside poked an awl through the hull and patch, followed by a 9 in (23 cm) needle and flax thread. The needle was pulled through from the outside with pliers and pushed back into the hull. In this bone-chilling manner, inch by inch, they laboriously patched the hull.

Over the next few days, the crew was aware of land nearby—floating seaweed, tree-logs, and more birds were all valuable tell-tale signs that would have also been used by the early voyagers. The *Brendan* was also in the rich feeding grounds off North America, and more humpback and pilot whales appeared. On the night of June 25th, they could see pin-pricks of light ashore and smell pine trees. The next morning, they made landfall on Peckford Island in the north of Newfoundland; it had taken 50 days to sail from Iceland.

Severin created renewed interest in early Atlantic navigation and especially in the voyages of medieval monks (of which the voyage by St. *Brendan* was only one). He also showed that early Irish monks could have sailed to America—but this did not prove they had actually made the voyage. There is plenty of circumstantial evidence to support his theory. St. Brendan wrote of seeing a Great Pillar of Crystal surrounded by a net of marble fragments, and of sailing to the Island of the Fiery Mountain; these could well refer to icebergs and Iceland, but the evidence is circumstantial. As Severin himself acknowledged, "…the only conclusive proof that it had been done will be if an authentic relic from an early Irish visit is found one day on American soil."

So far, that has not happened.

≈≈≈≈≈≈≈

The weather was not good in Lindisfarne on the east coast of England on the morning of June 8, 793 A.D. The monks were celebrating St. Médard's day in memory of a bishop who was martyred a couple of hundred years previously. Many people believed that bad weather on St. Médard's day would continue for weeks on end; unfortunately, some of the monks would never find out—for they would never live to see another day.

That morning and without warning, a flotilla of sleek Norse longships appeared over the horizon and slipped on to the sandy beach of the sacred island. The English historian, Simeon of Durham, wrote a graphic account of the raid:

> "They came to the church of Lindisfarne, laid everything waste with grievous plundering, trampled the holy places with polluted steps, dug up the altars, and seized all the treasures of the holy church. They killed some of the brothers, took some

away with them in fetters, many they drove out, naked and loaded with insults, some they drowned in the sea..."

The massacre on that summer's day is generally regarded as the beginning of the Viking Age in the British Islands, and the ruthless attack by Norsemen on the defenseless monks of Lindisfarne is typical of the popular notion that these Scandinavian raiders were bloodthirsty marauders who respected neither property nor people. Historically, this was the beginning of 300 years of bloody Viking raids in Britain and Ireland, and the monk's lament, "From the Fury of the Northmen deliver us, O Lord" has echoed down through the years.

Most of the accounts of Viking attacks were written by the clergy, often several centuries after the event, and historians do not consider their records to be either objective or reliable. There is no doubt that the Norsemen had their bloodthirsty moments, but new archaeological research reveals a more complex and fascinating culture, suggesting the Norsemen (and women) were bold explorers and resourceful traders. Within 60 years of the Lindisfarne raid, the Vikings had voyaged to northern France and Germany, and east into what is now Russia and Ukraine, opening up trade routes for 2,000 miles (3,218 km) across Europe.

The Norsemen sailed long, narrow, lightweight clinker-built vessels called longships, although they came in many different sizes. The most common vessel used for warfare was the snekkja (or snekke) with at least 20 rowing benches, and typically 56 ft (17 m) long, with a beam of 8.2 ft (2.5 m), and a shallow draft of 1.6 ft (0.5 m). The vessel carried a crew of around 40 fighting men. These ships were fast, achieving up to 10 knots, although under ideal conditions they could reach 15 knots; this made them ideal for lightening raids up rivers. Even larger warships called skeids were built with around 30 rowing benches and carried a crew of up to 80 warriors.

Their trading ships, called knarrs, were very different. These had a smaller crew, and the hulls were wider, deeper, and shorter. They were usually about 54 ft (16.5 m) long, with a beam of 15 ft (4.6 m), and capable of carrying up to 25 tons of cargo. These ships transported trading goods like timber, wool, wheat, furs, and pelts, and supplied distant warriors and traders with weapons, armor, and food.

The Icelandic sagas told of daring voyages in knarrs—even across the Atlantic—and historians have long deliberated where the Vikings might have landed. The old Norse name of "Vinland" often cropped up in the sagas and the name was thought to refer to wild grapes. Most historians assumed that the Vinland region existed somewhere along the Massachusetts coast, which was about as far north that grapes will grow naturally.

However, in 1960, Norwegian archaeologists discovered the remains of a Norse settlement in northern Newfoundland at a fishing hamlet called L'anse aux Meadows, and the site was carbon-dated to between 990 and 1050 A.D. It was an exciting find and confirmed the Norsemen had arrived in North America at the turn of the millennium. Today, the old Norse word "vin" is thought to mean pasture-land and not grapes.

The sagas confirm the scientific dating of the settlement, and tell how Leif Erikson (second son of Erik Thorvaldsson, aka Eric the Red) was blown off course on his way from Norway to Greenland and landed in Newfoundland by accident—by most accounts around 1000 A.D., or slightly earlier. Here Erikson founded a community on the north coast of Newfoundland that became home to between 70 and 90 people—there were a few women, but mostly men who worked on boat repair, iron smelting, and smithing. L'anse aux Meadows was not a colonizing site, but a base to explore and exploit natural resources—timber, furs, walrus tusks, and luxury food such as walnuts and berries to ship back to Greenland.

Erikson went on to record two further landings on the coast: one he called "Helluland"—the land of the flat stones, and the second he described as flat and wooded and named it "Markland." Neither of these two locations has been identified with any certainty, although Helluland is thought to be Baffin Island and Markland somewhere along the coast of Labrador.

The period around 1000 A.D. marked the middle of the Medieval Warm Period when global temperatures were milder than today and the North Atlantic was about 1.8 deg F (1 deg C) warmer. The Norsemen took advantage of these conditions, and this made it possible to colonize southern Greenland and then Newfoundland.

They made long ocean voyages of up to 1,000 NM (1,852 km) in their open longships. Navigating such distances in the open ocean was fraught with danger and there is inevitably no record from the many ships that were lost. Yet the Norsemen were intuitive sailors who used several techniques to find their way, including watching for migrating birds and whales, observing celestial bodies, wave patterns, clouds, and wind direction. The clear polar air and the Arctic Mirage or Hillingar effect also helped with navigation. The sailors also kept cages of ravens aboard, and if they thought land was nearby, they would release a bird. If the raven returned, they did not expect to find land soon; if the bird flew off, then the ship followed in the expectation of finding land.

A partially-built replica longship showing the overlapping clinker planks; when the wood becomes wet it expands, making the vessel watertight.

The Norsemen also carried sundials that were calibrated to show the direction of the North Pole. Some archaeologists also believe they used a "sunstone" or "larvikite" to aid navigation, although others are skeptical. The sunstone is a translucent crystal such as calcite that polarizes light, even on cloudy days. When it is rotated, sunlight passing through the crystal is brightest when the crystal is aligned with the polarization rings in the atmosphere—essentially, the crystal becomes brightest when pointing directly at the sun, even if the sun is hidden behind clouds.

The three centuries of Norse trading and colonization is an important part of Scandinavian history, and it was inevitable that the crossing from Norway to Newfoundland would one day be reconstructed. In March 2010, the oak keel was laid for the biggest Viking longship ever built in modern times—the *Draken Harald Hårfagre* (named after the first Norwegian king. This Norse skeid was 115 ft (35 m) long, with a beam of 26 ft (8 m) and a draft of 8.2 ft (2.5 m).

By any standards, the *Draken* was a big ship. The clinker hull was planked in oak, with more than 10,000 nails securing the timbers. The 79 ft (24 m) mast was hewn from a solid piece of Douglas fir and weighed more than 2.5 tons. The spar supported a huge single mainsail made of silk, with an area of 2,800 sq ft (260 sq m)—the area of a tennis court. In good conditions, the vessel could make 14 knots under sail. The skeid also carried 25 pairs of oars, each powered by two crew members, making a rowing crew of 100. Under sail, during ocean voyages, the ship was limited to a crew of about 32 because of maritime safety regulations.

The Vikings left almost no record about how they built their ships or how they sailed them. So, the organizers claim the *Draken* is not a replica ship, but a re-creation of a vessel the Vikings called a "Great Ship," used for long ocean voyages. The ship was built using old boatbuilding traditions, based on the legends from the Norse sagas. Experts in traditional boatbuilding techniques contributed to building a ship with the seaworthiness that characterized these ocean-going longships. In this way, you not only have the adventure of sailing an historic ship but you also learn something of the problems faced by the early shipbuilders, and by the sailors who managed these vessels at sea.

The *Draken* was launched in the summer of 2012, and for the next two years, the crew sailed along the Norwegian coast, learning how to get the best out of such a large vessel. These were not easy boats to sail, for the lack of any substantial keel and the huge square mainsail made it impossible to sail close to the wind. The Norwegian coastline is a lee-shore for the prevailing south-westerly winds—a thousand years ago the Norse sailors could have relied on one-hundred oarsman to get them out of trouble if the wind dropped or blew from the wrong direction. Instead, the *Draken* relied on powerful diesel engines—something that was also a legal requirement for safety reasons.

For reasons of common sense and safety, the *Draken* also made full use of modern electronics, including a satellite phone, VHF radio, Wi-fi boosters, all manner of safety beacons, ditch bags, and so on. The ship also had a marine head (WC) that would have puzzled the original Vikings; the tiny, cramped compartment below the deck did not offer full standing headroom, but somehow a single toilet managed to serve a crew of 32, usually half male and half female.

The *Draken* made her maiden passage in the summer of 2014, sailing from her home port in Haugesund, Norway, to Liverpool in England. The Norsemen originally arrived in this part of England in 902 A.D. where they left not only their genes (up to 50 percent of people in parts of the north-west of England have Norse origins) but also many place names such as Toxteth on the banks of the River Mersey (most likely "Toki's landing-place") and Kirkby (or Kirkjubýr, kirk being Norse for church).

The passage to Liverpool was not without incident. Three days out, the ship's mast snapped. Too much wind and the constant whip-lash effect from sailing into big waves caused the rig to fail, and one and a half tons

The elaborately carved figurehead (above) was based on remains from archaeological excavations. The originals were intended to strike terror in the hearts of anyone under attack.

The Draken (below) under full sail in the Atlantic, on her way to Newfoundland.

of top spar and sail crashed to the deck, with half the huge mast falling to port and the other half to starboard. The crew had been carefully watching the rig because they knew it was under strain, and that is probably why nobody was hurt. The crew was trained to have an immediate roll call in the event of an emergency, but one crew member was missing—it was the first mate, who was trapped in the head's compartment wondering what was happening above him on deck.

With a single mast on such a large vessel, the sailing rig on these big longships had to be kept light in order to be raised and lowered. So, it is possible that the original vessels had similar problems with failure, and the Norsemen would then have resorted to rowing. The *Draken*, however, only had its regular crew of 32, so they had no option but to start the engines and motor to Lerwick in the Shetland Islands.

With valuable lessons learned from their shake-down cruise, the *Draken Harald Hårfagre* and her crew were ready to take on the North Atlantic. The ship left Norway in April 2016 and laid a course west to the Shetland Isles as her predecessors had done a thousand years before. After a brief stopover, the ship sailed to the Faroe Islands, and then on to Reykjavík in Iceland. The next section to Qaqortoq in southern Greenland was more than 1,000 NM (1,852 km) and involved rounding Cape Farewell, Greenland's most southerly point, where strong winds and confused seas create treacherous conditions. The *Draken* also had to dodge sea ice that could puncture the hull.

Between Qaqortoq and Newfoundland, the ship encountered icebergs drifting south on the Labrador Current, just as Tim Severin and his crew had 40 years previously in the *Brendan*. A thousand years ago during the Medieval Warm Period, it is likely the original Vikings would have encountered more benign conditions and less sea ice.

Norse longships are open boats with little space below deck for anything but ballast and bilge water, and the *Draken* crew had to live, eat, and sleep on deck, just as their forefathers did a millennium before. The crew was able to shelter under an awning-like structure stretched over the deck, but their predecessors relied primarily on heavy woolen clothing and animal skins for protection and slept in the open.

Carrying enough supplies is always a challenge on long sea journeys, but the Vikings tended to keep their ocean crossings short and rarely planned to be at sea for more than a week. There is little written in the sagas about what was eaten aboard, but food would most likely have been coarse bread, dried or salted meat and fish, perhaps supplemented with fruit and berries. The Norsemen would have drunk water, beer, or sour milk. One specialty was a dried fish, called tørrfisk, that could last for up to 15 years if kept dry, but was so hard that it had to be broken with an ax and then soaked for a couple of days before being eaten. The Norsemen probably did not cook aboard, so this delicacy would have to wait until they had landed.

On June 1, 2016, the *Draken* completed her historic Atlantic crossing and sailed into St. Anthony in Newfoundland, close to the Norse settlement of L'anse aux Meadows. The voyage raised several more issues with the design. One of the shrouds holding up the mast broke and had to be replaced at sea, again highlighting the vulnerability of the mast on the longship. Another issue was the engines—the ship's design dated back more than a thousand years, and the constant mechanical vibrations caused problems. Motoring at full speed was possible in calm conditions, but the planks began to open up if the ship motored too fast into a significant head sea.

From Newfoundland, the *Draken* headed up the St. Lawrence Seaway to Montreal and Toronto. Here their voyage was halted—not by weather or gear failure—but by bureaucracy. When the longship passed from Canadian to American waters in the Great Lakes, they were informed that they would have to take on a professional pilot. The organizers were told by Canadian officials that they did not need a pilot in their waters, but the regulations were different in the United States. The Norwegians argued they could not afford $400 an hour for a pilot—a bill that was expected to reach $400,000. The U.S. Coast Guard would not budge and argued that because the organizers charged for people to come aboard (a payment that helped to defray the cost of running the ship), they were classified as a commercial vessel and required a pilot.

After four months of ocean sailing covering more than 3,500 NM (6,500 km), it was red tape, bureaucracy, and the threat of an unexpected bill that finally halted the latest invasion of North America by the Vikings.

The Atlantic Auto Route

Saturday, December 2, 1950, Ben and Elinore Carlin were nine days out from the Azores and three-quarters of their way across the Atlantic; their situation was not looking good. They had already spent nearly six wretched weeks at sea—more than twice as long as Carlin had anticipated. Now they were facing their first real storm. Outside, the waves were building to an alarming size—over 40 ft (12 m) high and increasing. Inside, everything was soaking wet; blankets, clothes, pillows. They were thoroughly miserable and Elinore wrote in her log:

> "1700: Used to think it was an exaggeration when people talked of seas 30, 40, & 50 ft. high... Bloody huge waves—& the wind she blew like hell."

The next morning, the wind moderated to under 43 knots (80 km/h), but still a severe gale-force 9 on the Beaufort Scale. The radio had not worked for days, but Ben tried once more in desperation to tap out a distress call. To his astonishment an operator in Madeira replied. He told Ben that the Portuguese navy had given them up for lost, thinking nobody could survive the storm.

The sea conditions would have been difficult to manage even in a well-found boat; however, Ben and Elinore Carlin had left Halifax in Nova Scotia to cross the Atlantic in an amphibious jeep, built for the U.S. Army to cross rivers, not oceans. Carlin took out his sextant and checked his position, and arranged for the Portuguese warship, the *NRP Flores*, to drop off two tanks of fuel for the jeep—without it, they could not make it to Madeira.

The story of Ben and Elinore Carlin's attempt to cross the Atlantic in an amphibious jeep is one of the most audacious ocean voyages ever taken. It was an idea that had been long in the planning, ever since Ben Carlin was in the army during World War II.

Carlin was a mining engineer from rural Western Australia and he had signed up with the Corps of Engineers at the outbreak of war and posted to India. It was here that he first came across the GPA Jeep (General Purpose

Amphibious jeep), an amphibious version of the successful GPW "Willys" jeep, built for the U.S. army by the Ford Motor Company. The GPA retained the jeep's two- and four-wheel drive capability, but it was designed to carry troops across rivers, lakes, and shallow bays; it was therefore fitted with a capstan winch at the front and a propeller and rudder at the back.

While in India, Carlin met Elinore Arone, an American Red Cross nurse from Watertown, Massachusetts. They were kindred spirits, each searching for adventure, although their on-off relationship was said to be turbulent. After his discharge from the army in 1946, Carlin stopped over in Hong Kong on his way to the United States, where he met up again with Elinore and they rekindled their romance. He was reluctant at first to tell her why he was on his way to North America; Elinore persisted, so he explained that he wanted to circumnavigate the world in an amphibious jeep.

Elinore made it clear that she had every intention of coming with him.

The GPA had a blunt bow welded to the front, and a simple folding bow deflector to stop water flooding back into the jeep.

On his arrival in the United States, Carlin set about finding himself a suitable vehicle. Construction of the GPA had begun in 1942, but the production vehicles were heavier than specified in the design brief. As a result, the GPA floated too low in the water; in fact, it only had a freeboard of 4 in (10 cm). The American troops hated the vehicle; it frequently became stuck in the mud, it was too heavy and unwieldy to drive on land, and its dangerously low freeboard meant it could not even cross rivers in safety. After the war, the U.S. Army sold most of its vehicles to the Soviet Union, but there were some still to be found in the US.

On January 30, 1947, Carlin found exactly what he needed in an army surplus yard in Aberdeen, Maryland. He handed over $901 and became the proud owner of a 1942 GPA amphibious jeep. It had been "well-used," which meant it was dented, decrepit, and barely running. He initially tried to persuade the manufacturers to sponsor his trip but the Ford Motor Company refused, believing the vehicle would never make it.

Undaunted, Carlin drove down to Annapolis, where he rented a slip in a local boatyard. The road trip of 60 miles (96 km) took two full days and he broke down several times. By the time he arrived the gasoline tank had dropped off, the fuel lines were clogged, and the exhaust was belching out filthy black smoke. It is just as well he was an engineer by training.

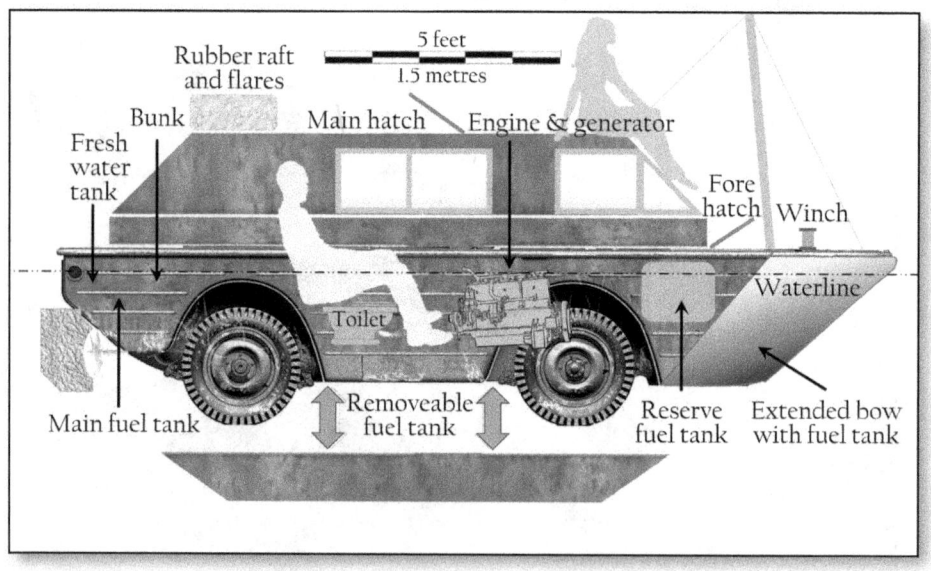

Ben Carlin's amphibious GPA in ocean-going form.

The choice of a failed amphibious jeep design for a global circumnavigation might seem total madness, but Carlin went about preparing the GPA methodically. He spent eight months in Annapolis reinforcing the vehicle, covering the outside with neoprene to prevent leaks, and fitting an extended bow section to house additional fuel tanks; this increased the length by an extra 3 ft (0.9 m) to 18 ft (5.5 m). He fitted another tank under the "belly" of the vehicle tied on with nylon ropes, increasing the fuel capacity from the original 12 U.S. gallons (45 liters) to 200 gallons (760 liters). He also built a cabin over the open interior that made the jeep look like a garden shed on wheels. All the windows were replaced with unbreakable acrylic glass.

The enclosed cabin was claustrophobic, just 10 ft (3 m) long by 5 ft (1.5 m). Carlin kept the two front seats and fitted a chemical toilet underneath. There was room for a narrow bunk behind, but it was not long enough to stretch out straight. He also fitted aircraft navigation instruments, a two-way radio, and a hatch in the roof as the only means of exiting the cabin.

Elinore had been living with her parents in Boston since returning from Asia, but the couple was impatient to be together and get started. Carlin knew the jeep was far from seaworthy, but by October 1947 the couple was down to their last $300, so he decided it was time for a test run and made plans to sail for New York. In early November, he gingerly edged down the slipway at the boatyard and set off north-east up the Chesapeake Bay; he drove briefly overland until he reached the top of Delaware Bay, before heading south towards the ocean. He then planned to motor-sail up the New Jersey coast to the Hudson River—all in the middle of winter.

Carlin found the jeep was difficult to steer on land and he only managed 1.6 knots (3 km/h) in the water. Progress was painfully slow and by day three, strong winds made further headway impossible. When the wind moderated, he continued down the estuary, but it was not long before the steering seized and the jeep began to go around in circles, with each circuit taking him closer inshore.

Carlin was also getting blinding white flashes in front of his eyes, he had a severe headache with nausea, and he was losing the feeling in his arms, feet, and face. Through his brain fog Carlin recalled that he had experienced these symptoms before when working in a Chinese coal mine—he was suffering from acute carbon monoxide (CO) poisoning. Somehow, this colorless, odorless gas was seeping into the cabin. He was now in a very dangerous situation, as inhaling CO reduced the amount of oxygen in his bloodstream. Unless he got fresh air quickly, he would pass out—and with the engine still running, that would be fatal.

Carlin struggled through the small escape hatch and collapsed on the cabin roof, gasping for air and thankful to be away from the deadly fumes. It was too dangerous to go below again to shut down the engine, so the jeep continued running in circles until it impaled itself on steel stakes on the shoreline, ripping a 1 ft (30 cm) gash in the port side below the waterline. It was time to come out of the water again, and he drove overland to New York

City where he continued work on the jeep. Meanwhile, Carlin continued to pester the British Consul for his back pay from the army; in April, a $1,800 disbursement finally arrived—at last, they had the funds to continue.

Carlin was certainly motivated by challenge and adventure, but he also had an eye on making money from the voyage. With cash in the bank, he was able to engage a press agent who suggested that a story about two carefree newlyweds setting out for their honeymoon across the Atlantic was an easy story to sell. So Elinore returned to New York and the couple married at the City Hall in early June 1948.

On June 16th, they began their transatlantic voyage—and their honeymoon. Unfortunately, Carlin misjudged the tides, and while newspapers reported that they were cheered on their way by "100 amazed wharf laborers," they actually disappeared in the opposite direction, and were swept upstream on a strong flood tide. The tide eventually turned, and they were swept back downstream and out into the Atlantic, where they chugged away at their cruising speed of 5 knots (9.3 km/h). Unfortunately, they failed to keep their scheduled radio contact and the U.S. Coast Guard initiated a search. They eventually came ashore in the Shark River after five days, just 34 NM (63 km) south of New York harbor.

They were still experiencing trouble with the rudder and they found steering for 24 hours a day was exhausting. Undeterred, they set out again on July 3rd, only to return within a few days with a cracked exhaust pipe that nearly asphyxiated them in their enclosed cabin. Their third attempt was aborted, this time due to more mechanical problems, and seasickness.

Ben & Elinore Carlin before embarking on their Atlantic crossing.

Most people would have given up by now, but not Ben and Elinore Carlin. They left New York for a fourth time on August 7th in blazing sunshine and managed to motor 260 NM (481 km) before a shaft bearing seized. Unable to sail under a jury rig, they drifted helplessly in the North Atlantic for ten days before being rescued by an oil tanker heading to Montreal. Enough was enough, and Carlin considered abandoning the entire project; it was the tanker's Norwegian captain who persuaded him to continue with the immortal words: "Hell, you're not going to leave that god-damned jeep lying around!"

The ship docked in Canada three days later, and while Carlin spent his time preparing the jeep for a road trip, his indefatigable wife went out drinking with the ship's crew. When the jeep was ready, they drove east to Halifax, Nova Scotia. It was now too late in the year to attempt the North Atlantic, so Elinore returned to Boston to find a job and Ben worked for a marine salvage company; here, he could rebuild the GPA in his spare time. They also named their pride and joy *Half Safe* after a deodorant commercial that was running on the radio: "Don't be half-safe—use Arrid to be sure."

By the middle of 1949, the couple was ready for a new attempt. This time the clutch burnt out and had to be replaced. More importantly, Carlin realized that he was not carrying enough fuel for the voyage, so he decided to tow a pair of additional fuel tanks. They also added an extra stabilizing rudder and painted their craft bright yellow to make themselves more conspicuous at sea. They set off again in September, but only got 30 NM (56 km) offshore before losing both their auxiliary fuel tanks on the first night. Perhaps it was just as well because September was a foolish time to begin an Atlantic crossing. Carlin was now exhausted trying to make *Half Safe* suitable, and he decided to give up, but Elinore persuaded him they should continue their dream.

Carlin spent the next six months making further modifications to *Half Safe*, including fabricating a purpose-built tank to be towed behind the GPA. This gave them a fuel capacity of 735 U.S. gallons (2,782 liters). Fortunately, gasoline was only 20 U.S. cents a gallon, so he was able to fill up for $150.

The couple waited for a high-pressure weather system to build from the west that would give them good weather for the start of their voyage. Then on July 19, 1950, they left, clearing customs without too much trouble, although the authorities were not really sure if it was legal for a floating jeep to leave. As Ben eased *Half Safe* away from the dock, Elinore sat back in the cabin and calmly lit a cigarette, sitting next to enough petroleum to cause an explosion that would wake every dozing inhabitant in Halifax.

In addition to the fuel, they carried 8 U.S. gallons (30 liters) of oil for the engine, enough food for six weeks, but only 30 U.S. gallons (113 liters) of drinking water. The tiny cabin was to be their home for the next month.

With the 60 hp 4 cylinder engine clattering away 24 hours a day, the cabin shuddered with the teeth-rattling ferocity of a hay cart speeding over cobblestones. Inside, the air was a fetid mixture of petrol, exhaust fumes, and raw sewage. Ben had installed 12-volt fans on each side of the dashboard, but all they did was churn the obnoxious smell around the cabin. Meanwhile, they had the tedious task of peering through the salt-encrusted windscreen to keep *Half Safe* on course.

Perhaps not surprisingly, the voyage to the island of Flores in the Azores was not without mishap. Elinore was seasick for the first week, before adjusting to the foul conditions. Next, they had their first engine trouble and Ben had to remove the cylinder head to scrape away the build-up of carbon on the engine valves. He had to "de-coke" the engine three times, replacing the head gasket on each occasion—no easy task in a vehicle bobbing around in a North Atlantic swell. Carlin decided to continue on reduced speed to reduce the strain on the engine.

Every time they needed to top up the main fuel tank, Carlin had to stop the engine and siphon petrol from one of the auxiliary tanks, a nauseating job. On one occasion, as they tried to cut the empty belly tank free, a rope

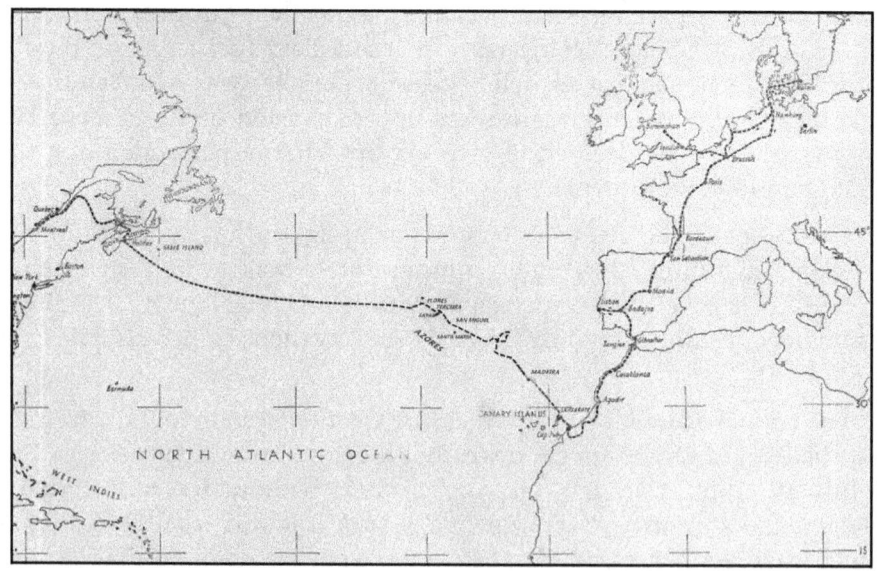

Ben Carlin's hand-drawn chart of their route across the Atlantic and north to England and Sweden.

hooked around the jeep, causing them nearly to capsize. They were lucky their GPA did not sink like a stone. Other problems included losing radio contact several times which led to newspaper reports that they were lost at sea; they could not dry their bedding in the moist, salty atmosphere, and the same humid conditions caused the labels to fall off their canned food. A combination of fumes and living in such enclosed conditions caused them to start hallucinating.

Usually, the couple drove without stopping, taking turns to steer and grabbing naps whenever they could in the hot, noisy cabin. But there were also light-hearted moments; the weather was generally warm and sunny, with only occasional rain squalls. On one occasion Ben caught a 3 ft (0.9 m) mahi-mahi (also called a dolphin fish). This large meaty fish makes excellent eating but the Carlins had no way of cooking it properly. Undeterred, Ben wrapped it around the exhaust pipe but without any great culinary success; the inside was burnt to a crisp, the outside remained raw, and only a small piece in the middle was edible.

After 29 days at sea, Carlin realized that one of the engine exhaust valves was burning through. This would require a complete engine overhaul that was impossible to do at sea, so he was forced to throttle back to a crawl. Three days later, they arrived in Flores after covering 1,480 NM (2,740 km)—just 46.4 NM (86 km) a day, or an average of under 2 knots.

On arrival, they became minor celebrities; LIFE magazine published several of their photos and ran a feature article on the couple, claiming that it was "certainly the most foolhardy, and possibly the most difficult transatlantic voyage ever made." The couple rested, ate, overhauled the engine, and raised money whenever possible. Their next leg to Horta, another island in the Azores archipelago, was just 126 NM (233 km) away, and they spent several weeks visiting other islands before starting their next leg.

They had originally intended to head straight for Lisbon in Portugal, but they prudently chose instead to island-hop via Madeira and the Canaries, then on to Morocco. It was a wise decision that probably saved their lives. Halfway between the Azores and Madeira, the Carlin's were caught in a tropical storm. Carlin steered east, hoping to outrun the track of the depression, but the north-westerly winds continued to batter *Half Safe*. Elinore became violently seasick and Ben found it almost impossible to steer in the rising seas; the wind increased to a storm force 10, with winds exceeding 48 knots (89 km/h). These conditions typically create waves 30-41 ft (9 m-12.5 m) high, but they estimated that some were bigger.

With fuel running low, Ben coaxed his erratic radio into life and sent a distress call, that was picked up in Madeira. The next day, the *NRP Flores*

Half Safe in Copenhagen, during their European tour.

naval ship found the floating jeep and took the couple aboard, where they showered, drank wine, and ate. The ship left them with enough fuel to make it to Madeira—they were back on schedule.

After a brief stop-over on the island, *Half Safe* continued to the Canary Islands and then Morocco without any further catastrophes. They eventually came ashore on February 23, 1951 at Cape Juby in the south of the country. They were elated—after three years of hard work their floating jeep *Half Safe* had got them across the Atlantic.

Back on terra firma, their problems were not over, only different. Carlin now had to drive through an empty quarter of the western Sahara, negotiating 50 ft (15 m) sand dunes. They had lost their spare wheel during the sea crossing and he worried about getting a puncture. Not knowing if there were any spare parts for the jeep in Morocco, Carlin drove cautiously. Daytime temperatures reached 170 deg F (77 deg C) inside the vehicle, so they drove mostly at night—no mean achievement along rough, unlit Moroccan roads.

Carlin gingerly nursed *Half Safe* 840 miles (1,352 km) to Tangier, followed by a short 13 NM (24 km) hop to Gibraltar, although strong currents in the straits meant the crossing took them six hours. The couple then drove through Spain and France, and eventually over the English Channel to London. Ben and Elinore stayed in England for nearly three years, rebuilding *Half Safe* and raising funds to continue. They left in early

1955 for the road trip through Europe to Turkey, across the Bosphorus, and on through Syria, Jordan, Iraq, Pakistan, and India, where they decided to ship the jeep to Australia.

After five years with *Half Safe* Elinore was tired of travel and constant seasickness. She decided to return home to the United States and divorced Ben later that year. She never remarried, nor did she ever speak publicly about her time in *Half Safe*.

Ben Carlin went on to complete his circumnavigation in *Half Safe*; it was a journey that took him eight years, he traveled 38,987 miles (62,744 km) overland and 9,600 NM (17,780 km) by sea. He finished the full circle back to Montreal on May 12, 1958.

In 1963, while in the United States, Ben Carlin married Cynthia Henderson; however, their marriage lasted only a year. He died in Perth in 1981 at the age of 69, and is survived by their daughter, Deidre Scott Carlin.

≈≈≈≈≈≈≈

Giorgio Amoretti was a photojournalist and something of an eccentric free spirit. In 1950, he rode around the world on a Lambretta scooter with a 125 cc two-stroke engine, three gears and a top speed of 44 mph (70 km/h). After being jilted in love in 1957 he decided he needed to prove his manliness by swimming the length of Lake Garda in mid-winter, covering 27 NM (50 km) in just under 24 hours. Twice he crossed the Sahara Desert, first with an all-terrain vehicle (quad bike), and then with a parasail. The Italian was inspired by Alain Bombard's 1952 crossing of the Atlantic in an inflatable dinghy, (see chapter *The Heretics*). In 1978, Amoretti attempted his craziest stunt yet—to cross the Atlantic Ocean in a Volkswagen Beetle filled with polystyrene; he called his car-boat *Automare* (Sea Car). He intended to follow Bombard's trade wind route and shipped his car to the Canary Islands. Once the authorities understood his intentions, they promptly confiscated his auto-craft.

Amoretti was not a man to forget, nor someone to give up lightly; 21 years later at the age of 67, he was diagnosed with terminal cancer and his dying wish was to cross the Atlantic in a car-boat convoy with his three sons, this time using two vehicles. He chose a 1987 Volkswagen Passat and a 1981 Ford Taurus. Surprisingly, given the madcap nature of their attempt, their extraordinary story has hardly been reported outside of Italy.

Giorgio Amoretti and his three sons went to work to convert their cars on their family farm in La Spezia, in north-western Italy. Everything was rushed as the father's medical condition was deteriorating. By late April 1999, they were ready, but Amoretti was not and he was taken into hospital, seriously ill. His three sons, Marco, Fabio, and Mauro, together with a family friend, Marcolino De Candia, wanted to honor Giorgio Amoretti's plans, so they shipped the car-boats out to the Canary Islands as planned. Meanwhile, Giorgio Amoretti remained hospitalized.

The two vehicles were far from state-of-the-art ocean vessels. The cars were already well-used, but this was not very relevant as they were no longer expected to function in the way their manufacturers had intended. Amoretti always claimed that making a car-boat was a simple process: "Just make the cabin water-tight by using welding, resin and expanding waterproof foam." The secret was to make sure there was enough foam in the vehicles for them to remain buoyant, even though everything below the headlights remained underwater.

The floating cars were reasonably well-equipped for the voyage. They lashed an inflatable rubber raft securely on the roof of each vehicle to use as living and sleeping quarters. The brothers carried a GPS navigation system and an Inmarsat satellite phone (a very expensive addition to their equipment in 1999), and this allowed them to keep in touch with their father. They also carried short-range VHF radios that allowed them to communicate with each other over short distances. They powered their 12-volt batteries with wind generators and solar panels.

Each boat-car had two steering wheels: the left steered the car when on land, and the other on the right controlled the rudder. The engine was removed to give room for an anchor and safety equipment, although this storage could only be accessed by first jumping into the sea. Inside the cabin were mooring lines and two 5.3-gallon (20-liter) fuel tanks for the outboard. Most of the inside of the vehicle was already filled with the foam, then packed tightly with food and water tanks.

As the sun rose over the still Atlantic Ocean on the morning of May 4, 1999, the four self-styled "Autonauts" pushed and steered their two car-boats into the sea in Las Palmas in the Canary Islands. They decided to leave at daybreak to avoid the Civil Guard, the very people who had prevented their father from achieving his ambition 21 years previously. It was probably a wise decision because no responsible maritime authority would ever have allowed the Italians anywhere near the water's edge if they had the legal power to stop them. The young men had no experience in sailing, no technical support, nor any sponsorship or outside funding.

Once in the water, they ran the outboards for as long as the fuel lasted. This at least got them away from land and the eagle eyes of the Civil Guard.

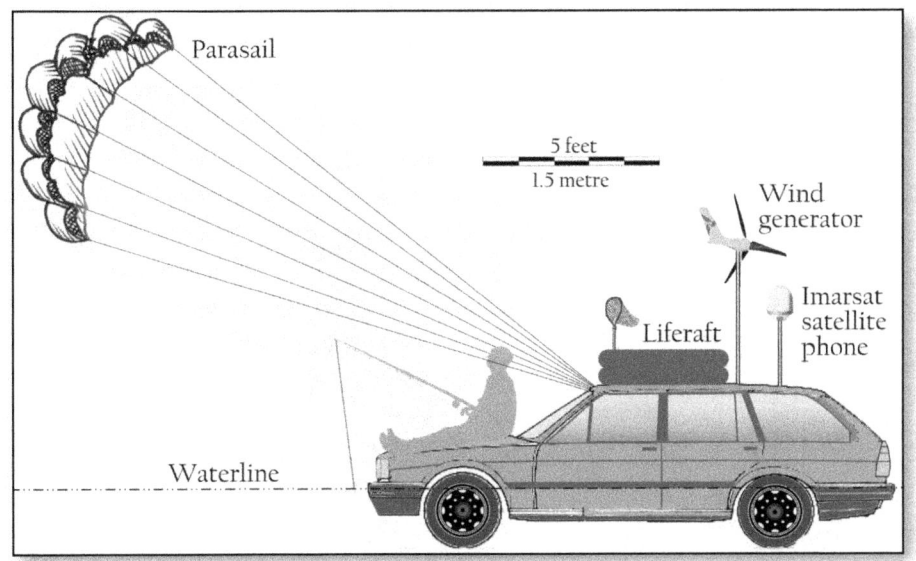

The Amoretti's floating 1987 Volkswagen Passat.

They then dumped both outboards and the empty fuel tanks over the side to give them more room aboard.

Their main form of propulsion was now parasails—parachute-like sails attached to the roof of their car-boats. These helped to lift the front of the car to prevent nose-diving, but they were only useful with the wind from behind, and strong enough to keep the parasail full (but not too strong to capsize you). Unfortunately, the winds were very light at first and they made little progress. Instead, they hoisted a square sail on a stubby mast mounted on the roof, and they slowly crawled west away from the islands.

It did not take long for the harsh reality of the voyage to sink home. The rolling, jerky motion was very unpleasant and soon induced seasickness. This was too much for the two younger Amoretti brothers, Fabio and Mauro, who were only 21 and 23 years old. They used their satellite phone to call up a helicopter rescue on May 14th, just 10 days into the voyage. They had to do this before they sailed outside the 54 NM (100 km) limit of the rescue services.

There is no record of the response they got from the authorities when they were picked up by the helicopter at great expense. Together with his friend Marcolino De Candia, Marco Amoretti stuck it out to honor his father's wish and continued the voyage. The price they paid for staying on the voyage was the usual catalog of gales, calms, lightning, sharks, whales, sunburn, and saltwater boils. Progress was slow, then on May 25th their

The floating VW had little freeboard and was inherently unstable.

Inmarsat satellite phone failed and contact with the rest of the world was lost. This resulted in them being reported as "missing at sea" by their local press, and tragically Giorgio Amoretti died just three days later thinking his son was lost at sea. When Marco managed to get the Inmarsat working five weeks later, his mother decided to say nothing, fearing the news would come as a devastating psychological blow when he still had a long way to go to complete the voyage.

Hurricanes form off the African coast during the summer, so the month of May is a little late to begin a crossing of the Atlantic along the southern trade wind route. The hurricane season officially begins in the West Indies on June 1st, and in 1999 there were five category four hurricanes in the Atlantic—a new record for a single season. It was not a matter of if, but when bad weather would arrive. It came in the form of Tropical Storm Emily—not quite a full-blown hurricane, but a nasty storm nevertheless, with sustained wind speeds of 46 knots (85 km/h) and huge breaking seas capable of rolling their car-boat. Their only option was to take refuge in the cramped interior of the vehicle and peer through the salt-caked windows of their VW Passat at the atrocious weather outside. In a floating "tub" with no stabilizing keel or proper protection, the conditions must have been nothing short of horrendous.

No matter how tough the conditions, or how inappropriate the vessel, there are always good times to be had sailing the Atlantic. Marco and

Marcolino passed their time fishing and playing their guitars. During good weather, they also experimented with Alain Bombard's ideas of survival at sea. They supplemented their freeze-dried food by fishing and collecting plankton in fine-mesh nets, which gave them extra protein and vitamin C; they also collected rainwater whenever they could.

On a good day, the two friends sailed 26 NM (48 km)—not much faster than the speed of the current taking them from east to west, so their car-boat was never going to break any speed records. After 108 days at sea, they crossed the path of an oil tanker, and the skipper of the *Chevron Atlantic* dropped welcome supplies over the side—but Marco had to swim out to recover the goodies as they had no dinghy.

The two friends eventually sighted the island of Martinique and they made landfall at the village of Tartane on August 31, 1999, after 119 days at sea. Their family was there waiting for them; only then did Marco find out that his father had died three months previously.

≈≈≈≈≈≈≈

Many crazy transatlantic crossings start as a wild dream, and over the years they develop into a reality—or a nightmare. This was certainly the case with Mait Nilson, an Estonian from Tallinn. Ever since he was a boy he dreamed of circumnavigating the world in a vehicle built by himself—a vehicle that was part car and part boat, that was unrestricted by geography and could take him across land, rivers, lakes, and even oceans.

Nilson grew up to become an engineer—the ideal training for such a venture. He claims that he spent 20 years dreaming, three years practicing, three years designing, two years building, and four years testing and refining before his *Amphibear* was ready.

Like Ben Carlin and Giorgio Amoretti before him, Nilson adapted an existing vehicle to meet his requirements, but that is where any comparison ends. Nilson was a mechanical engineer working in the early twenty-first century, and he had materials and technologies available to him that the earlier pioneers could only have dreamed about. He could then develop sophisticated and complex solutions to build his car-boat.

Nilson built his *Amphibear* in his spare time and covered the cost entirely from his own resources, but he also raised modest sponsorship and crowdfunding to cover the cost of his trip. He developed his own website and blog to keep his followers up-to-date on his progress: (http://www.amphibear.com/). His approach was first to take one of the toughest and most reliable off-road vehicles around—a Toyota Land Cruiser 120 4D4. This solved the on-road part of his journey; to cover the watery bits, the

Nilson and his Toyota Land Cruiser ready for the road. The rubber front fender was required to conform to modern safety laws.
Photo: Pille Russi

Land Cruiser was designed to sit on a catamaran built from two hulls, or "sponsons." It would have been much simpler to carry the hulls on a trailer towed behind the off-roader; the boat section could then be assembled when needed. But Nilson chose not to take the easy route, preferring instead to take on the engineering challenge of making the *Amphibear* completely self-contained.

The Estonian chose to permanently attach the sponsons to the Land Cruiser with aluminum cantilevered arms that allowed the two hulls to be lifted up and carried over the roof of the vehicle. Nilson then used the vehicle's winch to lower the sponsons into the water before launching. At the rear of each sponson were lifting sterndrives and propellers, powered by the Land Cruiser's engine, using oil pumps and a hydraulic system.

In the 1960s, the U.S. Navy developed a design principle with the acronym KISS—"Keep it simple, stupid." The KISS approach maintains that most systems work best if they are kept straightforward and avoid over-complication—simplicity should be a key goal in any design and needless complexity avoided. Mait Nilson, however, wanted to indulge his training and he looked on the project as a personal engineering challenge. His design broke all the KISS principles and became overly complicated for a project that was already a considerable challenge.

Nilson claims his biggest problem was to keep the overall weight of the *Amphibear* within legal limits for road use, while also making the car-boat strong enough to withstand the ocean crossings. The Toyota Land

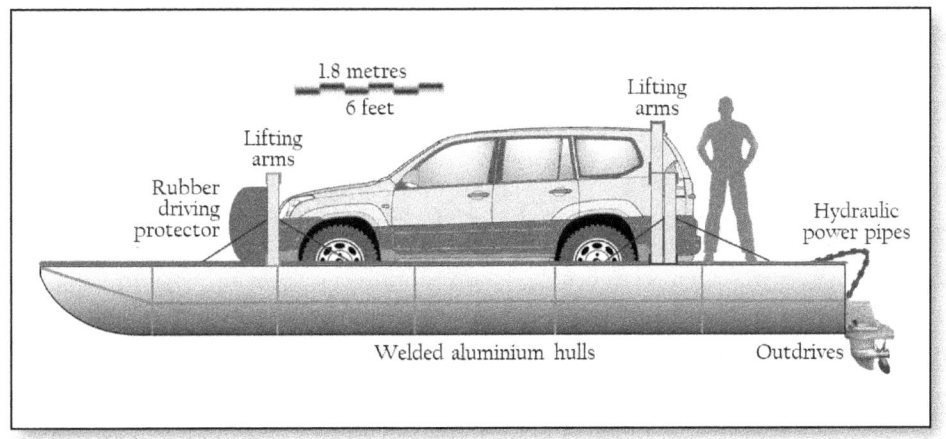

Matt Nilson's Amphibear.

Cruiser weighs 2.54 tons with an empty fuel tank and no extras; once Nilson added the sponsons and mechanical arms, equipment, hydraulics, and sterndrives, food, water, and fuel, the weight doubled. The 4x4 is also a big vehicle, 16 ft 3 in (5 m) long, but with the sponsons, the final length of the *Amphibear* doubled to 32 ft 10 in (10 m).

Technically the *Amphibear* was certainly a very clever solution, but the engineering required to construct a cantilevered flotation system of this size, attached to a Land Cruiser, and capable of sustaining an ocean crossing, was anything but straightforward. The car-boat also had to be road legal and meet a variety of restrictions in many different countries. He also had to fit a large, rubber fender to the front of the Land Cruiser to meet legal requirements for the protection of pedestrians.

In its completed form and fully fueled, the *Amphibear* weighed 4.5 tons. Toyota recommends a Gross Vehicle Mass (GVM) of 3.35 tons, leaving a payload of about 0.75 ton, so the vehicle was overloaded for road use and top-heavy. On the road, the *Amphibear* was 10 ft 10 in (3.3 m) high and 8 ft (2.46 m) wide; with its standard 3-liter diesel engine it was capable of a maximum speed of 68 mph (110 km/h), but in its original form the Land Cruiser could reach 109 mph (175 km/h).

On the water, the catamaran hulls kept the wet surface area low; this helped to reduce drag, and the two hydraulically powered sterndrives pushed the car-boat along at a maximum speed of 8 knots (15 km/h). By putting one propeller ahead and the other in reverse it was possible to turn the catamaran hull in its own length. The hulls were 32 ft 10 in (10 m) long (including the sterndrives) and 2 ft 7 in (0.8 m) in diameter; the two sponsons therefore, gave a total buoyancy of around 9 tons, or about twice

Amphibear during lake trials.
Photo: Pille Russi

the weight of the amphibious vehicle. With the hulls lowered in their seagoing configuration, the *Amphibear* was 15 ft 7 in (4.75 m) wide.

Compared to Carlin's amphibious jeep or Amoretti's floating VW Passat, living conditions aboard the *Amphibear* were positively luxurious. Nilson could sleep full-length on a bunk over storage boxes; inside he had a portable toilet and a stove mounted on the rear door. Other equipment included a radio-scanner, road navigation GPS, marine plotter GPS, camera screens, a VHF radio, a CD player, and an autopilot. He was able to monitor the hydraulic power system and other essential mechanical systems from instruments on the Land Cruiser's dashboard. He even fitted exterior waterproof cameras on the front of the hulls, as well as a camera inside the cabin.

Safety equipment included a bilge pump, an ocean life raft, rescue flares, and an Emergency Position Indicating Radio Beacon (EPIRB). He fitted a diesel heater for cold nights, and rather than carry large quantities of fresh water on long voyages, he also fitted a desalinator. All this equipment, of course, added weight.

Nilson decided that a boat of no less than 29 ft 6 in (9 m) was really the smallest size that would be suitable for an ocean crossing. He acknowledged that an amphibious vehicle like *Amphibear* had some disadvantages when compared to an ocean-going catamaran or a monohull—for example, it had a higher center of gravity and less room for equipment and crew. To compensate, he argued, the *Amphibear* had lower wind resistance, and that meant there was less risk of the vehicle capsizing in big seas compared to a sailing or power catamaran.

Nilson took advice from wave scientists who confirmed that "normal waves" were not dangerous for the *Amphibear*, but that any breaking wave bigger than 13 ft 5 in (4.1 m) could cause problems. It was inevitable that he would eventually have to face waves even bigger than this during the ocean crossings, and his plan was to trail a sea anchor behind him when wind and wave conditions became dangerous. He considered his cruising speed and overall weight were low compared to typical power and sailing boats, so the structural demands on the *Amphibear* were not excessively high and he was confident his assembly had an adequate safety margin to withstand an ocean crossing.

The biggest design challenge was to attach the floats to the Land Cruiser using cantilever arms. The catamaran platform was very wide, so huge twisting forces are created when a wave passes under it; first one part of a hull is lifted, then as it falls back so the other sponson is lifted, creating significant stress. This is not a problem in lakes and rivers where waves are relatively small, but once in the open ocean, the twisting from passing waves could become a significant structural problem—and the motion never stops for as long as you are at sea. Only proper trials in the open ocean could show whether his design would work.

After seven years of planning, construction, and testing, Mait Nilson left Tallinn in Estonia on November 2, 2013, with his *Amphibear*; he expected the circumnavigation to take him 9 months, and anticipated covering more than 32,400 NM (60,004 km). He expected to be joined by several co-pilots on different legs of the journey. He had a co-driver on the motoring section from Estonia to Senegal, a distance of 4,660 miles (7,500 km). However, he could not get anybody to accompany him on the ocean sections—he found his friends with time on their hands had no money, and his friends with money had no time.

His first stage went through Europe to Spain, before crossing the Straits of Gibraltar to Morocco. As part of his preparations, Nilson had already put in 200 hours on the water, but none of that time was testing on the open ocean. When he arrived in Spain, he prepared the Amphicar for the crossing to Morocco, but the authorities refused to allow him to launch the car-boat. He presented his official documentation to the police, and they became much more helpful.

When Nilson eventually landed in Ceuta in Morocco after making the short crossing, there were hundreds of people on the beach watching his arrival. However, the authorities would not allow him to take the *Amphibear* over the border from the Spanish enclave of Ceuta into Morocco, so he had to return by ferry to Spain, and then take another ferry back to Tangier in

Morocco. He then drove to the border with Ceuta so that he could claim to have properly completed that section of his circumnavigation.

The next stage continued south through Mauritania and Senegal. This was only the beginning of his circumnavigation; once he had crossed the Atlantic, he intended to drive through Brazil, Argentina, Chile, Peru, Colombia, Panama, Nicaragua, Honduras, Guatemala, Mexico, the United States, Canada, and Russia—still with his catamaran hulls suspended over the roof.

By mid-December, Nilson was in Senegal and ready to face the Atlantic. Being an experienced engineer, he must have had his doubts about whether the cantilever arms and aluminum floats would cope with conditions in the open ocean. A month before leaving Tallinn, he wrote to the Canadian manufacturer of the sponsons asking if the floats were up to the job. Their reply was not encouraging:

> *"As aluminum welding does not tolerate vibration, or repeated bending forces, some engineers have proposed it can crack as a result of repeated wave forces (develop micro-cracks that later lead to a structural break in a pontoon)."*

The manufacturer went on to suggest that vibration on the road sections could also create minute fractures in the aluminum welds, and on his arrival in St. Louis, Senegal, Nilson found that he had to re-weld sections of the pontoons and add reinforcement plates. These are not the sort of repairs that you want to be doing before embarking on a solo ocean crossing to the Cape Verde Islands, but Nilson put aside his concerns and prepared his *Amphibear* for the ocean.

While in St. Louis, Nilson was frequently asked if he had seen the breaking waves which form where the flow from the Senegal River meets the ocean. Intrigued, he drove to the end of the peninsular and saw the twisting channel and white breakers for himself; it did not look encouraging. He decided to take a closer look from the deck of a local boat, but the captain became too nervous to sail as far as the breakers and they turned back before they even reached the rough water.

Nilson's plan was to wait for the best weather forecast at the start of his voyage, and hope the conditions would remain favorable for the second half. On December 1, 2013, he drove the *Amphibear* into the Senegal River and headed downstream towards the Atlantic Ocean. He wisely left at high water, which allowed him to be swept downriver on the ebb tide; he could also watch the local fishing boats navigate the winding channel as they returned from a night's fishing. These boats—all of them bigger than the *Amphibear*—were rolling heavily in the white breakers.

Nilson now found himself heading into these alarming conditions in an untested boat. By following the route of the incoming fishing boats, the *Amphibear* zigzagged her way out towards the open ocean and the first of the breakers. They looked terrifying through the spray-splashed windscreen of the Land Cruiser, but the *Amphibear* rose to the challenge and powered through the white water. They were soon through the worst of the conditions, and the surface of the ocean became flat.

It was an encouraging start, but the optimism did not last. The waves off the West African coast seemed to be completely random, and Nilson described them as "rolling miniature hills." The autopilot reacted too quickly to the motion, and the constant rudder corrections made progress jerky and uncomfortable. There was no rhythm to the movement, and Nilson had to hold on constantly, even when lying in his bunk. As night fell, there was no moon and heavy fog lay over the ocean; even though the waves were slight, Nilson succumbed to seasickness.

The sun rose the next morning on a new problem. The engine cooling fan had worked well until now, but it was intended to function with the Land Cruiser driving on a road. They were now in the topics and moving very slowly at sea; the engine temperature soon climbed over the recommended maximum of 194 deg F (90 deg C). Nilson had to go on deck every two hours in the pitching *Amphibear*, open the bonnet, and then attend to the over-heating engine; this was particularly difficult (and dangerous) in the pitch-black darkness of night.

On December 3rd, Nilson tweeted that he was halfway to the Cape Verde archipelago. He noted that he had used 55 gallons (210 liters) of fuel, which was less than a third of the total. The waves were small and choppy; the water temperature was 26 deg C (79 deg F), and air temperature 25 deg C (77 deg F).

The next day—the fourth day at sea—the hydraulic system powering the sterndrives developed an oil leak; Nilson shut the engine down and searched for the source of the problem. Once again, this was a difficult and dangerous task to do alone. As most of the hydraulic tubing was underwater, this involved taking a swim with an adjustable wrench to test all the connections, but he could not find the leak. Darkness comes early in the tropics, so Nilson deployed his sea anchor and went to sleep. The next morning, he found the source of the trouble and the leak could easily be accessed over the left front wheel—so no more swimming.

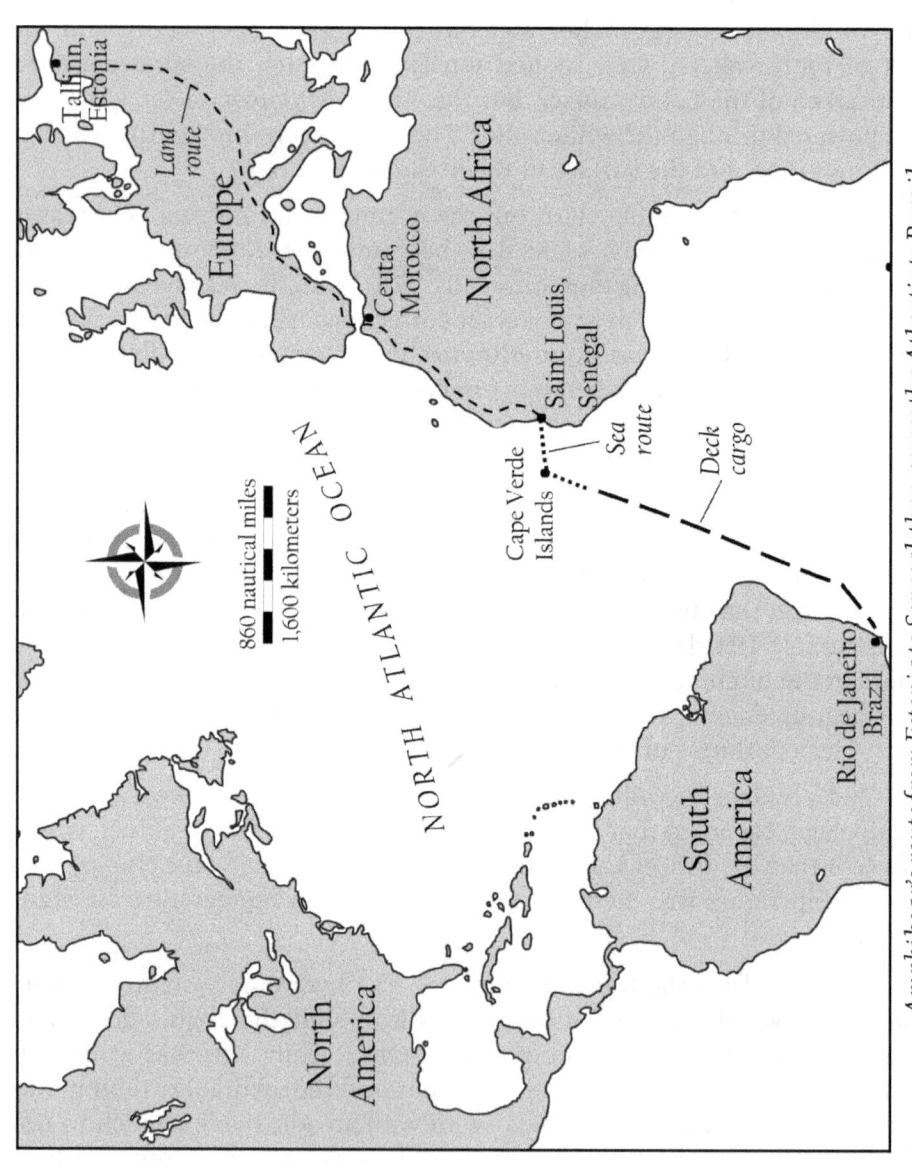

Amphibear's route from Estonia to Senegal, then across the Atlantic to Brazil.

194 · DAREDEVILS OF THE ATLANTIC OCEAN

There were now several problems developing with the mechanical systems, so Nilson decided to ease the strain on the engine and throttle back to 4.3 knots (8 km/h) for the final 24 hours. As he approached Santiago, the main island in the Cape Verde archipelago, the swell was running at over 6 ft (2 m). The weather forecast predicted stronger winds, so Nilson headed immediately into the safety of Praia harbor.

The *Amphibear* had passed her first ocean test, but it had not been an easy crossing. Nilson found sleeping to be very difficult because of the unpredictable rolling and incessant noise of the diesel engine, and he always wore a safety harness whenever outside the cabin. When on deck—even in good weather—he quickly became drenched from the constant slapping of waves on the vehicle's wheels and sponsons. It was possible to fish and cook, but the biggest problem he faced was a lack of sleep.

Nilson spent his time in Praia harbor overhauling the *Amphibear* and preparing for the 1,620 NM (3,000 km) crossing to Recife in Brazil. He hoped the conditions would be easier on this section, with the wind and waves behind them. As with his departure from Senegal, he waited for a favorable weather forecast before starting; once he committed to the voyage, the *Amphibear* would not have the power to turn around and motor back against wind and waves to the Cape Verde Islands.

It took only a few days on the second leg before small cracks appeared in the aluminum hulls. Nilson realized he could not continue and put out a distress call. He was answered by the *MS Haru*, a 394 ft (120 m) Panamanian registered cargo ship. The *Amphibear* was only a speck in the big ocean, and the crew of the *Haru* came within 1 NM (1.85 km) of the car-boat before they saw her. Nilson carefully maneuvered alongside, but the rolling swell caused the *Amphibear* to slam against the side of the ship. Sudden impacts like this can cause brittle aluminum welded joints to fracture, and more cracks to develop; the sponsons now began to take in more water, and one of the sterndrives was put out of action.

The captain of the *Haru* offered to hoist the *Amphibear* on deck, but the ship's crane could only handle 3 tons; Nilson knew that he had no option but to abandon his dream and climb aboard the cargo ship; the *Haru* resumed her course south, and before long, Nilson was tucking into a welcome lunch of meatballs and rice. By an extraordinary stroke of luck, the *MS Haru* was notified that the *MS Geoholm* was passing close to the *Amphibear*'s last known position. This 282 ft (86 m) offshore supply vessel had a very large crane, and the Norwegian captain generously offered to lift the amphibious vehicle on deck; his concern was not the challenge of picking the *Amphibear* out of the Atlantic in big ocean seas, but the fact that the car-boat was not on his customs manifest.

The *Geoholm* was on passage to Rio de Janeiro in Brazil, and when they arrived, the captain's worst fears were realized—the Brazilian customs authorities took one look at the strange craft on deck and impounded it. The *Amphibear* was eventually released and Nilson could make a detailed inspection of the damage. He found multiple cracks in the aluminum hulls, including the internal bulkheads.

The *Amphibear* had made it as far as Brazil, but her days as an ocean voyager were now over.

≈≈≈≈≈≈≈

If cars can cross the Atlantic, then why not a bicycle—well, a pedalo to be precise? Ever since he was ten years old, a young American, Dwight Collins dreamed of making an Atlantic crossing, and during his high school years he assembled a clippings file of transatlantic voyages. When he got to a university, he had an inspiration: "In life everything is gray," he claimed, "but the idea of pedaling the Atlantic was clear, simple, straightforward, and it had never been done."

Two-and-a-half years later and after logging nearly 4,000 hours on an exercise bike at home, and combining his savings of $30,000 with another $30,000 raised from sponsors, Collins was able to build his pedal boat.

Dwight Collins left Newfoundland on June 14, 1992, and took 40 days to pedal across the Atlantic..

This was a far cry from anything that you might have experienced on your local town pond. The craft was 24 ft (7.3 m) by 4.5 ft (1.4 m), weighed 850 lbs (386 kg), and named the *Tango* after its bright orange paintwork. This sophisticated, watertight, and self-righting craft was made from carbon fiber and cedar strips and built by Goetz Marine Technology (renowned for building America's Cup boats) in Bristol, Rhode Island. The belt-drive pedal system was assembled from bicycle parts, and the craft carried the usual array of modern electronics powered by solar panels.

Collins left St. John's, Newfoundland on June 14, 1992—the starting point of so many Atlantic crossings. As he pedaled away from the island, he caught the Labrador Current, which proved to be stronger than he anticipated, and he was swept too far south. It was tough going, and even pedaling 17 to 20 hours a day, he initially made little progress; during one depressing 17-hour stretch, he covered just 8.6 NM (16 km).

Two weeks later, a four-day gale brought strong winds from the southwest, but at least the *Tango* was heading in the right direction as she slid down the front of 30 ft (9.1 m) waves. More storms continued to speed him across the Atlantic. "By the end of the trip, I had gone through so many gales I could hardly keep track," he recalls. "When the weather was bad, it was important to take advantage of the following sea, so I pedaled as hard as I could and coasted down these huge waves. It was exhilarating." During his best 24-hour period, he covered 80 NM (148 km).

Halfway across, Collins paused in the middle of a foggy night to repair his pedal-drive system. At 2:00 a.m., a bright light flickered through one of his portholes, illuminating the inside of his cabin—a short distance away was a fishing trawler heading in his direction. He was not entirely comforted by earlier assurances from the boat's designer that even if it was cut in half, his boat would still float. The trawler finally caught the pedal boat in its spotlight and veered off, missing a collision by just 200 ft (60 m).

After 40 days at sea and weighing 30 lbs (13.6 kg) lighter, Collins pedaled his way into Plymouth harbor in the west of England on July 24, 1992. He had crossed over 1,836 NM (3,400 km) of open ocean in a pedal boat, averaging 46 NM (85 km) a day.

The *Tango* is now on display at Mystic Seaport Museum, in Mystic, Connecticut.

The Heretics

*I*n the early 1950s, it was estimated that 200,000 people died every year at sea; of these, 50,000 survived the initial disaster and reached their lifeboats but subsequently perished. The French physician, Alain Bombard had researched human resistance to privation, and especially the hardships experienced by political deportees, prisoners, and people suffering from malnourishment, and he became an expert in understanding survival under adversity.

Bombard was, however, perplexed by one specific area of his research—this poor survival rate of people from a shipwreck. Why, he asked himself, did so many people die having taken to lifeboats when all around them was the means to stay alive? He pointed to the survival of Captain Bligh and his crew in 1789, who spent 40 days afloat in the South Pacific on eight days of rations, and sailed 3,618 NM (6,701 km) to safety.

By contrast, there was the notorious case of the French frigate, the *Méduse*, that ran aground on a sandbank off the West African coast in 1816. There were not enough lifeboats and at least 146 men and one woman were off-loaded onto a hastily-constructed raft and given limited provisions, including two barrels of water and six of wine. All the officers who stayed aboard the *Méduse* survived the shipwreck, but it was a very different story for the wretched souls on the raft. By day four only 67 remained, at which point they resorted to cannibalism. By day eight, the strongest pitched the weak and wounded over the side. After 13 days at sea, 15 men remained to be rescued, and ten of those died soon afterward.

Bombard delved further into the statistics of shipwrecks and found that 90 percent of survivors died within three days of taking to the lifeboats—even though it takes much longer than that to perish from hunger and thirst. He concluded that these people died long before they met the limits of their biological endurance; their problem was not physical, but psychological. These people were dying from despair, which he concluded was a ruthless and efficient killer.

Bombard became obsessed with this dilemma, and he took a logical and systematic approach to finding unorthodox ways to extend survival rates for those who find themselves adrift at sea. In October 1951, he began research at the Museum of Oceanography in Monaco, where he was given full access to their well-equipped laboratories. He studied previous shipwrecks and what lessons could be learned from these incidents. He also studied how best to catch fish in the deep ocean, and how they could be eaten by a shipwrecked survivor. He was also keen to understand the wind and water circulation patterns in the oceans, and how these might best be used to aid survival.

The "Raft of the Medusa" (Le Radeau de la Méduse) by Thédore Géricault. This highly controversial painting did much to bring the tragedy to the publics' attention. It can be seen hanging in the Louvre in Paris.

Bombard understood the human body needs three classes of food: protein, fat and carbohydrates (sugars), and he analyzed the nutrition offered by a wide variety of fish. Protein was easy to obtain from fish, although the flesh of rays and sharks benefits from washing to remove excess urea and ammonia. Fish also offered abundant fats, so the second food group was also fulfilled. This left carbohydrates, and this became a concern to Bombard. Although the livers of many fish generate glucose, eating too much gives you dangerously high levels of vitamins A and D.

Bombard concluded that you would need to rely on your body's own ability to manufacture the necessary carbohydrates—something that the human body is quite capable of doing; after all, the Inuit (he called them Eskimos) survive quite healthily during the six winter months on a diet of meat and fat, and drinking melted sea-ice water.

The French doctor concluded there was adequate nutrition available in the ocean for survival providing you had a fine mesh to filter plankton, lines with hooks, and harpoons to catch fish. In theory, at least, he believed there was every chance of maintaining a balanced diet by living off the sea following a shipwreck. Even scurvy—that great fear of sailors for centuries—he believed was not a big problem. Baleen whales, he reasoned, ate only plankton that provided these marine mammals with enough vitamin C to survive. He was confident that plankton would provide the necessary supplement for humans as well.

His one remaining concern was finding enough fresh water to survive. A human can live for 30 days without food, but only ten days without water. It is well-known that drinking seawater in large quantities results in death. Yet the human body also needs a regular intake of salt and Bombard calculated that drinking 1.6 pints (0.75 liters) of seawater a day would provide the optimum amount of salt, although after five days there was a risk that nephritis (inflammation of the kidneys) could become a problem. However, five days would give you valuable time to catch fish and collect rainwater, both offering a good supply of fresh liquid.

Bombard had no solution, however, to what he thought was the biggest killer of all: despair. It formed no part of a study on nutrition, but he knew that thirst would kill quicker than hunger, and he believed that hopelessness would kill quicker than thirst. He began to realize that if his theory would ever move beyond the stage of a hypothesis, he would have to test his ideas in the real world.

≈≈≈≈≈≈≈

This was the ultimate experiment for a scientist—Bombard was prepared to put his life on the line and take a long sea journey to test his theory. His practical preparations were as thorough as his theoretical work. He wanted to isolate himself for a period of one to three months, and his route must have favorable winds and currents. He did not want to be close to any busy shipping routes in case he was tempted to abort his experiment. He decided that the Trade Wind route from east to west across the Atlantic would meet all these criteria.

Bombard also had to decide how he was going to extract the nourishment he needed from the ocean. Almost every day, he went out in one of the museum research boats to catch different fish species, which he pressed to extract fresh liquid. He discovered that a simple fruit press was the best gadget to use.

He also had to choose a survival craft. At an early stage, he decided on a standard ship's lifeboat, but he abandoned this idea in favor of a catamaran with two open hulls where he and a crew member could sit, and that supported a simple sail. During a test in the bay of Monte Carlo, a breaking wave flooded one of the pontoons and the craft turned turtle; Bombard had to swim ashore and scraped his thigh climbing over sharp rocks. Soon the local police were involved, having received reports that a naked, bleeding man was seen lurking about in the woods: such are the trials of an experimental scientist.

So far, his work had been more-or-less secret, but the newspapers began to get wind of his work and articles appeared in both France and Britain—many of which grossly distorted the facts. One benefit, however, was that Bombard received offers of help from volunteers. Some were more appealing than others: one gentleman proposed that Bombard should take his mother-in-law because his life-saving experiment could start by rescuing his marriage; another tried to make his candidature more appealing by offering himself to be eaten should Bombard's survival ideas fail; yet another had failed to commit suicide on three occasions and asked to come, as he thought the voyage would be a more reliable method of achieving his objective.

After his disastrous trial sail in a catamaran, Bombard settled on a 15 ft (4.57 m) inflatable dinghy, 6 ft (1.83 m) wide. The French company, Zodiac, had developed the modern U-shaped inflatable boat with a wooden transom in 1937, using techniques and materials used to manufacture airships. The company patented the design in 1943, and by the 1960s Zodiac had licensed production to a dozen companies in several countries.

Because of the width of the inflatable tubes, space inside the boat was limited to just 3 ft (0.9 m). The sponsons were divided into five individually sealed compartments for safety, each with a valve to allow the segment to be inflated separately; an outside valve also allowed air to pass from one compartment to another. The boat had a shallow inflatable keel to help keep it tracking in a straight line, and wooden slats raised the floor so the occupants were not sitting directly on the rubberized hull. Bombard also fitted a small 27 sq ft (2.50 sq m) sail to allow downwind sailing. In a sardonic nod to his detractors, Bombard named his boat *L'Hérétique*—'The Heretic.'

Bombard also decided on his crew member. All mothers-in-law, reckless adventurers, and those with a death-wish were bypassed in favor of a single, experienced sailor. His name was Herbert Muir-Palmer, better known as Jack Palmer. He was an English-born naturalized citizen of Panama and a proven navigator, having sailed his 30 ft (9.1 m) yacht from Panama to Cairo, then back to Monaco. As the two men worked to prepare *L'Hérétique* for the voyage, Bombard grew to like Palmer more and more. But at the back of his mind, there was the niggling uncertainty about how his crew member would respond when things got difficult. How would he react to gnawing pangs of hunger, day-after-day? And what if the two men fell out? They would never be more than a couple of feet apart for weeks at a time. In the end, Bombard decided that a trial sail was a prudent beginning.

≈≈≈≈≈≈≈

The little harbor in Fontvieille in Monaco lies less than a mile south of Monte Carlo, but Alain Bombard and Jack Palmer were gambling higher stakes than anyone in the casinos as they prepared for their trial sail. At dawn on Saturday, May 24, 1952, the two men launched their Zodiac and began to

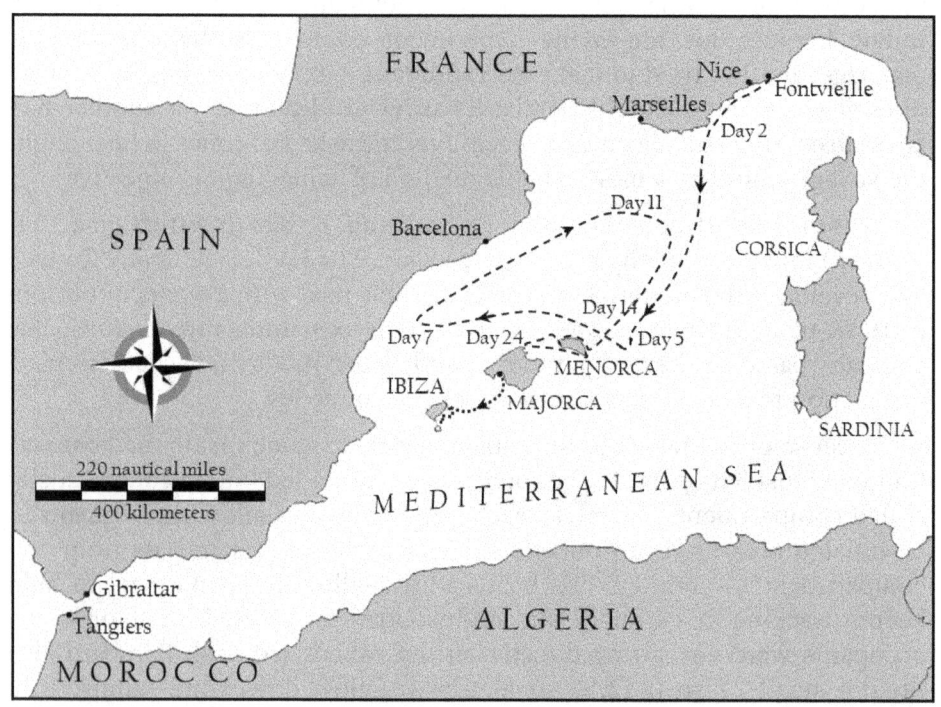

Bombard's trial sail in the Mediterranean: the dashed line shows May 25th to June 18th, the dotted line from Majorca to Ibiza lasted from July 6th to July 15th.

load their equipment. At 2:00 p.m. in the afternoon an official arrived to put his seal on their jerrycans of water—these would only be used in an emergency. The two adventurers were constantly pestered by journalists and photographers, but interest waned when it became clear the wind direction would not allow them to get away, and they postponed their start until the next day.

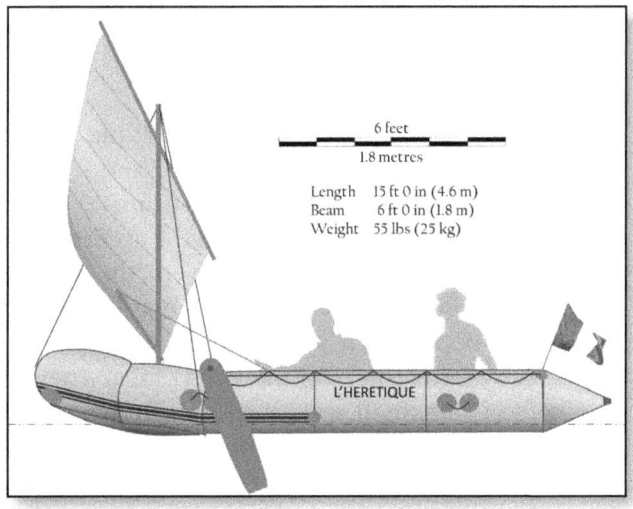

L'Hérétique in offshore trim, with a small sail forward and a pair of leeboards on either side to assist steering.

Meanwhile, one gentleman in a wide-brimmed hat sidled up to Bombard: "young man," he proffered, "I know something about this business. I just got back from South America. There is no point in being squeamish. If your companion dies on the way, don't throw him overboard. Eat him. Anything serves as food; I have even eaten shark!" Bombard politely thanked the man; he was never short of advice from strangers.

Bombard and Palmer went down to the harbor the next morning at dawn. *L'Hérétique* was intended to be nothing more than a floating life raft and the dinghy was never expected to sail anywhere except downwind. Bombard had therefore arranged to be towed out to sea by a motorboat. Once they cast off, their well-wishing flotilla returned to the harbor and they were left alone. The wind increased, the waves built, and the two men sat almost motionless in dispirited silence. What had they done? Could they brave the elements and survive on nothing more than what the sea and sky could provide?

Before they even had a chance to hoist their small sail, the wind increased, the waves grew, and the two sailors were soon completely soaked. The conditions became too much for their feeble mast, so they deployed their sea anchor to limit drift. Cleverly, Bombard had made his parachute-like drogue to double as a net for collecting plankton, thus saving space and weight. As the sun rose the next day, they could see they were dangerously close to the rocky shoreline; the headlands of Cap Ferrat and Cap d'Antibes, and the Lérins Islands to the south of Cannes, jutted out like traps to catch unfortunate vessels on a lee shore. The wind had now reduced, so for the first time they hoisted sail—and it proved to be a struggle in their overcrowded inflatable.

To their immense relief, *L'Hérétique* began to move through the water—not very fast, perhaps only 1½ knots (less than 3 km/h), but at least the movement gave them some control over their direction. By 11:00 a.m. on their first morning, they rounded Cap Ferrat, only to have the wind die. As the dinghy wallowed in the swell, the enormity of their commitment hit home. Their response was to organize themselves and allocate every minute of the day to a specific task. A couple of fishing lines were trailed as a step towards catching their next meal; they set watches so that at least one person remained awake and vigilant; they also towed their plankton net. After an hour they caught two tablespoons of what Bombard called "pap," which tasted like lobster purée (or so he zealously claimed) and was certainly filling. Palmer had never tried raw plankton before, and he was dubious about the meal being offered, but to his surprise, he found it quite palatable. Bombard smugly enjoyed his small victory.

The weather was typically warm for late May in the Mediterranean, and the two men were soon thirsty. Bombard sipped small quantities of seawater, but he had less success persuading his crew member to do the same. Palmer had fully supported Bombard's theory when they were ashore, but now faced with the reality of testing his ideas at sea, he refused. Bombard thought this was illogical and he considered it to be a striking example of how a deeply-rooted taboo of generations of seafarers prevented survival at sea. Here were two men in the same situation, one who retained the classic inhibitions of a castaway, and the other who embraced heretical ideas.

By nightfall, an offshore wind carried them away from land and into the relative safety of deep water. This is exactly what they hoped would happen; as the land cools at night, so a land-sea breeze is created, blowing offshore. During the daytime, the opposite occurs as the land warms up, the air rises, and cooler air is drawn in from the sea, creating an onshore breeze. They needed to use the night breeze to get well offshore and give themselves as much sea room as possible before the wind reversed direction in the morning.

That first night they settled into a routine, with Bombard taking the first watch from 8:00 p.m. until 1:00 a.m. in the morning. That night they saw at least ten ships, but their dinghy was low in the water, their riding light only offered a feeble glimmer, and they worried they would not be seen. If a ship came too close, they shone a torch on their sail making their boat look like a shimmering, ghostly apparition. In practice, Bombard thought they were probably not noticed at all.

The next morning the wind changed direction as expected and it began to blow on-shore. They lowered the leeboards to limit sideways drift, and this allowed them to maintain a safe distance offshore. Both men suffered hunger pains and Palmer in particular was feeling ill. Bombard gave him a comprehensive medical examination: his tongue was dry and coated, he had developed a rash on the back of his hands, and although his pulse was strong, it was slow. He was becoming dehydrated, yet he still refused to drink seawater. Bombard was in better shape, he believed because he was drinking his allocated ration of salt water. They were both constipated, making the chamber pot they had brought along yet another piece of redundant equipment. Worse than thirst was hunger. They had eaten nothing for two days except for a few spoons of plankton, and there was no sign of fish on their lines.

Later that afternoon, Palmer agreed to sip some seawater, and by next morning his signs of dehydration had disappeared—much to Bombard's relief. Over the next few days, they also found nearly a pint (0.5 liter) of water in the bottom of their boat. They had not shipped any waves and the water was fresh—it came from the warm, humid air condensing on the bottom of their boat that was in contact with the colder seawater.

On the afternoon of day three, Bombard caught their first fish—a good-sized grouper, sometimes called a sea perch. The raw pink flesh almost made them vomit at first, but it became more palatable with each mouthful—after all, it was the freshest sashimi you can get. The rest of the fish was pressed for its liquid and the flesh laid out to dry in the sun: their next meal tasted almost cooked. Like most fish, the grouper carries parasites including digeneans (parasitic flatworms), isopods (a relative of the woodlice), nematodes (roundworms), and cestodes (where the adult is commonly known as a tapeworm). Not all fish parasites are dangerous to humans, but some species can cause serious gastrointestinal problems and lung infections. Normally these parasites are destroyed by cooking, but Bombard did not have that luxury on *L'Hérétique*. As a doctor, Bombard must have been familiar with the risk to humans from fish parasites, yet surprisingly, he never mentions the problem in his book, *The Bombard Story*.

The grouper, with whatever parasitic infestation it might have had, was soon consumed and they were back to sipping seawater and gulping plankton. Fish were in short supply, but the winds were favorable and Bombard held a course for Menorca in the Balearic Islands. After one night's watch, he became aware of grey shadowy objects in the pale dawn light. At least ten whales came to visit, their 60-100 ft (18-30 m) bodies dwarfed the tiny dinghy. They were playing with *L'Hérétique*, sometimes swimming right up to the boat before diving underneath, leaving their tail visible on one side and their head on the other. Bombard found the cetaceans to be quiet, friendly, and docile, although Palmer was less generous towards them as he recalled tales of small boats being attacked when they had accidentally run into whales sleeping on the surface.

Towards the end of the fifth day, they could see the outline of Mount Toro in the distance, the highest peak in Menorca. They had eaten nothing but a couple spoonfuls of plankton for two days and were wracked with hunger. They could think of little else but the meal that awaited them on shore, but they had an unpleasant surprise. First, the wind dropped, and then the sail began to shiver. The sky grew overcast and they could see a squall approaching from the south-east. They quickly dropped all sail and put out the sea anchor. Bombard likened the experience to being on a wet Ferris wheel, but he had every confidence in the seaworthiness of the inflatable that seemed to stick to the surface of the ocean like a limpet. The storm blew them away from the island and their eighth day dawned with a rough and confused sea and fog so dense that they could not even see the bow of the dinghy 10 ft (3 m) away. Their fear now was that they would be driven ashore on the Spanish coast, south of Barcelona.

On June 2nd, the sky cleared and the wind went around to the south-west. They had eaten nothing for five days. Their stomach pains had gone, but the two men were in poor shape with sunken cheeks, baggy eyes, and swollen faces. To their amazement, a 10 lb (4.5 kg) grouper swam alongside the dinghy. Bombard had his harpoon out in no time and the fish was soon inside the boat. They needed liquid more urgently than food, so Bombard made an incision behind the dorsal fin that runs along the backbone of the fish, and the two men desperately sucked at the fresh liquid. They now had food for two days, but they found the raw fish difficult to digest.

By June 5th, 11 days into the voyage, the weather had calmed but the sailors were exhausted. A school of tuna brought hope of more food, but even though Bombard managed to spear a large fish, it took off with his harpoon still quivering in its side. With no food for several days and only seawater and plankton to survive on, the days grew monotonous, and Bombard fully understood that hunger was giving way to starvation. They tried to signal passing ships with a mirror—not to be rescued but to inform their families that they were still alive. They tried several times, but without success.

Just after dawn on June 7th, they sighted a ship in the distance. This time they used their precious distress flares and they were spotted. The cruise liner *Sidi Ferruch* turned around and came alongside. They asked the captain to report their position and they accepted emergency rations. That day, they gorged themselves on sea biscuits, bully beef, condensed milk, and fresh drinking water. Bombard later regretted accepting the supplies.

Later that day the wind strengthened and blew them towards Menorca. On June 8th, two weeks into the voyage, the summit of Mount Toro appeared again on the horizon, looking much the same as it had when they last saw it eight days previously. Fishing too had improved and Bombard was spearing more fish than they could eat. It took two more days to get close inshore, but there was nowhere to land on this inhospitable coastline. By day 18 they found themselves a few miles off the village of Ciudadela on the western side of Menorca. They hailed a fishing boat and asked for a tow, and soon they were tied up safely in the little harbor.

From Menorca, the two men then sailed on to Majorca. Bombard had accomplished his "shake-down" cruise, and apart from a few repairs and needing some extra equipment, he was pleased with their achievement. Jack Palmer was also an excellent crew member; unfortunately, the same could not be said of Bombard's relationship with journalists. Once word got out about them taking supplies from the *Sidi Ferruch*, the press announced that his great experiment had failed. He also got the news that his sponsor had declined to help any further—claiming that he did not want to be an accessory to his suicide.

Undeterred, the two men sailed on to Ibiza and then shipped *L'Hérétique* to Ceuta on the coast of Morocco; they then sailed on to Tangier. It was time to replace the inflatable that had already carried them more than 900 NM (1,668 km) and was now three years old. Bombard knew his sponsor had ordered a replacement, but he refused to release it. His patron then had a change of heart and agreed to ship the new boat, then changed his mind again. In the end, Bombard got a replacement direct from the manufacturers.

Unfortunately, the time spent procuring his new dinghy in Paris had a more serious consequence—Jack Palmer was losing enthusiasm. While waiting for the winds to become more favorable, Palmer went into Tangier to make some last-minute purchases: by 6:00 p.m. the wind was perfect to leave, but there was no sign of the missing crewman. Frustrated, Bombard scribbled a note to Palmer and left alone, sailing through the busy Straits of Gibraltar at night. It took him seven days before he arrived in Casablanca—and he made the most of the passage to teach himself how to navigate with a sextant.

Bombard arrived in the Moroccan port on Wednesday, August 20th, only to read a headline in the morning paper: "*L'Hérétique* lost in the Gulf of Cadiz." It seemed that nothing he could do would make reporters take him seriously. He could not wait to leave, and he set sail for the Canary Islands after just four days. It was an important passage down the North African coast because he still claimed to be a complete novice at ocean navigation, and he feared he would miss the Canary Islands completely and sail into the South Atlantic. Six days into the passage, he stopped a Portuguese boat to confirm his position, but he refused their offer of supplies. He was catching large quantities of mackerel and claims that Atlantic seawater tasted "absolutely delicious" and less salty than Mediterranean water.

Eleven days sailing brought him to Castillo del Romeral, a small harbor a few miles south of Las Palmas. Within a few days, he received a telegram: "Happy to announce the birth of Nathalie. Our congratulations to *L'Hérétique*." Alain Bombard was a father. He flew to France to be with his wife and daughter for a few days, and then returned to prepare for his grand experience. Neither parenthood nor the pleas from his friends was going to stop him from leaving.

Bombard was still smarting from adverse comments in the press and he was determined not to give them any more fuel for criticism. So although he took food and liquid for use in an emergency, they were sealed in a locker by none other than the French Consul in Las Palmas. Bombard hoped he would never have to fall back on these rations.

By Sunday, October 19th, the wind had swung around to the north-east and conditions were ideal to leave. Once outside the small fishing harbor, he cast off his tow and hoisted his small square sail; he found he could make a respectable 3½ knots (6.5 km/h). Until it rained, he had nothing to drink but seawater, and until he caught fish or plankton, he had nothing to eat at all. Despite this, his morale was high.

Bombard soon settled into the usual routine of sailing the Trade Winds, with a steady breeze alternating with periods of calm and squalls. On the fourth day, strong winds shredded his new sail, and he spent a whole day laboriously sewing it back together. A week into the voyage and his morale began to falter:

> "*...because increasing tiredness and exhaustion led me to expect the worst, and this in its turn made me weak and*

cowardly. From this moment on I was prey to an inner conflict of morale, quite as vital as that with the elements."

He did not catch his first fish until the end of his first week—it was a dorado, sometimes called a mahi-mahi or a dolphin fish. He trailed his plankton net for his "lobster purée," and he even caught a shearwater bird, which he ate raw. For the rest of the voyage he found anything up to 15 flying fish in his dinghy every day—these too he ate raw.

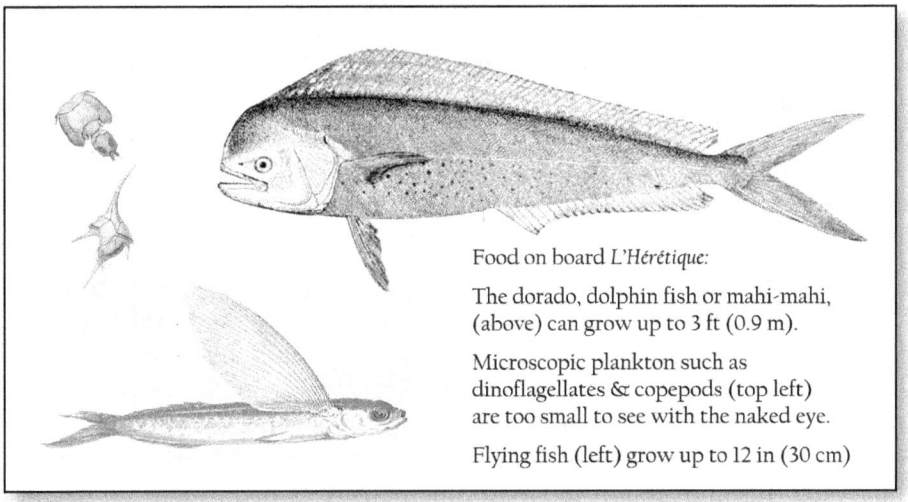

Food on board *L'Hérétique:*

The dorado, dolphin fish or mahi-mahi, (above) can grow up to 3 ft (0.9 m).

Microscopic plankton such as dinoflagellates & copepods (top left) are too small to see with the naked eye.

Flying fish (left) grow up to 12 in (30 cm)

Bombard had two other daily preoccupations; one was maintenance and checking the dinghy for chafe and wear, for the slightest friction could lead to a leak in the rubberized fabric; the other was exercise, which he did for 30 minutes every day. He was aware of the risk of edema (swelling) in his ankles, and although it was too unstable to stand up in *L'Hérétique*, he did knee squats to compensate.

It was not until 24 days into the voyage that it rained—a surprisingly long time in the sub-tropics. Until this point, he had relied solely on drinking seawater and the juice squeezed from fish to hydrate himself; he was also desperately in need of a proper wash to rinse the salt off his body. The rain allowed him to store several gallons of fresh water for future use. Generally, he was in good physical condition, although he was losing weight and had lost four nails from his toes—probably as a result of constant dampness.

On Wednesday, December 10th—53 days into his crossing—Bombard sighted his first ship; it was the *MS Arakaka*, a passenger-cargo vessel out of Liverpool. Initially, Bombard asked only for his position and he was told he was still over 540 NM (1,000 km) short of his goal. The captain invited him aboard and offered to take him and L'Hérétique to Georgetown in British Guiana. Bombard refused; he was then offered a hot meal, and he refused again. But his resolve weakened, and after more persuasion, he sat down to a fried egg, a small piece of liver, cabbage, and some fruit—no gastronomic feast by any stretch of the imagination, but a welcome break from raw fish and plankton. He would regret the meal—not only for the worst stomach trouble he experienced during his entire journey, but also for accusations of breaking his self-sufficiency.

Bombard reached Barbados on December 23, 1952, after a 2,376 NM (4,400 km) crossing that had taken him 65 days. He was emaciated and was found to be anemic, but he was still able to walk two miles to the nearest police station. He had endured fear, solitude, despair, storms, and shark attacks. His belief that humans can survive by drinking small quantities of seawater was vindicated. But even more important than water or food, he said, was mental attitude: "The survivor of a shipwreck," he wrote, "deprived of everything, must never lose hope."

He joined the French Socialist Party in 1974, and was elected to the European Parliament, and became a formidable campaigner on environmental issues, ranging from nuclear power to the culling of baby seals. His outspoken opposition to force-feeding geese for pâté de foie gras earned him and his family death threats. A journalist once asked what motivated his conversion to environmentalism: "I had fought on behalf of man against the sea," he replied, "but I realized that it had become more urgent to fight on behalf of the sea against men."

He died on July 19, 2005, at the age of 80, and was survived by his wife, Ginette (who he married in 1952), and by three sons and two daughters.

≈≈≈≈≈≈≈

Shortly after Bombard completed his Atlantic crossing, another medical doctor became involved in the heated debate about survival at sea. Hannes Lindemann was a German physician born near Hamburg in Germany in 1922. Like Bombard, he specialized in the effects of survival at sea on the human body, and like Thor Heyerdahl (see chapter The History Men) he became interested in the possibility of early migration by Europeans or Africans to the New World.

Lindemann met Bombard in Morocco in 1952, just before the French doctor embarked on his transatlantic crossing. Bombard explained his theory that you could drink limited amounts of seawater when freshwater was not available, but Lindemann was not convinced. This eventually set them on a head-on collision of opinion over how best to survive at sea. Lindemann then went on to work in a clinic in Liberia in West Africa, and as he approached the end of his two-year contract, he decided to build a traditional African dug-out canoe or pirogue, and sail across the Atlantic to test his own ideas about survival at sea.

Lindemann's first canoe—called *Liberia*—caught fire when he tried to kill wood-boring insects by "smoking" the hull over a fire. Now short of time he bought a canoe—essentially a hollowed-out tree trunk, 23 ft 6 in (7.2 m) long and just 2 ft 6 in (0.76 m) wide. He wrote that "It had holes in the stern and bow, and in the bottom where it had lain on the ground fungal growth had softened the wood somewhat." Undaunted, he thought the mahogany hull was essentially sound and decided to repair it.

The pirogue weighed over 600 lbs (272 kg), to which Lindemann added a 250 lb (113 kg) lead keel, and decked over most of the hull with plywood, fitted waterproof compartments, internal iron frames, and then fiberglassed the outside of the hull. He also fitted 10 in (25 cm) thick cork sponsons along the waterline to reduce rolling. Together with its sailing rig, the pirogue must have weighed nearly half a ton—a far cry from the

Dugout canoes similar to the one purchased by Hannes Lindemann.
Photo: Grace Rengifo

simple native craft he had originally bought. In memory of his first ill-fated attempt, he christened his new canoe *Liberia II*.

His initial sea trials were not a great success. Lindemann found the lead keel was inadequate to counter-balance the weight of the mast and sail, so he filled three large sacks with sand to use as extra ballast. He then spent the next few weeks making sailing and fishing trips, getting used to how best manage the sailing rig. Lindemann's description of the rig is sketchy; he apparently fitted an ironwood mast that was stiff enough to "run even in the Gulf of Guinea without a backstay."

Lindemann also had a choice of two mainsails: he used a square sail for running downwind, and a gaff sail when sailing with the wind on the beam. Both were very modest, just 9 sq yds (7.5 sq m) and used with a tiny 3 sq yds (2.5 sq m) jib. He also fitted a rudder controlled with cables that could be steered either by a tiller or by foot. His 3 hp outboard was ruined when the boat capsized at the dock before the start of his voyage, so he dumped the engine but made no other improvements to the craft's stability.

In early February 1955, he loaded three-months of supplies into the *Liberia II* and set sail from the little harbor of Harper in southern Liberia, destination Haiti in the Caribbean—3,750 NM (6,945 km) away. This was not a sensible time to leave because his arrival in the West Indies would coincide with the start of the hurricane season. Once at sea, he found his canoe was unstable and prone to excessive rolling; the rudder was also too small to maintain direction with the wind on the beam. He also found sleep was difficult, as his shoulders would not fit in the narrow cockpit, and he was unable to get comfortable. These are all problems that should have been resolved before leaving.

The ferocious tiger shark has a very well-developed sense of smell and has a reputation for attempting to eat almost anything.

Weather in the first couple of weeks was typical of the tropics, with little wind interspersed with squalls and lightning. A long period of calm was broken by the visit of a 9 ft (2.7 m) tiger shark. Although sharks rarely attack humans, the tiger shark has a reputation for a large proportion of fatal shark-bites and it is certainly one of the most ferocious of shark species. It also has the reputation for swallowing almost anything it finds, and objects recovered from their stomachs include bottles, tires, clothing, cats, pigs, and even a whole horse's head. A shark of that size would certainly have been able to capsize a narrow canoe.

Eight days into his voyage, Lindemann had a relapse of malaria. He found his drugs, but it would be 24 hours before they took effect:

"For a night and a day I was held tight in the grip of nightmare and hallucination. I recovered with the setting sun and with only a hazy recollection of what had happened, but then I realized immediately that I had been active during the time; crates of cans, a copper container with flashlight batteries, my last rubber cushion, and other important possessions had disappeared. I had thrown overboard everything that was in my way. It was a cruel awakening."

Lindemann was in no position to continue his voyage, and he turned back and headed for Ghana. Within sight of land, a tropical storm with lightning and torrential rain forced him to take down all sails. The next morning, he found a large ray had somehow become caught in his sea anchor. Fearing the fish would capsize his canoe, he cut the line. He eventually waded ashore in Takoradi, 17 days after leaving Liberia.

He had used his time at sea to experiment with drinking seawater, but found that within two days his feet began to swell; the condition became worse and the swelling extended to his knees. When he stopped drinking seawater, his legs returned to normal.

Undeterred by his abortive attempt, Lindemann shipped the *Liberia II* to a boatyard in Hamburg where shipwrights replaced the internal ballast with additional external ballast, added a larger rudder, plus a 4 in (10 cm) combing around the cockpit for comfort. He then shipped the (much heavier) canoe to Oporto in Portugal and set off in May 1955 for his second transatlantic attempt in four months, optimistically hoping to arrive in Haiti in June or July—still the height of the hurricane season.

This attempt was no more successful than the first. From Oporto, he sailed south down the Portuguese coast, heading for Safi in Morocco. He encountered stormy conditions off Mazagan, just 80 NM (148 km) short of his destination, and he decided to head for the safety of the harbor there. Large breaking waves swamped his canoe and he eventually made it into the harbor, soaking wet and with his pirogue full of water.

Lindemann had continued with his experiment by drinking seawater when on passage, together with other liquids, including evaporated milk and mineral water mixed with red wine. But he was not convinced with Bombard's conviction that is was safe to drink even small quantities of salt water:

> "During the past eleven days at sea, I had drunk a daily ration of seven fluid ounces [200 ml] of salt water and almost a quart and a half [1,420 ml] of other liquids. By the second day, edemata [edema] had developed, which soon extended to my knees... I had proved to myself that there is no advantage to drinking salt water; it can in fact, weaken a sailor's physical condition at a time when he needs all his strength."

His medical experiment was damaging his health and he was convinced it was a dangerous idea. This started a heated debate between Lindemann and Bombard over the wisdom of drinking seawater for survival.

After more adaptations to the *Liberia II*, Lindemann set sail for the Canary Islands but was forced to put into Safi for more rudder repairs. He left again for the Canaries, but yet another gale broke his reinforced rudder. The storm lasted four days, by which time he was swept past the Canary Islands by the offshore currents. Now steering with only a paddle, he had little option but to run downwind to the nearest port on the African coast, Villa Cisneros (now called Dakhla) in Western Sahara. By the time he arrived, he had sailed 760 NM (1,407 km) down the coast of Africa, mostly without a rudder.

Lindemann was still determined to complete his transatlantic voyage and his physiological experiment. He spent three weeks in the harbor before a mail steamer passed through and took the *Liberia II* as deck cargo to Las Palmas in the Canary Islands. Here he had a boatyard fit an enlarged rudder—this time massively reinforced. He also fitted new sails, a spare mast and paddle, and a canvas spray cover with an iron frame. He relaunched in October—just eight months after his first failed attempt from Liberia. On October 26, 1955, he left for Haiti for the third time. The hurricane season would soon be over in the West Indies and the Trade Winds were blowing at their strongest. With a good following wind, he hoped the crossing would take two months. If only...

Lindemann had bought a paraffin stove in Las Palmas, and on his first day out he tried cooking at sea. On first lighting, the stove flared up and set fire to a wooden crate of food. In desperation, he jabbed the prongs of his harpoon into the stove and hurled the flaming contraption over the side. He and his canoe were safe, but he now had no means of cooking for the rest of the voyage.

For the first 18 days, he relied only on fluid from the juice of apples and oranges. When the fruit was used up, he switched to a daily liquid intake of 0.85 pint (402 ml) of evaporated milk with a mixture of 1.82 pint (860 ml) of mineral water and slightly more than 0.5 pint (236 ml) of red wine. He also ate a raw onion daily which, he maintained, contained enough vitamins to prevent scurvy. His other food was limited, comprising a can of meat (eaten cold) and a few spoons of honey a day, with other canned rations and whatever fish he caught—which he ate raw.

A few days after leaving the islands, he found himself becalmed in a smooth sea with a heavy swell rolling in from the north. Sailing was out of the question, and as Lindemann watched Madeira petrels swoop between the troughs in the swell he caught sight of a large brown object in the water. When it next appeared, he realized he was looking at a giant squid floating on the surface. He estimated it was at least twice as long as his canoe—the female is the larger of the two sexes and can grow up to 43 ft (13 m) long. (Claims of specimens of up to 66 ft (20 m) have not been scientifically documented). Giant squid are shy creatures that live most of the time in the deep ocean, but they are widespread throughout all the world's oceans, and it is not uncommon for them to be sighted by ocean sailors.

It took two weeks before Lindemann sailed out of the fickle winds and into the Trade Wind belt proper. In these more boisterous conditions, the pirogue was uncomfortable to sail and rolled badly. His life was now completely dominated by wind conditions. When no progress was possible because of strong winds, he slept until dawn; when the wind was favorable, he woke at 2:00 a.m., bailed out his canoe, hauled in the sea anchor, and set the square sail.

In the narrow confines of the canoe's cockpit, exercise was difficult. However, every day he did knee bends, massaged his legs, and somehow managed to execute stationary military marching while standing in his cockpit. He would have taken a swim, but early in the voyage a 15 ft (4.6 m) shark nudged alongside and broke one of the steering cables to the rudder; after that, he prudently decided to stay in the boat.

The Trade Winds were favorable for much of the voyage, bringing 18-24 ft (5.5-7.3 m) waves, but during stronger winds, the waves would build to 30-40 ft (9.1-12.2 m) high—a terrifying experience in a small, low pirogue at sea. It also became obvious that his estimate of 40 days for the passage was optimistic, and he feared he would run out of food in mid-ocean—after all, he was still only halfway across. He decided it would be prudent to head

The Fishermen Battle with the Giant Squid, dated 1881.
Drawing by Victor Nehlig (1830-1909).

for a closer island in the Caribbean, and settled on St. Thomas in the Virgin Islands.

By now Lindemann was lapsing into depression. He was short of liquid because his canoe was too narrow to catch much rainwater, and besides it rolled too much. The *Liberia II* was also too narrow to have the bonus of flying fish landing on deck. Apart from dehydration and a lack of food, he was suffering from exposure to sun and constant drenching from salt water. The calluses on his hands had worn off, leaving painful open wounds. His skin was also breaking out in boils, making it impossible to sit comfortably.

On Christmas morning Lindemann sighted two lights in the west, but he could not tell if they were from a ship or the two lighthouses on the Atlantic coast of Antigua. As the sun rose, he realized the island was dead ahead and he left it to the currents to take him north or south of Antigua. The next day he was south of Nevis, but the wind changed direction making it impossible for him to make landfall in St. Thomas as planned. On December 29th, a day after his 33rd birthday, he sailed into Christiansted, the largest town on the island of St. Croix, after a passage of 65 days. After such a long time in such cramped conditions, he was in remarkable condition:

"My knees were weak; the ground under my feet felt as liquid as the sea; I found I had difficulty walking in a straight line. But, on the whole, I felt extremely well, and above all, jubilant at my safe arrival."

Lindemann spent ten days on St. Croix recovering from his crossing, then took off again (weathering a vicious storm) to fulfill his ambition to sail from the first African republic in the Old World (Liberia) to the oldest republic in the Caribbean (Haiti). With the voyage now over, Lindemann had time to think about what to do next.

Like Alain Bombard, the German physician was haunted by the horrors of the sinking of the French frigate *Méduse* in 1816, when at least 147 people were abandoned to a raft, and only 15 were still alive 13 days later. On another occasion in 1897, the *Ville de St. Nazaire* went down off Cape Hatteras in a hurricane, and only 4 of the 38 people who boarded the lifeboats survived. As a physician, Lindemann understood that in a temperate climate, castaways can survive for more than a week without food or water. So why, he asked himself, did so many people die unnecessarily?

Bombard had asked himself the same question and he believed the solution was to maintain nutrition and hydration by catching and eating fish and plankton, and by drinking small quantities of seawater if fresh liquid was not available. Lindemann thought the problem was more of a psychological issue, and this set the two doctors apart. During his first voyage, Lindemann had come to understand that self-doubt and hesitation were his worst enemies; if you could manage this, he believed, your chances of survival were dramatically increased.

In his search to understand the issue better, Lindemann became interested in a form of self-hypnosis called autogenic training, advocated by the German psychiatrist, J. H. Schultz. This technique trains your body to respond to your verbal commands, by literally "telling yourself" to relax and control your breathing, blood pressure, heartbeat, body temperature, and so on. The goal is to achieve deep relaxation and reduce stress.

≈≈≈≈≈≈≈

Ten months after landing in Haiti, Lindemann was back in Las Palmas making preparations for a second voyage across the Atlantic to help confirm his ideas about survival at sea. This time his choice of craft was even more extreme—a standard production Klepper Aerius II folding kayak (introduced in 1952 and still in production today). In this way, he believed he could recreate the conditions of a lonely castaway. Despite being short of money, Lindemann insisted on paying for the kayak himself—perhaps a snub to Alain Bombard who had accepted sponsorship for his crossing.

Lindemann named his craft the *Liberia III*; it was 17 ft 1 in (5.20 m) long, 3 ft (0.9 m) wide, and weighed 60 lbs (27 kg). The kayak was light because it comprised a simple plywood frame that folded out to support a skin of five-ply rubber and canvas, with air tubes built into the gunwales to give added buoyancy. It weighed so little that it could literally be carried under one arm.

Lindemann made very few changes to the standard craft. He had a sailmaker in Las Palmas make him two tiny square sails; the fore-mast was supported by a pair of backstays, and the mizzen was simply a paddle stuck in a socket. He also added an extra spray cover and strapped a small inflatable outrigger to the port side, to give the kayak some stability.

Several weeks before departure, Lindemann practiced his self-hypnosis and induced in himself a state of complete self-confidence. He wrote: "I had a feeling of cosmic security and protection and the certainty that my voyage would succeed."

On October 20, 1956, Hannes Lindemann cast off from Las Palmas, expecting the crossing to take 70 days. It is difficult to understand how he could carry enough food and liquid to sustain himself for that period. However, he had deliberately fasted for 36 hours before departure to prepare his body for a starvation diet, and he also believed that self-hypnosis would nullify hunger pangs:

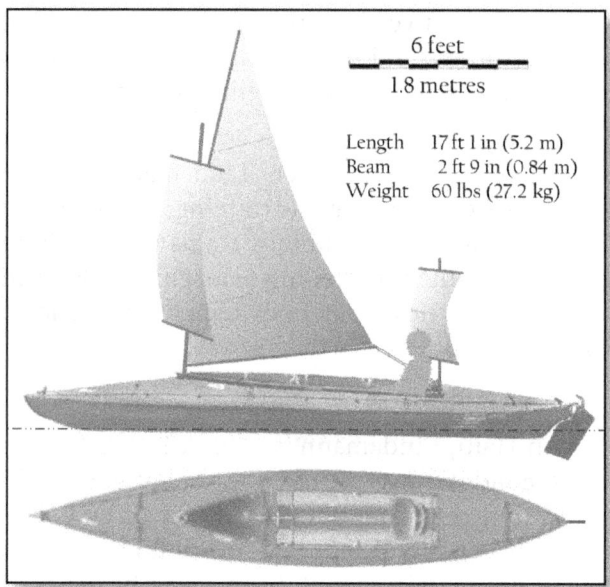

Liberia III weighed just 60 lbs (27 kg) unladen.

"*I knew myself well and knew that after the problem of thirst would come the problem of morale. I had to keep my sense of humor and a relaxed outlook; I had to remain cheerful, unconcerned, and emotionally stable.*"

After his previous voyage, Lindemann understood the problems he would have to manage. On his second day, he found the sprayhood leaked and he was forced to bail out his kayak regularly with a rubber syringe. He found the craft was overloaded and threw 22 lbs (10 kg) of perfectly good fruit over the side; the boat was still too heavy, so he threw a similar weight of canned food over the side—this left him with just 154 lbs (70 kg) of food and liquid for the whole voyage. He supplemented this with whatever fish he could catch, eaten raw because of no cooking facilities. He caught his first fish—a dorado or dolphin fish—on his eighth day: "First I drank its blood, then I ate its liver and roe, which actually tasted better than the flesh of the fish, as well as being richer in vitamins and minerals." That fish saved him a whole day of his sparse rations.

When the weather allowed, Lindemann would strip off his damp clothing and bask in the warmth of the sun—first peeling off his thin rubber jacket, oilskin trousers, shorts, a thick sweater, and his undershirt. He called it his "hour of hygiene and preventative medicine."

For the next several weeks his voyage was much as he expected: periods when the Trade Winds blew steadily, followed by calms, squalls bringing rain, and the occasional serious blow. For several days the wind went frustratingly around to the west, pushing him back towards the Canary Islands. Perhaps surprisingly, there was quite a lot of bird-life out there in the middle of the Atlantic, 1,350 NM (2,500 km) from the nearest land—mainly Madeira petrels, Mediterranean shearwaters, Tropicbirds, and Manx shearwaters; he also had visits from the occasional whale, dolphins, and several inquisitive sharks.

On the night of November 17th, 28 days into the voyage, the wind freshened and thunder rumbled across the horizon lit with lightning flashes. Lindemann was battered, wet, and cold. When breaking waves overtook him from behind, they at least lifted his tiny kayak and carried it that little bit closer to the West Indies. But when a wave broke over the kayak from the side, the *Liberia III* literally disappeared under a mountain of white froth and foam. He then had to bail out every hour, his hands bleached white from the cold and constantly being wet. His rudder also broke and he had to wait a day before it was safe to replace it.

On day 36 the *MS Blitar* out of Rotterdam stopped and offered him assistance and supplies, but Lindemann asked only for his latitude and longitude to check against his own calculations. He found his latitude was exact, but his longitude was one degree too far west. This was quite an achievement, not only did the sharp movement of the kayak make taking a sun sight difficult, but being so close to sea level also made taking accurate readings a challenge. He must have passed through the shipping lanes, because the following day he saw a second ship, although the ship did not see him.

On December 15th, 56 days into the crossing, the voyage very nearly ended. The conditions were so rough that he dared not sleep; nor did he risk trailing his sea anchor because the line snagged his rudder. At 9:00 p.m., a huge wall of water appeared out of the darkness, picked up his kayak and tossed it sideways, capsizing it; Lindemann was thrown into the sea. He could see his kayak was upside down in the water, and he managed to climb onto the slippery bottom of the boat. With one wave after another washing over the capsized kayak, all he could do was hang on until daybreak and hope the wind would drop. During the night he began to hallucinate. He first heard church bells, then a voice invited him over to have a drink and a soft bed in a farmhouse. "Where is the house?" he asked. "Over there, in the west, behind the hill" came the reply.

Lindemann waited seven hours before dawn brought enough light to allow him to salvage his kayak. The wind had not abated, but he knew he had to get out of the wind chill—by now he must have been suffering from advanced hypothermia. He fixed a line to the outrigger and pulled the kayak upright. The boat was full of water, the mizzen mast had broken, and the rudder was gone. As he bailed frantically, the water level inside slowly went down, making the craft more stable. He checked the kayak and found all his food was gone—all he had left were 11 cans of emergency milk, and he still had more than 432 NM (800 km) to go.

On December 21st he found hope—Frigate birds circled overhead; these birds soar for hours over the ocean, but they return every night to roost in trees. Land could not be far, but it took another nine days before he sighted an island. He eventually staggered ashore through the surf at Phillipsburg Bay in St. Maarten, after 72 days at sea. He had lost over 25 percent of his body weight, and on arrival, his pulse was down in the mid-30s.

≈≈≈≈≈≈≈

After their voyages were over, a debate began over the different experiences encountered by Bombard and Lindemann. They were two remarkably determined men, both doctors, who subjected themselves to extraordinary privations to test on themselves the psychological effects of being alone at sea, and whether it is possible to survive by drinking seawater. The two men fundamentally disagreed.

Bombard was convinced that as long as you did not succumb to sharks, madness, or exposure, you could survive for long periods at sea by drinking modest amounts of seawater and the less saline juice pressed from fish—all supplemented by whatever rainfall you could catch. After his voyage, Bombard had no doubts that he had proved his theory and wrote in 1953: "I claim to have proved that the sea itself provides sufficient food and drink to enable the battle for survival to be fought with perfect confidence."

Lindemann also used his voyages to examine the physiology and psychology of enduring long periods alone at sea, but his experience was very different from Bombard's. The Frenchman believed the key was to gradually start drinking seawater as soon as fresh water no longer became available and before you become seriously dehydrated, but Lindemann was skeptical. During his voyages on the *Liberia II*, his legs swelled up from edema, and he put this down to drinking seawater. Later, when he avoided drinking seawater, he did not suffer from swelling.

The sailing conditions experienced by the two men were very different. Lindemann was restricted mostly to his cockpit, although he did as much static exercise as possible. Bombard did suffer several physical ailments during his Atlantic crossing, but he reported little edema swelling. It does make you wonder whether Bombard's ability to move around his inflatable more freely might have helped his circulation. Also, the physiology of individuals varies significantly, and it is also possible that Bombard was simply less prone to edema than Lindemann.

The disagreement between the two sailors might also be related to their priorities. Bombard was primarily interested in the human body's ability to survive on limited food resources that could be obtained from the sea—hence his emphasis on collecting plankton and drinking small quantities of seawater. In this respect, his approach was very scientific.

Lindemann, on the other hand, had a more spiritual approach to survival, and he openly acknowledged the benefits he received from prayer. His interest in self-hypnosis certainly helped him through his darker moments at sea. He concluded that the biggest risk to survival at sea came from the mind, not the body:

"I know now that the mind succumbs before the body, that although lack of sleep, thirst, or hunger weakens the body, it is the undisciplined mind that drives a castaway to panic and heedless action. He must learn to command of himself and, of course, of his boat."

Whichever side you might be tempted to take in the debate there can be no dispute that both men were highly focused and dedicated, and were prepared to subject themselves to great danger and extreme hardship in the pursuit of medical science.

Stranger Things Have Happened at Sea

Once in a while, somebody crosses the Atlantic in a craft that defies most criteria for what would normally be considered either a sensible or seaworthy vessel. This happened again in 2002, in what was neither sailboat, motorboat, rowing skiff, nor kayak—it was not even an automobile. It floated, it had a 130 hp two-stroke petrol engine, and it was 9 ft (2.7 m) long and 3 ft 7 ins (1 m) wide: the craft was called Numancia, an off-the-shelf "jet ski" made by Bombardier of Canada.

The craft was ridden by Count Álvaro de Marichalar y Sáenz de Tejada, an aristocratic adventurer born in Pamplona in Spain in 1961. As a young man, de Marichalar became a pilot with the Spanish Air Force before a traffic accident forced his retirement. He then moved into real estate and telecommunications, where he made enough money to indulge in a variety of marine expeditions, including a solo voyage in an 11 ft (3.4 m) sailboat from Florida to Panama. He claims to hold 11 Guinness World Records.

On February 23, 2002, de Marichalar set off from the River Tiber in Rome aboard his Sea-Doo XP personal watercraft (PWC). When asked why he decided to cross the Atlantic in a PWC—or a "water scooter" as he preferred to call it—de Marichalar declared it was the smallest vessel he could imagine that would allow him "to experience the ocean in a very unique way. I'm not above the water, rather I'm one with the water."

After leaving Rome, he headed west across the Mediterranean towards Gibraltar, and then out into the open Atlantic Ocean. In support was a large motorboat with a crew of six, who supplied him with food, fuel, and spare parts; he also slept aboard. The Sea-Doo traveled much faster than the support boat, so de Marichalar had to stop every four hours to allow the mother ship to catch up and refuel his PWC. He spent 12 hours a day powering across the ocean before going aboard the bigger vessel to eat and sleep.

Despite the significant assistance he received from his support crew, it was an impressive accomplishment to cross the Atlantic in such a small and unsuitable craft. Traveling at speed, the hull slammed into the ocean waves, forcing de Marichalar to spend most of his time standing up. He claimed that on average, he was thrown off the watercraft 10 times a day. The Sea-Doo XP is capable of over 50 knots (93 km/h), and traveling at such high speeds in a big sea always brings the risk of pitchpoling, where the PWC could literally cartwheel.

The main Atlantic crossing from the Canary Islands to the West Indies took him 18 days, and he then continued on to Miami where he arrived on June 22nd; the total voyage from Rome was more than 4,600 NM (8,500 km). De Marichalar rested a few days in Florida before continuing for another 1,000 NM (1,852 km) to New York. After the voyage, he claimed: "The most difficult part was the cold … Between Rome and Naples, it was really terrible."

≈≈≈≈≈≈≈

Over the last couple of centuries, the North Atlantic has been crossed by an eclectic group of people: determined fishermen and dynamic millionaires, stalwart sailors and skilled airline pilots, hard-nosed entrepreneurs and soft-handed journalists, and of course a Spanish aristocrat on a "water scooter." Despite this unusual mixture of adventurers, their voyages had one thing in common—they all had some form of propulsion. Many crossed the Atlantic under sail, some had engines to drive their vessels, others chose to tax their arms and even their legs. Having your own means of propulsion not only hastens your journey, but it also gives you some independent control over where you might be heading. With your own propulsion, you might also be able to avoid bad weather, and you can certainly steer away from a potential collision with other vessels.

Just suppose for a moment that you throw convention to the wind and dare to be different. Just suppose that you decide not to use any form of propulsion, but instead to simply drift across the Atlantic Ocean, abandoning yourself to the whims and vagaries of the wind and currents. You would have no means to control where you might arrive, or even be able to move away from immediate danger.

Crazy? Well perhaps… Possible? Well probably… Did anybody try it? Well yes.

On December 26, 2018, the Frenchman, Jean-Jacques Savin, decided to challenge even the most fundamental requirement for an Atlantic crossing of being able to steer a course. He claims he was inspired as a young boy by Alain Bombard's Atlantic crossing in an inflatable dinghy in 1952, and Savin cast off from the Canary Islands in a wooden barrel with the intention of gently drifting west towards the West Indies.

He hoped to end his journey on a French Caribbean island such as Martinique or Guadeloupe on practical grounds, "that [it] would be easier for the paperwork and for bringing the barrel back [to France]." When he cast off on Boxing Day from the island of El Hierro—wisely choosing the most westerly island in the archipelago—he expected the voyage of 2,600 NM (4,800 km) to take about three months. But it was not going to be quite that simple.

The 71-year-old Frenchman had plenty of experience surviving in adverse conditions: he was a triathlete, a long-distance swimmer, and a former paratrooper, he had sailed the Atlantic four times before, and climbed Mont Blanc (the highest mountain in Europe).

Savin raised $65,000 (approximately £50,000) through crowdfunding and sponsorship from a French barrel maker. He then spent several months building his bright orange, barrel-shaped capsule of resin-coated plywood that he claimed was strong enough to withstand the battering from waves and potential attacks from orcas (killer whales). The barrel gave him about 65 sq ft (6 sq m) of inside living space, including a small galley with a stove, and a manual water maker, together with a single bunk. Most of his food was freeze-dried, although he did pack a bottle of Sauternes white wine and some pâté de foie gras to celebrate New Year's Eve, plus a bottle of St.-Émilion red wine to celebrate his 72nd birthday in January.

The barrel had four portholes for light and to allow Savin to see out, plus two underwater windows to give him endless amusement. A weighted keel kept the barrel from inverting, but without any forward propulsion through the water or sails to give a steadying effect, the barrel inevitably rolled in even a moderate swell, and he needed to lash himself into his bunk with straps to stop himself from being thrown out.

Technically, the barrel was very well-equipped. A pair of solar panels generated power for his iridium satellite phone, VHF radio, and GPS positioning equipment. With this gear, he was able to update his coordinates daily on his website and Facebook page. Savin's safety equipment was equally comprehensive and included a life raft, life jacket, personal locator beacon, emergency flares, sea anchor, and a bilge pump. He also dropped markers during his voyage to help oceanographers better understand ocean currents, and he cooperated with medical researchers to help them understand the effects of solitude in closed confinement. In this respect, he floated across the Atlantic in the wake of Alain Bombard and Hannes Lindemann, in support of medical research.

Even though he had no sails to trim or engines to maintain, Savin found himself busy during daylight hours. He spent 3 to 4 hours a day simply

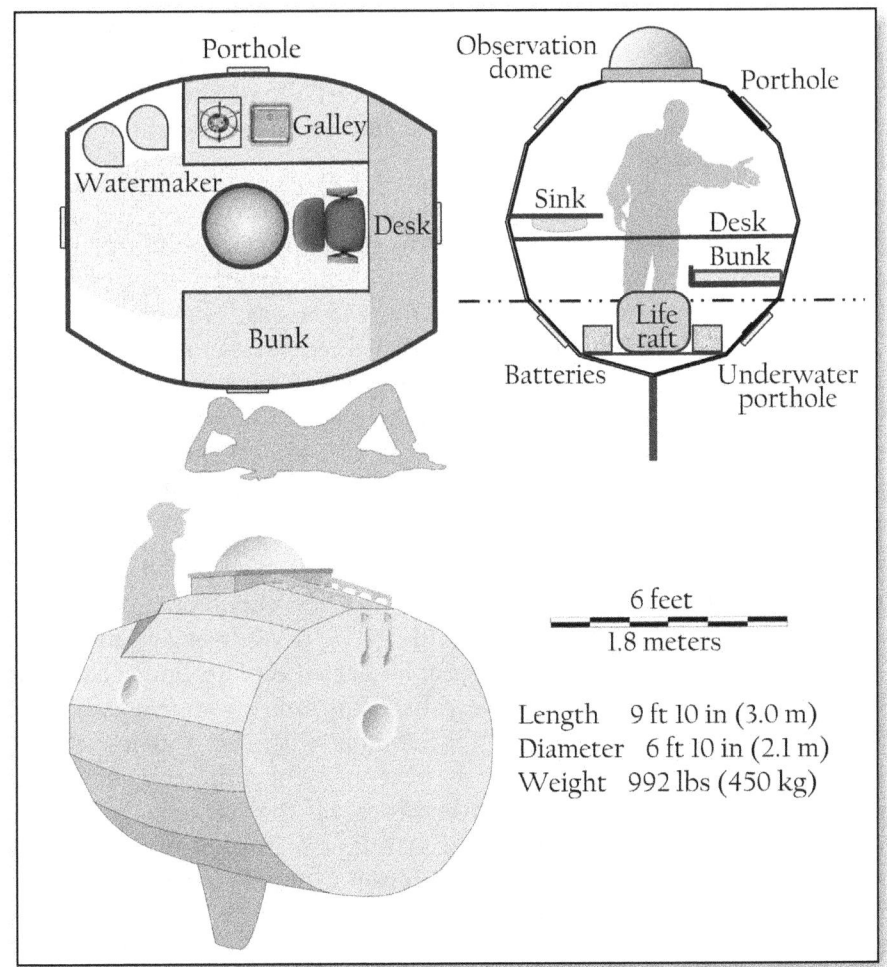

Jean-Jacques Savin's Atlantic barrel

replying to email messages and updating his online log, he swam and caught fish to supplement his diet, he played his mandolin, and he read lots of books. However, he underestimated the time the voyage would take, and the American oceanic research vessel *NOAAS Ronald H. Brown* was asked to rendezvous with his barrel in mid-Atlantic; it was his 62nd day at sea, and the crew brought him fuel, fresh fruit, and other supplies.

His voyage almost ended disastrously on two occasions—both through collision. The first, an oil tanker, was on a collision course with Savin's barrel, but the Frenchman was able to contact the ship on his VHF radio and the vessel turned away at the last minute. On the second occasion, he was unable to make radio contact. The ship was again on a collision course, and it came within 650 ft (200 m) before Savin set off a flare in desperation; only then did the vessel alter course slightly, and it missed his barrel by about 65 ft (20 m)—much too close for comfort. On neither occasion could Savin independently change course, but had to rely on warning others to take avoiding action.

Savin's most difficult moment, though, was his arrival on May 2, 2019, after 122 days at sea. His barrel was drifting quickly with a strong following wind, and with no control over his direction he was in danger of running aground on a coral reef. Fortunately, the U.S. Coast Guard was keeping a close eye on his progress and they contacted a passing oil tanker, the *Maritime Kelly Anne*, to take him in tow. He was dropped off healthy and in good spirits on the tiny Dutch-speaking island of St. Eustatius; a few days later he made his way to Martinique. He described his voyage as a "crossing during which man isn't the captain of his ship, but a passenger of the ocean."

On January 1, 2022, Savin set off a second time to cross the Atlantic, this time in a 26 ft (8 m) rowing boat. He was now 75 years old, and claimed he was making the voyage "to laugh at old age." On Wednesday January 19th, less than three weeks into the crossing, he posted on Facebook that he was experiencing strong winds that were blowing him off course, but added: "Rest assured, I'm not in danger!" All contact with him was lost the next day, when he activated two distress beacons. The following day, Friday January 21st, his boat was found overturned off the Azores, and his body was recovered from inside the vessel. A follower posted on his Facebook page: "Unfortunately, this time the ocean was stronger than our friend, who loved sailing and the sea so much."

≈≈≈≈≈≈≈

You might imagine that the ingenuity of adventurers hell-bent on crossing the Atlantic in weird and wonderful ways might be exhausted, but far from it. Why, for example, do you even need a boat?

On July 16, 1998, 31-year-old Frenchman Benoît Lecomte waded into the surf off Cape Cod in Massachusetts wearing nothing more than a wet suit, snorkel and face mask and headed for the open ocean. He intended to swim across the Atlantic. Lecomte was about as well prepared as you can be for this extraordinary feat of endurance. He was an experienced long-distance swimmer and had been training for six years. He was also accompanied by a support boat that created a 25 ft (7.6 m) electromagnetic field to protect him against sharks. His intention was to swim for up to 8 hours a day in sessions of two to four hours, then rest and sleep on the

40-foot (12 m) sailboat. He had to spend four hours every day eating to replace the 9,000 calories he burned.

Lecomte, who was based in Austin, Texas, was also highly motivated. His father had died of colon cancer seven years previously, and he was swimming to raise money for a Scottish-based cancer charity. Before he left, he also asked his girlfriend Jenny, to marry him—but she told him to ask her again "on the other side."

Even though Lecomte was swimming in mid-summer, the water temperature was still low as the Labrador Current brings cold water south into the North Atlantic from Greenland. He also had to swim through storms that brought 45-60 knot (83-111 km/h) winds and 10-20 ft (3-6 m) waves; the electromagnetic field was effective against sharks, but he still had to contend with sea turtles, inquisitive dolphins, and jellyfish.

He was exhausted by the time he reached the Azores, and he took a week's break to recover. While there, he picked up the phone and asked his girlfriend again to marry him—she declined to give him an answer. By the time he reached Quiberon in Brittany, France on September 25th, he had been at sea for 73-days and had covered 3,229 NM (5,960 km). On his arrival, his first words were "never again." His girlfriend was waiting for him, and this time his proposal was accepted. He also raised £100,000 for his cancer charity in memory of his father.

No sooner had Lecomte completed his marathon swim, however, and controversy began to surround his achievement. His transatlantic crossing was not recognized by the Guinness World Records because the organization claimed there was no standard definition of "swimming across the Atlantic." Questions were also raised about the distance that Lecomte had actually covered while swimming, rather than resting on the sailboat; although the yacht did not sail when he was aboard, it did drift with the prevailing (favorable) currents. According to an analysis by the ROCKY MOUNTAIN NEWS, Lecomte needed to average 7 knots (13 km/h) to swim the entire distance—this is 3 to 4 times faster than other long-distance swimmers.

A similar controversy surrounded an Atlantic swimming attempt by Jennifer Figge, a 56-year-old athlete from Aspen, Colorado. Figge slipped into the water in Brava in the Cape Verde Islands on January 12, 2009, and took just 24 days to swim to Chacachacare Island in Trinidad, where she arrived on February 5th. She woke most days around 7:00 a.m. and ate a high carbohydrate breakfast of pasta and baked potatoes while she and her crew assessed the weather. Her longest period in the water was about eight hours, and her shortest was 21 minutes. The crew threw bottles of energy drinks into the water as she swam, but if the seas were too rough, divers would deliver them in person. At night she ate a high protein meal of meat, fish, and peanut butter, replenishing the estimated 8,000 calories she burned every day.

Figge spent most of her time swimming inside a shark cage. Inevitably, she had to cope with strong winds and waves up to 30 ft (9.1 m). During her crossing, she saw a pod of pilot whales, several turtles, dozens of dolphins, plenty of Portuguese man-of-war, but fortunately no sharks. "I was never scared," she claimed. "Looking back, I wouldn't have it any other way. I can always swim in a pool."

The controversy surrounding Figge's crossing was that she covered 2,186 NM (4,048 km) in a little over 3 weeks. Even if she had swum for a full 8 hours every day, she would have to cover 91 NM a day (169 km), averaging more than 11 knots. An Olympic swimmer can maintain 4.5 knots (6.5 km/h) for short periods, so clearly there was something wrong with the sums.

Part of the problem arose because several major media outlets erroneously reported that she swam the whole distance. For example, the reputable British newspaper, THE DAILY TELEGRAPH, ran the headline: "U.S. athlete Jennifer Figge is the first woman to swim the Atlantic Ocean in 24 days." In an interview with the ASSOCIATED PRESS, Figge clarified her achievement by claiming that she "never intended to swim the Atlantic," but that she only ever intended to swim sections of the ocean. It later transpired that Figge swam a total of just 139 hours, covering a cumulative total of 300 NM at an average speed of 2.15 knots—a much more realistic swimming speed.

Despite the controversy surrounding both Atlantic swimming attempts, there is no doubt that both Ben Lecomte and Jennifer Figge were extraordinary athletes whose sheer determination and tenacity is to be applauded.

Despite claiming "never again" Lecomte attempted to swim across the Pacific Ocean. He left Chōshi on the east coast of Japan on June 5, 2018, heading for California—4,800 NM (8,900 km) away. Part of the reason for his swim was to raise awareness about sustainability and the impact of excessive human garbage polluting the world's oceans. Speaking to THE JAPAN TIMES, he explained his motivation:

"I have a deep connection with the environment—but unfortunately within my almost 40 years of swimming, I've seen big changes. There is plastic everywhere; clean beaches I walked on when I was a child now have plastic. Do I sit back and not care about it? Or do I use my passion to shine a light on the issue?"

This time, Lecomte planned a "staged swim," where he used a GPS tracking device to resume swimming every morning in the exact location in which he left the water the previous day. He intended to swim for eight hours a day and average about 35 NM (64 km) a day with the help of a favorable current.

After swimming nearly 1,500 NM (2778 km), the mainsail of Lecomte's support boat had been repeatedly torn by heavy winds and could no longer be repaired. Fearing for the safety of his crew, Lecomte decided to cancel his attempt.

≈≈≈≈≈≈≈

If you can swim the Atlantic, then why not walk it? It might sound far-fetched, but is it possible? Well maybe...

On April 1, 1988, the 39-year-old French entertainer, Rémy Bricka, left Tenerife in the Canary Islands with a pair of long polyester floats strapped to his feet. "I am not crazy," he claimed before leaving. "I want to fulfill one of man's oldest dreams, which is to walk on water." He managed to leave despite being banned by the Spanish Navy. (To be precise, Bricka did not actually walk on water, but rather paddled himself while standing on floats).

Apparently, Bricka spent three years planning his crossing. He used a double-bladed oar and towed a rubber raft in which he slept during his voyage. He claims to have survived on vitamin pills, flying fish, plankton, and distilling seawater. Given Bombard and Lindemann's experiences several decades before, this sounds overly-optimistic of what might be possible; Bricka does not, for example, claim to have caught fish with a hook and line, but instead waited for flying fish to leap into his inflatable dinghy.

At the end of May, a Japanese freighter picked him up about 40 NM (74 km) off the coast of Trinidad and he was taken to a hospital for a medical check-up. According to the Canary Islands' newspaper, DIARIO DE AVISOS, Bricka lost 44 lbs (20 kg) in weight, was found to be malnourished and suffering from vision problems, but otherwise, his condition was satisfactory. Yet Bricka would have needed to have consumed 5,000 to 6,000 calories to sustain paddling all day, and this would have been difficult to maintain while living off flying fish and plankton, as Bombard and Lindemann showed on previous voyages. So in many respects, it is remarkable that he was not in worse physical condition on arrival.

If his account is true, then Bricka's crossing was an extraordinary test of determination and resilience by somebody who had no record of endurance training. On April 24, 2000, at the age of 50, he is reported to have attempted to cross the Pacific Ocean but was rescued south of Hawaii after five months at sea on his ski-floats. Yet, these "voyages" inevitably raise the question of whether it really is possible to "walk" such long distances in the open ocean. Even balancing on the floats in still water is a challenge; exactly how he managed to remain steady in an ocean swell or during bad weather is difficult to imagine.

*Rémy Bricka,
perhaps more entertainer than adventurer.*

In 2016, a Polish inventor called Krzysztof Rogus developed a working "Float-Ski" for recreational use, which allowed people to walk on water by combining the latest surfboard materials with modern aviation technology. His floats incorporated an intricate set of fins, flaps, hinges, and small stabilizing floats on each side of the floats. Rogus found that an experienced user could walk on water at around 3 knots (5.5 km/h), and with paddles, this increased to about 4 knots (7.4 km/h)—at least for relatively short periods.

Could Bricka have achieved this on heavier, cruder floats some 18 years previously?

The straight-line distance from the Canaries to Trinidad is 2,830 NM (5,240 km), and Bricka claims to have spent 61 days at sea; therefore, he had to average over 46 NM (85 km) a day. Assuming he paddled for 12 hours a day for the duration (in itself a remarkable achievement), he would have to average 3.8 knots (7 km/h)—that is the speed of a very brisk walk and impossible for anyone to sustain on water for 12 hours a day for 61 consecutive days. Previously, all other transatlantic voyages along this route had encountered bad weather, big waves, contrary currents, sun exposure, dehydration, and hunger—all this would have slowed him down.

To put Bricka's 61-day crossing into context, it took Hannes Lindemann 65 days to sail the slightly shorter distance from the Canaries to St. Croix in the Virgin Islands in his canoe, and he was able to sail for more than 12 hours a day without much physical exertion. It took the experienced Aleksander Doba 196 days to paddle his kayak from mainland Portugal to Florida in 2014—three times longer than Bricka (who admittedly took a slightly shorter route). Perhaps an even better comparison was the supremely-fit Chris Bertish, who took 93 days to power his stand-up paddleboard from Morocco to English Harbour, Antigua, in 2017. Bertish averaged 38 NM (70 km) a day—significantly slower than Bricka's claimed average of 46 NM (85 km) a day. Bertish found his paddleboard difficult to handle, but it must surely have been easier than having your feet strapped to a pair of polyester floats and towing an inflatable dinghy.

Except for his departure from the Canary Islands and his rescue 61 days later off the coast of Trinidad, there are no witnesses who can verify Rémy Bricka's crossing. Nor is there any independent evidence of how long Bricka spent on his floats and how much time he spent resting in his inflatable. If he had really "walked" across the Atlantic in 61 days, then it would have been a truly outstanding achievement. Yet Bricka was primarily an entertainer, not a survival expert.

Perhaps the secret behind his voyage lies in the date of his departure—April 1st.

Glossary

Abaft
 Toward the stern, usually relative to an object such as "abaft the mast."

Abeam
 The location of anything beyond either side of a vessel.

Aboard
 To be on or in a vessel.

Adrift
 Afloat and unattached in any way from the shore or seabed.

Aft
 Towards the stern of the vessel.

Aground
 Resting on or touching the ground or bottom.

Ahead
 Anything forward of the bow.

Aloft
 Above the ship's uppermost solid structure; overhead or high above.

Alongside
 By the side of a jetty, pier, or another ship.

Amidships (or midships)
 The middle portion of a ship, along the line of the keel.

Anchor
 An object designed to prevent or slow the drift of a ship, attached to the ship by a line or chain; typically a metal, hook-like object designed to grip the sea bottom.

Anchorage
 A suitable place for a ship to anchor. Area of a port or harbour.

Anchor chain or cable
 Chain and/or rope connecting the vessel to the anchor.

Astern
 Toward the stern; an object or vessel that is abaft another vessel or object.

Awash
 So low in the water that the water is constantly washing across the surface.

Bank (seafloor)
 A large area of elevated seafloor.

Beam
 The width of a ship at its widest point.

Bear away
 Turn away from the wind, often with reference to a transit.

Bearing
 The horizontal direction of a line of sight between two objects on the surface of the earth.

Bermudan rig
 A modern fore-and-aft sail configuration in which the mainsail is triangular.

Bilge
 The lowest point inside the hull of a vessel where water collects so that it can be pumped out at a later time.

Boatswain (or bosun)
 A non-commissioned officer responsible for the sails, ropes, and boats on a ship.

Boom
 A spar on which the bottom of a fore-and-aft sail is attached.

Bosun
 See Boatswain.

Bottom
 The outside surface of the hull below the waterline.

Bow
 The front of any hull.

Bowsprit
A spar projecting from the bow used as an anchor for the forestay and other rigging.

Broach
A sudden movement when a vessel running with the wind from behind, suddenly and accidentally turns into the wind; potentially a dangerous event in strong winds.

Bulkhead
An upright partition within the hull of a ship, often load-bearing and watertight.

Bulwark
A raised side above the level of weather deck designed to keep water off the deck.

Cabin
An enclosed room on a deck.

Capsize
When a ship or boat rolls over, exposing the keel; on large vessels, this often results in sinking.

Capstan
A large rotating hub (wheel) mounted vertically on deck and used to wind in anchors or other heavy objects.

Catamaran
A vessel with two hulls.

Centerboard
A lightweight hinged keel, that when lowered is used to resist leeway.

Centerline
The center of a boat running from bow to stern, exactly halfway between either side.

Chine
The angle in the hull where (usually) plywood panels are joined, as compared to the rounded shape of most traditional boat hulls.

Cleat
A fitting that secures or locks a sheet or running rigging.

Coaming
The raised edge of a hatchway used to help keep out water.

Cockpit
The area from which the sailors control the boat.

Compass
A magnetic instrument that revolutionized navigation where an arrow always points to magnetic north.

Crew
A person or persons who help sail a boat and who take orders directly from the skipper or helmsman.

Current
The horizontal flow of water.

Daggerboard
A type of centerboard that moves vertically into the water.

Decks
The structures forming the approximately horizontal surfaces within a ship's general structure.

Downwind
A location in the leeward direction, i.e. literally "downwind."

Draft
The depth of a ship's keel below the waterline.

Draught
See draft.

Fathom
A unit of length equal to 6 ft (1.8 m), roughly the distance between a man's outstretched hands.

First mate
The second in command of a ship.

Following sea
Wave or tidal movement going in the same direction as a ship.

Foot
The bottom of a sail.

Fore
Towards the bow (of the vessel).

Forestay
Long wires or cables from the front of the vessel to the top of the mast, used to support the mast.

Freeboard
The height of a ship's hull (excluding superstructure) above the waterline.

Furl
To roll or wrap a sail around the mast or spar to which it is attached.

Gaff
The spar that holds the upper edge of a fore-and-aft or gaff sail; also, a long hook with a sharp point to haul fish aboard.

Gaff rig
A sailing rig in which the mainsail is four-cornered and set fore-and-aft.

Galley
The kitchen of the ship.

Gangplank
A movable plank or bridge used to board a ship when alongside a jetty.

Global Positioning System (GPS)
A satellite system that provides continuous worldwide coverage to enable air, marine, and land users to identify their position.

Gunwale
The upper edge of the hull.

Halyard or Halliard
Ropes used to raise a sail.

Headsail
Any sail flown in front of the most forward mast; includes jibs and foresails.

Heaving to
To stop a sailing vessel by lashing the helm in opposition to the sails; the vessel will gradually drift to leeward and comfortably ride the waves.

Heel
The tipping, tilting, or leaning of a sailing boat towards the leeward side due to the pressure of the wind on the sails.

Helmsman
A person who steers a ship.

HMS
A British abbreviation for "Her Majesty's Ship" or "His Majesty's Ship"; always a naval warship.

Hogging or hog
The distortion of a hull where the ends of the keel are lower than the center; this can result from a weak hull flexing as waves pass beneath.

Hull
The body of the boat to which everything else is attached; the hull displaces water which allows the boat to float.

Jib
A triangular staysail at the front of a ship.

Jib sheet
The line that controls the jib.

Keel
The central structural backbone of the hull. A keel might be weighted to lower the boats center of gravity and help prevent heeling.

Lee helm
If the helm was centered, the boat would turn away from the wind (to the lee). Consequently, the tiller must be pushed to the lee side of the boat in order to make the boat sail in a straight line. Not a good characteristic in a sailing boat. (See weather helm).

Lee side
The side of a ship sheltered from the wind. (See the weather side or windward side).

Lee shore
A shore downwind of a ship. A ship that cannot sail well to windward risks being blown onto a lee shore and grounded.

Leeway
The angle that a ship is blown to leeward by the wind. See also weatherly.

Leeward
In the direction towards which the wind is blowing.

Length overall (loa)
The overall maximum length of a vessel (usually including the bowsprit).

Lifeboat
A small steel or wood boat located near the stern of a vessel. Used to get the crew to safety if something happens to the mothership.

LOA
See length overall.

Luff
The forward edge of a sail.

Mainmast (or Main)
The tallest mast on a ship.

Mainsheet
A line that controls the mainsail.

Mast
A vertical pole (either wooden or metal) on a ship that supports sails or rigging.

Mizzen
The sail flown from a mizzen mast.

Mizzen mast
A smaller mast stepped aft in a ship, but ahead of the rudder post.

Oilskin
Wet-weather gear worn by sailors.

Pilot
A navigator who is especially knowledgeable and qualified to navigate a vessel through difficult waters, e.g. harbour pilot etc.

Pitch
A vessel's motion, rotating about the beam axis, so the bow pitches up and down. (See roll).

Pooped
Swamped by a high, following sea.

Port
Towards the left-hand side of the ship facing forward; denoted with a red light at night. (See starboard).

Privateer
A privately-owned ship authorized by a national power to conduct hostilities against an enemy

Radar
Acronym for RAdio Detection And Ranging; an electronic system that transmits radio signals and receives reflected images to determine the bearing and distance of another vessel or the coastline.

Radar reflector
A fitting that reflects a radar signal, thereby enhancing the image of the vessel on radar.

Reef
To temporarily reduce sail area, usually in response to strong winds; also, a rock or coral shallow enough to endanger a vessel.

Rigging
The system of wires and lines on ships and other sailing vessels that support the sails and spars.

RMS
A prefix used on British seagoing vessels that carry Royal Mail under contract to the British government; the designation dates back to 1840.

Roll
A vessel's motion rotating from side to side, about the fore-aft axis. (See pitch).

Running rigging
Rigging used to control sails, spars, etc. See standing rigging.

Sea anchor
A parachute-shaped drogue deployed in the water to assist in heaving to in heavy weather; this acts as a brake and keeps the hull in line with the wind and waves.

Sheer
The upward curve of a vessel's longitudinal lines as viewed from the side.

Sheets
Lines used to control the sails.

Shoal
Shallow water that is a hazard to navigation.

Shrouds
Standing rigging running from a mast to the sides of a ship. (See forestay).

Skipper
The captain of a ship.

Spar
A wooden (and in later years a metal) pole used to support various pieces of rigging and sails; both a mast and boom are classified as spars.

Standing rigging
Fixed wires that are used to hold the mast upright. See running rigging.

Square-rigger
A traditional sailing ship where the yards (booms) lie at right-angles to the vessel. (See fore-and-aft).

SS
A prefix used on merchant vessels indicating that the ship runs on steam propulsion.

Standing rigging
Fixed rigging that supports masts and spars. (See running rigging).

Starboard
Towards the right-hand side of a vessel facing forward, denoted with a green light at night. (See port).

Stern
The rearmost part of any hull.

Strake
One of the overlapping boards in a clinker-built hull.

Topsides
The part of the hull between the waterline and the deck.

Tiller
A horizontal bar (usually wooden or occasionally metal) attached to the top of a boat's rudder and used for steering.

Transom
A generally flat surface across the stern of a vessel.

USS
Abbreviation for a commissioned ship of the United States Navy.

Weather helm
If the helm was centered, a boat will turn towards the wind (weather); the tiller must therefore, be pulled to the windward side of the boat in order to steer the boat in a straight line. Moderate weather helm is considered a good thing in a sailing boat. (See lee helm).

Windward
In the direction from which the wind is blowing.

Windlass
A winch mechanism, usually with a horizontal axis, that is used to raise the anchor.

Yard
The horizontal spar from which a square sail is suspended.

Yawl
A sailing boat with two masts, where the smaller mast is aft of the rudder post.

Bibliography

Chapter 1: Big Ocean, Little Boat

Andrews, W. A. & Macaulay, J. (1880). *A Daring Voyage Across the Atlantic Ocean: by Two Americans, the Brothers Andrews: The Log of the Voyage.* Boston, MA: E. P. Dutton.

Crapo, T. & Cowin, W. J. (2019). *Strange, but True. Life and Adventures of Captain Thomas Crapo and Wife.* Sydney, New South Wales: Wentworth Press.

Essex Journal and New Hampshire Packet, (1787, May 2).

Garland, J. E. (1998). *Lone Voyager; the Extraordinary Adventures of Howard Blackburn, Hero, Fisherman, of Gloucester.* New York, NY: Simon and Schuster.

Longyard, W. H. (2003). *A Speck on the Sea.* New York, NY: International Marine/McGraw-Hill.

Morris, R. (2003). *Alfred Centennial Johnson: the Story of the First Solo Atlantic Crossing from West to East in 1876.* Cardiff, UK: Y Crofft.

Chapter 2: The Space Race

Ellam, P. & Mudie, C. (1953). *Sopranino: 10,000 Miles Over the Ocean in a Midget Sailboat.* New York, NY: W. W. Norton.

Manry, R. (1966). *Tinkerbelle.* New York, NY: Harper & Row.

McClean, T. (1983). *Rough Passage: a Life of Adventure.* London, UK: Hutchinson.

Riding, J. C. (1968). *The Voyage of the Sea Egg.* Boston, MA: Pelham.

Smith, S. & Smith, C. (1952). *The Wind Calls the Tune: the eventful voyage of the Nova Espero.* Robert Ross.

Vihlen, H. (2019) Personal correspondence.

Vihlen, H. & Kimberlin, J. (1997). *The Stormy Voyage of Father's Day.* London, UK: Marlor Press.

Chapter 3: Steam Across the Atlantic

Braynard, F. O. (1988). *S.S. Savannah. The Elegant Steam Ship.* Dover, GA: University of Georgia Press.

Flayhart, W. (2003). *Perils of the Atlantic: Steamship Disasters, 1850 to the Present.* New York, NY: W. W. Norton.

Fox, S. (2003). *The Ocean Railway: Isambard Kingdom Brunel, Samuel Cunard, and the Revolutionary World of the Great Atlantic Steamships.* New York, NY: Harper Collins.

Stanton, S. W. (1965). *Steamboats of the River Hudson. Upper Montclair, New Jersey.* Kingston, NY: Hudson River Maritime Museum.

Chapter 4: The First Atlantic Yacht Race

Jefferson, S. (2016). *Gordon Bennett and the First Yacht Race across the Atlantic.* London, UK: Adlard Coles.

O'Connor, R. (1962). *The Scandalous Mr. Bennett.* New York, NY: Doubleday.

Samuels, S. (2012). *From the Forecastle to the Cabin (Seafarers' Voices).* Annapolis, MD: Naval Institute Press.

Sacramento Daily Union. (1866, November 6). (vol. 32, #4870).

Chapter 5: The Arms Race

Bray, P. (2004). *Kayak Across The Atlantic.* Worcestershire, UK: Polperro Heritage Press.

Clarke, J. (2017, March 9). Chris Bertish Becomes First to Cross Atlantic by Paddleboard. *New York Times.*

Naydler, M. (1968). *The Penance Way: The Mystery of Puffin's Atlantic Voyage.* London, UK: Hutchinson.

Rackley, A. (2014). *Salt, Sweat, Tears; The Men Who Rowed the Oceans.* New York, NY: Viking.

Ridgway, J. & Blyth, C. (1967). *A Fighting Chance; How We Rowed the Atlantic in 92 Days.* Philadelphia, PA: J. B. Lippincott & Co.

Shaw, D. W. (2003). *Daring the Sea: The True Story of the First Men to Row Across the Atlantic Ocean.* New York, NY: Citadel Press.

Weil, E. (2019, March 22). Alone at Sea. *New York Times.*

Chapter 6: The History Man

Ashe, G. (1962). *Land to the West: St. Brendan's Voyage to America.* New York, NY: Collins.

Clements, J. (2005). *A Brief History of the Vikings: The Last Pagans or the First Modern Europeans?* Philadelphia, PA: Running Press.

Heyerdahl, T. (1972). *The Ra Expeditions.* West Bengal, India: Signet Press.

Richards, J. D. (2004). *Viking Age England.* Cheltenham, UK: The History Press.

Severin, T. (2000). *The Brendan Voyage: Sailing to America in a Leather Boat to Prove the Legend of the Irish Sailor Saints.* New York, NY: Modern Library.

Chapter 7: The Atlantic Auto Route

Carlin, B. (1955). *Half-Safe: Across the Atlantic in an Amphibious Jeep.* New York, NY: Harper Collins.

Nilson, M. (2019). Personal correspondence.

Tempo D'Estate (1999, August 25) Gli autonauti al capolinea.

Chapter 8: The Heretics

Bombard, A. (1986). *The Bombard Story.* New York, NY: Sheridan House.

Lindemann, H. (1958). *Alone at Sea: a Doctor's Survival Experiments of Two Atlantic Crossings in a Dugout Canoe and a Folding Kayak.* New York, NY: Random House.

Index

A

Abercastle, Wales 11
Ader, Bas Jan 48
Adventure, HMS (British gunship) 1
Aga II (sailboat) 35, 36
Aga (sailboat) 35, 36
Airex 54
Aitutaki, Cook Islands 50
Albert, Prince 79
Allaire Iron Works of New York 65
Allum, Don 129, 130
Allum, Geoff 129, 130
Ambrose Lightship 82
America (dory) 27
American Samoa 48
America's Cup 95, 197
Amoretti, Giorgio 183–187
Amoretti, Marco 184–187
Amphibear 187–196
amphibious jeep 40, 174–176, 190
amphibious vehicle 190, 195
Amphitrite - goddess of the sea 83
Andrews, Asa 16, 17
Andrews brothers 20, 115, 117
Andrews, William 16–18, 22–28
Angus, Colin 130
Anisor (sailboat) 52
Antwerp, Belgium 25
April Fool (sailboat) 45–48, 51, 53, 57
Aquitania, SS 33
Arakaka, MS (passenger ship) 209
Archimedes, SS 78
Arctic Mirage 161, 162, 168
Around the World in Eighty Days 75
Arranmore Island, Ireland 51
Artemis Investments (rowing boat) 131

Atlantic Challenge (rowing boat) 130
Atlantic Rally for Cruisers (ARC) vi
Autonauts 184
Aymaro Indian boatbuilders 149
Azores 32, 43, 94, 180, 181

B

Baltic Light (bulk carrier) 136
Baltic Sea 133
Bates, Sir Percy 84
Bath, Maine 21
Bay of Biscay 32
Beaufort Scale 34, 174
Belderrig Co., Mayo, Ireland 132
Belgium 25
Bennett Jr, James Gordon 88–92, 94, 96, 105, 108, 110–112
Bennett Sr, James Gordon 98
Berlin (sailboat) 36
Bermuda 42, 135
Bermudian rig 37
Bertish, Chris 137, 138, 231
Beverly, Massachusetts 16
Big C (sailboat) 52, 53, 60
Bishops Rock Lighthouse 59, 82, 120, 131
Black Ball Line 69
Blackburn, Howard 26, 114
Bligh, Captain 198
Blitar, MS (cargo ship) 219
Blond, Pascal 130
bloodboats 69
Blue Riband 81, 84, 86
Blyth, Chay 130
Blyth, Sergeant Chay 122–128
Bombard, Alain 187, 198–210, 214, 217, 220–224, 229
Bombard, Ginette 210
Bombard, Nathalie 208
Bordeaux, France 2, 4

Boston Daily Globe 23
Boston Herald 24
Bosun (dog) 8, 9
Bradford Boat Services, Yorkshire 122
Branson, Richard 86, 87
Bray, Peter 131–134
Brendan (medieval sailboat replica) 154–166, 172
Brendan's Head, Ireland 44
Brendan, St. 44, 150, 151, 157, 160, 166
Bricka, Rémy 229–231
Bright and Co. 80
Britannia (rowing boat) 129
British and American Steam Navigation Co. 70–76
British and North American Royal Mail Steam-Packet Co. 77
British Merchant Navy 7
British Queen, SS (steamship) 72–77
British Royal Navy 68
Brittany 227
Brooklyn Daily Eagle 99
Brown, Captain Dick 95, 96, 109
Brown, Ronald H. 225
Brude, Ole 29
Brunel, Isambard Kingdom 70–81
Buckley, J. C. 8
Bulgaria, SS (steamship) 20

C

Cadiz, Spain 60, 208
Cairo Museum 146
Cambria (racing schooner) 111
Canada 27, 28
Canary Islands 51, 57, 59, 60
Candia, Marcolino De 184
Cape Ann Historical Society Museum 12
Cape Cod, Massachusetts 12, 54, 91, 123
Cape Hatteras 36, 44, 123, 124
Cape Horn 26, 48

Cape Ortegal 3
Cape Shoalwater (USCG cutter) 47
Cape Verde Islands 46, 192, 193, 195
Cap Horn (sailboat) 44
capsize 10, 11, 25, 32
Caribbean 52, 130
Carlin, Ben 174–180, 183, 187
Carlin, Elinore 174–183
Casablanca, Morocco 46, 208
Castle Garden Immigration Depot, NY 113
Centennial (sailboat) 10–12
cetacean (whale) 43, 59, 158, 159, 206
Charlemagne, Emperor 160
Charleston, South Carolina 36, 63
Chatham 12
Chaudière, HMCS (warship) 128
Chay Blyth 130
Chevron Atlantic MS (oil tanker) 187
Christopher Columbus (sailboat) 25
Citta di Ragusa (sailboat) 7–9, 20
City of Bath (sailboat) 21, 22
Classic Boat Museum in Cowes, Isle of Wight 37
Claude Girdwood & Co. 73
Clermont 61, 62. *See also* North River Steamboat of Clermont
Clermont, Camille 111
Cleveland, Ohio 38, 39, 42
clinker 33, 115, 167, 169
Coconut Grove 45
Collins, Dwight 196
Columbia (packet boat) 69
Columbia, SS (steamship) 82
Columbus, Christopher 5, 143, 150
Commodore 91
Cook Islands 50
Cornwall 16, 18, 21, 25, 50, 152
Coverack, Cornwall 25

Cowes, Isle of Wight 20, 37
Crapo, Joanna 12, 14, 16
Crapo, Thomas 12, 14, 16, 21, 115, 117
Crawford Auto Aviation Museum 42
Cuban pirates 67
Cunard Line. *See* British and North American Royal Mail Steam-Packet Co.
Cunard, Samuel 76, 92
Curling and Young (engineers) 73

D

Daily Express 35
Dark Secret (sailboat) 22, 23
Dartmouth, Devon 34
Dauntless (racing schooner) 111
day sailer 33, 40
Dayton, Captain George 95, 96, 102–105, 108
dead reckoning 118, 125
De Candia, Marcolino 184, 185
Delta Airlines 45
Dhow, Arab 16
Diario De Avisos 229
Dickinson, Wayne 50, 51
Dicuil (chronicler and geographer) 157, 160
Doba, Aleksander 133–137
Doldrums 5
Doree (sailboat) 26
dory 10, 20–23, 26, 27
double-ender 18
Draken Harald Hårfagre (Norse longboat) 170–173
Dreadnought (packet boat) 93, 94
Dunlop, Bill 50
Durano, SS 26

E

EchoMax system 137
Elbruz, SS, (steamship) 25

Ellam, Patrick 37, 38, 152
Emergency Position Indicating Radio Beacon (EPIRB) 190
Emma L. Rich 8
Enchantress (sailboat) 50
England 42
English Channel 18, 20, 34, 36
English Rose III (rowing boat) 124, 126, 127
Eric the Red. *See* Thorvaldsson, Erik
Erikson, Leif 168
Essex Journal and New Hampshire Packet 2
extra-tropical storm 59

F

Fairfax, John 129
Fairhaven 27
Falkland Islands Co. 80
Falmouth, England 37, 48, 57, 59
Falmouth, Massachusetts 40, 42, 50
Father's Day (sailboat) 53–59
Fava, Teresia 30
fiberglass 45, 54, 211. *See also* glass reinforced polyester (GRP)
Fickett & Crockett shipyard 65
Figge, Jennifer 227, 228
Finnmen. *See* Innuit (Eskimo)
First Edition (motor yacht) 47
fishing schooner 27
Fiske, Stephen 98–109
Fleetwing (racing schooner) 89–92, 95, 96, 97, 100–111
Flores, Azores 32, 180
Flores, NRP (Portuguese warship) 174
Florida 45
Flying Dutchman 26
foam-sandwich 60
Fort Lauderdale News 47
Fox, Richard Kyle 115, 116, 120

Fox (rowing boat) 114, 118–120, 123
Fox, Uffa 129
France 227
Fulton, Robert 61–64
Funchal, Madeira 57

G

gaff rig 3, 7, 10, 16
Geoholm, MS (offshore support vessel) 195, 196
Gibbs 80
Gibraltar 28
Giles, Laurent 37
Giltspur (sailboat) 49, 50, 129
glass reinforced polyester (GRP) 36, 38, 60
Gloucester, Massachusetts 10, 12, 16, 19, 20, 26, 29
God's Tear (sailboat) 50, 51
Goetz Marine Technology 197
Golif (sailboat) 38
GPA jeep (general purpose amphibious jeep) 174
Grand Banks 10, 11, 14, 26, 57, 96, 101, 102, 104, 114, 117, 118
Great Barrier Reef, Australia 50
Great Britain, SS (steamship) 75, 78–81
Great Republic (sailboat) 27
Great Western (sailboat) 26
Great Western, SS 73
Great Western, SS (steamship) 72–75, 79, 82
Great Western Steamship Co. 71, 75, 78, 80
GRP (glass reinforced plastic) 36, 38, 60. *See also* fiberglass
Guardia Fiscal 56
Guen, Joseph Le 130
Guinness Book of World Records 128, 222
Gulf Stream 47, 81, 101, 104

Guppy 13 (sailboat) 48

H

Hales, Sir Harold Keates 83, 86
Hales Trophy 83–87
Half Safe (amphibious jeep) 179–183
Halifax, Nova Scotia 18, 20, 33, 179
hallucinations 43, 181, 213, 220
Hamill, Rob 130
Harbo, Anine 113–115, 120
Harbo, George 113–118, 120, 123, 131
Harbo, Grace 114
Haru, MS (cargo ship) 195
Hasler, "Blondie" 44
Hasler wind vane 44
Haustellum (tanker) 126
Hayter, E. R. W. 8, 9
Henderson, Cynthia 183
Henrietta 109, 110, 111
Henrietta (racing schooner) 89–110
Heyerdahl, Thor 145–150
Hibben, Frank C. 143
Higgins & Gifford of Gloucester 16, 18
Hillingar effect. *See* Arctic Mirage
Hippocampe (sailboat) 37
H. K.. *See* Hales, Sir Harold Keates
Hoare, John 121–128
Homestead, Florida 45
Horse Latitudes 4, 5
Hull, Massachusetts 50
Hurricane Alex 132
Hurricane Alma 44, 125
Hurricane Andrew 56
Hurricane Faith 127, 128
Hurricane Floyd 59
Hurricane San Felipe Segundo 31

I

ImpiFish (paddleboard) 137
inflatable dinghy 40

Inmarsat. *See* satellite phone
Innuit (Eskimo) 164
International Small Craft Center 48
Ireland 8, 9
Irish Press 36
Isle of Wight 20, 33, 35, 37, 42

J

jeep, GPA 40, 174–183, 190
Johnson, Alfred 10–12, 47, 115, 117
Johnstone, David 121–128

K

Kaiser Wilhelm der Grosse, SS (steamship) 82
Kawau Island, New Zealand 43
kayak 131, 133
Kennedy, Robert 46
King Jr, Martin Luther 46
Kiwi Challenge (rowing boat) 130
Klepper Aerius II (folding kayak) 217
Klepper (kayak) 30
knarr (Norse longboat) 167
Kon-Tiki (raft) 145, 146
Korean War 45

L

Labrador Current 57, 104, 172, 197, 227
Lacombe, Jean 37, 38, 44
La Coruña, Spain 48
Lafayette, USS, (ocean liner, previously the SS Normandie) 85
Laird, Macgregor 70, 72
Land's End (England) 20, 24, 86
lapstrake 18, 19, 33, 39
lateen rig 16, 17
Lawlor, Josiah 23–25
Lecomte, Ben 226–229
leg-of-mutton sail 12
Le Havre, France 18, 22, 116, 120
Leland, W. Ted, Rear Admiral 54

L'Hérétique (inflatable dinghy) 201–210
Liberia (canoe) 211
Liberia II (folding canoe) 212–216, 221
Liberia III (folding kayak) 217–219
lifeboat 6, 7, 8
Lindemann, Hannes 210–221, 224, 229, 231
Lisbon, Portugal 134
Little One (sailboat) 48
Little Western (sailboat) 18–20, 40
Liverpool, England 51, 52, 54, 60
Liverpool Museum 9
Livingstone, David 111
Lizard Point, Cornwall 25
Lorillard, George 97, 98, 102, 104, 108
Lorillard IV, Pierre 89, 90, 95, 97, 111
Lucania, SS (steamship) 82
Lyons, Captain Martin 92
Lysistrata (steam yacht) 111

M

Maine 1, 21
Maine Marine Museum 22
Manry, Robert 38–42, 121
Manry, Victoria 38
Maritime Kelly Anne (oil tanker) 226
Marshall, Deborah 1
Marshall, Eleanor 1
Marshall, Samuel 1
Marty, Christian 139, 140
Massachusetts 10, 12, 16, 27, 29, 40, 50
Maudslay, Sons & Field 73
Mauretania, RMS (ocean liner) 82
McClean, Tom 49, 50, 129
McNally, Tom 51–60
McVickar, Commodore William 91
Mechanic Falls, Maine 50
Médard, Saint 166
medieval boat 44, 153
Méduse (French warship) 198, 199, 217

Melville, Herman 159
Mermaid (sailboat) 23–25
Miami Seaquarium 48
micro-cruiser 20, 21, 37, 42, 52, 53
milk run vi
Minnesota Historical Society 49
Mitchell, Samuel 12
Monroe, President James 67
Montauk Point Long Island, New York 48
Montezuma (packet boat) 70
Mudie, Colin 37, 38, 122
Muir-Palmer, Herbert. See Palmer, Jack
Müller, Aga (Agatha) 35, 36
Müller, Paul 35, 36
Mullion Cove (Cornwall) 18
Murden, Tori 130
Museum of Oceanography, Monaco 199
Mystic Seaport Museum 197

N

Nab Tower, Isle of Wight 42
Napier, Robert 73, 76
Napoleon Bonaparte 68
National Maritime Museum (Falmouth England) 59
National Police Gazette 115–117, 120
Nautilus (sailboat) 16–18, 22
Nautilus (submarine) 61
Navigation 151, 152, 157, 159, 160
Neptune - god of the sea 83
New Bedford, Massachusetts 12
New Bedford (sailboat) 12
Newport, Rhode Island 37
New York Herald 96
New York Yacht Club 89, 90, 111
Nonoalca (sailboat) 44
Normandie, SS (ocean liner) 84, 85
Norman, Frederick 18, 20, 115, 116
Norse longship 166, 172

Norsemen 143, 150, 160, 164, 167–173
Norse sailors 164, 170
North River Steamboat of Clermont 61, 62
North Star (steam yacht) 89
Nova Espero 33, 35
Nova Scotia 18, 20, 33

O

Observer Single-handed Transatlantic Race 38
Ocean Pier, Boston 24
Ocean Wave (sailboat) 48
Ohio 38
Old Town (sailboat). See also Whitecap (sailboat)
Olo (kayak) 133, 135, 136
Olsen, Ivar 21
Osgood, George 88–90, 95–97, 111
OSTAR. See Observer Single-handed Transatlantic Race

P

packet boat 63–66
packet company 69, 75, 77
Palmer, Jack 202, 207
paras 123–127
Pearl (rowing boat) 130
pedal boat 196, 197
pedalo. See pedal boat
Penzance, Cornwall 16
Peter, Eric 51
Peyron, Stéphane 140, 141
Phantom Ship (sailboat) 26
Phoenix (steamboat) 62
Pichavant, Alain 140, 141
Pillar of Crystal 165, 166
Pink Lady (rowing boat) 132
Plain Dealer 42
Point of Pines, Boston 22, 23

Portsmouth, New Hampshire 1
Portugal 130
Portuguese-man-of-war 41, 228
Potter, Maud 111
President, SS (steamship) 75, 76
Primorac, Nikola 6–10, 20
privateer 1
Puffin (rowing boat) 122–129

Q

QE3 (rowing boat) 129, 130
Quaker merchants 69
Queen Elizabeth, RMS (ocean liner) 85
Queen Mary, RMS, (Royal Mail Ship) 42, 84, 85
Queenstown, Ireland 8
Queen Victoria 9, 95

R

Ra II (papyrus sailing boat) 149
Raleigh, USS (naval warship) 1
Ransome, Arthur 28
Ra (papyrus sailing boat) 147–150
Razzle Dazzle (cocktail) 88
Recife, Brazil 52, 195
Red Cross Line (packet boats) 92
Reuter, George de 111
Rex, SS (ocean liner) 83–85
Ridgway, Captain John 121–129
Riding, John 42, 43
River and Rowing Museum 129
River Queen (river steamboat) 98
Rogers, Moses 62–68
Rogers, Steven 65
Romer, Franz 30, 31
Rosie. *See* English Rose III (rowing boat)
Royal Air Force 33, 85
Royal Humane Society 133
Royal Mail Steam Packet Co. 75
Royal Navy. *See* British Royal Navy
Royal Yacht Squadron Regatta 95

S

Sailing Alone Around the World 28
Sambro Island, Halifax 28
Samson (steam tugboat) 79
Samuels, Captain Samuel 92–96, 99–105, 108, 110
Samuelson, Frank 116, 118, 120, 131
Sapolin (sailboat) 25, 26
satellite phone 184, 185
Savannah, SS (steamship) 65–68, 73
Savannah Steamship Co. 65, 67, 69, 73
Savin, Jean-Jacques 223–226
Scarborough & Isaacs of Savannah 65
Scarborough, William 65–67
Schultz, J.H. 217
Schulz (river steamboat) 98, 99
Scotia, SS (steamship) 77
Sea Egg (sailboat 42, 43
Seaman, William 115
Sea Serpent (sailboat) 23–25, 40
sergeant 122
Severin, Dorothy Sherman 150, 151
Severin, Tim 150–157, 160, 161, 164, 166, 172
Shackford, Josiah 1–7
Sidi Ferruch (cruise ship) 207
Simeon of Durham (historian) 166
singlehanded 5, 10, 12, 18, 26
Sirius, SS (steamship) 74, 75, 81, 82
skeid (Norse longboat) 167, 169
Slocum, Joshua 27, 28
Smith, Colin 33, 34
Smith, Junius 69–73, 76
Smith, Stanley 33–35
snekkja (Norse longboat) 167
Sobraon, SS (steamship) 24
Sopranino (sailboat) 37, 38, 122, 152
Special Air Service (SAS) 49, 131

Speedwell Ironworks of New Jersey 65
Spiess, Gerry 41, 49
Spray (sailboat) 27, 28
Squirrel (sailing trade ship) 1
Stanford, Professor Dennis 144
Stanley, Henry Morton 111
Staples, Ernest 103, 107
St George Steam Packet Co. of Cork 75
Stubbs, Phil 130
Suriname 2
Swallows and Amazons 28

T

Tango (pedal boat) 197
Tench, USS (submarine) 40
The Japan Times 228
The Times of London 7, 70, 110, 121
Thomas, Captain Albert 96, 103, 106, 107
Thomas, George 18, 116
Thorvaldsson, Erik 168
Time Magazine 83
Tinkerbelle (sailboat) 39–42
Tonikay Nou (sailboat) 51
trade winds 3, 5, 37, 45, 46
Trans-Atlantic Yacht Race 42
Traynor, John 21
Trenton, USS (US warship) 18
Trepassey, Newfoundland 21

U

U-boat 32
United States, SS (ocean liner) 85, 86

V

Vanderbilt, Cornelius 88, 89, 111
Vera Hugh 54, 55
Vera Hugh-Cancer Research (sailboat) 59, 60
Vera Hugh-Pride of Merseyside (sailboat) 52–57
Verity, Bill 43, 44

Verne, Jules 75
Vesta 91, 95, 96, 101–110
Vesta (racing schooner) 97, 102, 103, 106
Vihlen, Hugo 45–48, 51–59
Vikings. *See* Norsemen
Violet, Charles 35
Virgin Atlantic Challenger 86
Virgin Atlantic Challenger II 87
Vraad (sailboat) 29

W

Wafaei, Julie 130
Wallace, Rev James 131
Wallis, William 48
Western Reserve Historical Society, Cleveland, Ohio 42
West Wight Potter (pocket sailing cruiser) 35
whaleboats 12, 14
Whitecap (sailboat) 39
William Patterson shipyard 72
Wind's Will (sailboat) 50
World War I 30, 83
World War II 9, 32, 36, 133

Y

Yankee Girl (sailboat) 49
Young, Harry 31, 32
Yuri Kostikov (fishing trawler) 52

About the Author

Peter Firstbrook grew up in England, and from an early age he developed a life-long passion for sailing. After studying oceanography at a university, he became a documentary film producer and worked for BBC Television for 25 years. Since then, he has developed a writing career, and his previous books include "The Voyage of the Matthew" (about the explorer John Cabot), "Lost on Everest" (about the climber George Mallory), "The Obamas: The Untold Story of an African Family, and "A Man Most Driven" (a biography of John Smith of Jamestown).

Over the years, Peter Firstbrook has sailed extensively from the Baltic to the Mediterranean, on both sides of the Atlantic, the Caribbean, and the Pacific and Indian Oceans—sometimes with a crew, and at other times single-handed. This experience has given him a profound respect for those who commit to long ocean passages, often sailing against the odds (and sometimes in totally unsuitable craft).

Firstbrook became fascinated by what motivates people to risk life and limb in pursuit of their dreams, and this led to extensive research needed to write "Daredevils of the Atlantic," in which he combines his love and expert knowledge of sailing, with a trained understanding of the weather and oceans, all told by a skilled and experienced story-teller.

"Lost on Everest" was translated into six languages, and won the prestigious International Trento Mountain Book Festival award. Peter Firstbrook has also won more than thirty international awards for his work in television. He sails his classic Vindö 40 out of Yarmouth on the Isle of Wight, southern England.

www.ingramcontent.com/pod-product-compliance
Lightning Source LLC
Chambersburg PA
CBHW050137170426
43197CB00011B/1867